HUMAN MOTOR BEHAVIOR:
An Introduction

HUMAN MOTOR BEHAVIOR:
An Introduction

Edited by

J. A. Scott Kelso
Haskins Laboratories
The University of Connecticut

 LAWRENCE ERLBAUM ASSOCIATES, PUBLISHERS
1982   Hillsdale, New Jersey   London

Copyright © 1982 by Lawrence Erlbaum Associates, Inc.
All rights reserved. No part of this book may be reproduced in
any form, by photostat, microform, retrieval system, or any other
means, without the prior written permission of the publisher.

Lawrence Erlbaum Associates, Inc., Publishers
365 Broadway
Hillsdale, New Jersey 07642

Library of Congress Cataloging in Publication Data
Main entry under title:

Human motor behavior.

 Bibliography: p.
 Includes index.
 1. Movement, Psychology of. 2. Psychology, Physio-
logical. I. Kelso, J. A. Scott.
BF295.H89   152.3   82-2512
ISBN 0-89859-188-0   AACR2

Printed in the United States of America

Contents

Preface

Why should anyone be interested in studying motor skills? One answer is that until quite recently many people were not. Psychologists for example might be the group of individuals to whom issues of how actions are generated might be the most germane. But by and large psychologists (of the experimental and physiological kind) have been of two types: one (sometimes called behaviorist) sees motor skill as a non-issue. Behavior is simply a function of "habits" or "response probabilities" developed by the number and strength of the stimulus-response reflex units built up through "experience." What matters is that a pigeon or a rat presses the bar; *how* the pigeon or rat does it is of no significance. The other type of psychologist (sometimes called cognitive) tends to ignore the problems of *motor* skill. After all, what is really interesting are things like perception, cognition and memory. "Translating" the results of these processes—organizing movements—seems pretty trivial by comparison.

This book is based on the contrary belief that the determinants of motor skill and the conjoint problems of how movements are coordinated and controlled are fundamentally important to anyone concerned with understanding human behavior. This includes psychologists, but applies even more especially to other disciplines—such as physical education and kinesiology—for which the subject of movement is particularly germane. In fact, this book is written primarily for undergraduates in kinesiology and physical education as well as psychology, and it may also be of interest to students in areas such as physical therapy, engineering and computer science.

It seems fair to say that the subject of motor behavior has a fairly chequered past both in terms of its relationship to science and with respect to its function in academic settings. Its traditional role—at least in physical education departments which are the main source of fosterment for the subject—was to familiarize future teachers, coaches, and rehabilitators with the gamut of factors that influence the acquisition of motor skills. Such factors were not always based on scientific data, but when they were they had to be gleaned from a huge and diversified data base obtained largely from applied settings. In short, not too long ago the area had a certain supermarket quality—plenty of isolated facts but little or no focus. Needless to say, without conceptual pegs to hang data on to, the student can walk away short-changed.

The present book sacrifices a comprehensive account of all the possible knowledge areas that might contribute to what we know about motor behavior, for a more coherent approach to some of the problems associated with acquiring, remembering, controlling and coordinating (usually simple) motor acts. It is coherent—not in the sense that all the contributors to the book agree on the solutions to these problems (they don't)—but rather on the way to approach the problems in the first place, namely through theory and experiment. The aim of the book is to familiarize the undergraduate (and perhaps the beginning graduate student) with some of the exciting conceptual developments of the last decade. Where possible, an attempt is made to illustrate the possible applications of concepts, although the reader should be aware that often the problems are sufficiently deep as to render any application strained, if not superficial.

The material of the book is organized in a logical and spiralistic fashion. The first two chapters by Kelso introduce the reader to past and present approaches to the topic and lay out some of the current concepts in the area to receive amplification in later chapters. In chapters 3, 4, and 5, information processing and closed-loop frameworks to motor learning and control are presented by Stelmach. These notions gained major status in the early seventies and still receive vigorous investigation. Stelmach presents new evidence that speaks to their strengths and weaknesses and provides us with an indepth treatment of motor memory. Keele provides a further analysis of information processing along with some of its applications for sports skills (Chapter 6) and then in Chapter 7 develops the concept of motor program—as an internal representation of a movement sequence. The important question of how these representations are built-up and how they interact with peripheral feedback receives the bulk of discussion. In Chapter 8, Schmidt expands on the notion of program by considering some of its properties and articulates a new model developed by himself and his colleagues to account for the acccuracy of rapid (programmed) motor acts. He proceeds to address in Chapter 9 the puzzling issue of how one produces "novel" movements and offers the motor schema construct as a mechanism for movement generation as well as movement storage. Some of the developmental implications of the schema view are discussed. Michael Turvey et al. change gears for the reader (who by now may be persuaded that it all makes sense) by offering a synthesis and elaboration of the problems of movement coordination first identified by the Russian physiologist, Nicolai Bernstein. Two of these, how the many variables (muscle, joints) of the motor system are regulated, and how the motor system achieves its goals in the face of changes in context receive the most attention. In the penultimate chapter, Turvey and colleagues address the question of how perception and action are related. This is a deep problem, but the beginnings of ways to approach it are offered, along with some compelling new data on the non-arbitrary relationship between what we see and what we do. In a final epilogue, Kelso offers a synthesis as well as a critique of some of the theoretical positions adopted in previous chapters. A brief glossary of some of the terms used is provided at the end of the book.

All the chapters, save the epilogue, are based on a series of lectures given during the spring semester of 1978 at the University of Iowa. The funds for carrying out the project were kindly provided by the National Science Foundation's program for local course improvement in undergraduate education (Project LOCI, Grant #SER77-02986). Any opinions, findings, and conclusions or recommendations expressed in this publication are those of the authors and do not necessarily reflect the views of the National Science Foundation. Additional funds were provided by the University of Iowa. Each contributor gave five lectures which were tape recorded and subsequently transcribed. Resulting transcripts were returned to the authors for 'tuning' (rewriting may be a more appropriate word). This is an arduous process for one and all but it has the benefit that any recent work of significance can be included until quite late in the production process. Nevertheless, it is crucial to emphasize that the area of motor behavior is in a state of flux—what seems right and just today may be grist for the mill tomorrow. In spite of the foregoing caveat, the concepts included here are part and parcel of that which defines the current state of the motor behavior area, and it seems certain that they will provide the springboard for future theoretical developments.

A number of acknowledgments are very much in order. To Sherry Yore who typed the original transcripts (and in doing so had to listen to many strange voices and even stranger words), I express my sincere thanks. Thanks also to David Goodman who served as a Graduate Assistant on the project and helped during all stages—often beyond the call of duty. To Haskins Laboratories who supported me through the final stages I extend my appreciation. Karl Newell and Dick Schmidt made many helpful remarks on an earlier draft of the manuscript. Thanks. Lastly, I am most grateful to those who participated in this project—not only for their final contributions but also for the many stimulating discussions we have had over the last few years. If anyone can be said to have had a role in bringing the motor behavior area to its present state, it is surely them.

J. A. Scott Kelso

PERSPECTIVES AND ISSUES IN MOTOR BEHAVIOR

Editor's Remarks (Chapters 1 and 2)

In Chapter 1 I develop the basic perspective that understanding movement means not only recognizing the *product* of skilled behavior—whether a particular goal was achieved accurately and efficiently—but also questioning how it is that such skilled movements are controlled and coordinated. The tools and concepts for the student of motor behavior emerge at several different levels. At the observational/experimental level we want to understand the key relationships between environment and performer that influence the development of skill. At the biomechanical/kinesiological level we seek to understand the physical basis for movement: how dynamic factors (the forces or torques generated by muscles and their viscoelastic properties) specify the patterning of limb segments in time. At the neurophysiological level we seek insights into the neural structures and their functional interactions that allow motor behavior to emerge. I argue in Chapter 1, that this interdisciplinary enterprise is necessary to fully understand movement *processes,* and, further, that movement processes—rather than being given secondary or negligible status—are an intrinsic aspect of understanding intelligent behavior.

In Chapter 2 I attempt to provide an inventory—a flavor as it were—of concepts that are expanded upon in later writings. But the chapter is not meant to be a haphazard presentation of isolated topics. It starts with a consideration of the sometimes synonymously used terms coordination, control, and skill in relation to the fundamental problem for any biological system; namely, how to regulate its internal degrees of freedom. For our purposes, the degrees of freedom can be considered to be the muscles of the body—792 of them at last count: How are they organized to produce skilled activities, and how does this organization come about? One answer, that receives much further elaboration in later chapters by Michael Turvey and colleagues, is that muscles are organized into functional combinations called coordinative structures that behave in a relatively autonomous way. Thus, the brain doesn't have to regulate every degree of freedom on an individual basis; that would create a tremendous computational burden. Rather, these lower-level muscle collectives can be "tuned" by higher centers to meet environmental contingencies. If this perspective has any validity, the motor system is not simply the slave of the senses: Perception and action are likely to be closely interwoven—not related to each other willy-nilly. Consider a skill that many of us take for granted—speaking. It is often fun (and some entertainers make a living out of it) to mimic other speakers, but imagine what this involves. Somehow, what we hear must *specify* how the speech muscles are to be organized in space and time if we are to mimic effectively. Information about the actions of others and about our own activities in relation to environmental demands must be crucial to the process of organizing skilled movements. With this premise in mind I go on to consider some of the basic properties of two major types of information—proprioceptive and visual—thought to be important in regulating movement. Guardedly, I refer to these sources of information as playing primarily a *feedback* role. But they can play a *feedforward* role as well. Thus, on the one hand, the performer has information about the results of activity as a potential aid to skill learning. On the other hand, skilled individuals seem able to use information effectively *prior* to executing a particular act. This "feedforward" information may be extrinsically defined—allowing the performer to "tune" or parameterize the system in accordance with changing environmental events. It may also take the form of patterns of neural activity within the nervous system itself, which can guide movement sometimes in the absence of peripheral information. As the reader sees, all these themes—in one guise or another—as well as many others receive further development in the chapters that follow.

1 The Process Approach to Understanding Human Motor Behavior: An Introduction

J. A. Scott Kelso
Haskins Laboratories and
The University of Connecticut

ORIENTATION

What is your conceptualization of skilled behavior? What does the word "skill" mean to you? Think about what *processes* underlie the exquisite coordination and timing of the ballerina, the perfectly executed pass from quarterback to wide receiver, the speed and gracefulness of a Pelé, the anticipation of a Mohammed Ali, the precision of a pianist. We all can recognize the *outcome* or the *product* of highly skilled performance, but how does this outcome materialize? What processes underlie the acquisition of skill and the control of movement? This is the overriding question that we are going to examine in some depth in the following chapters, and one that not only myself but my fellow contributors place at the forefront.

Throughout this discourse we make an implicit assumption. Namely, that striving to understand the underlying processes in acquiring skill will enable you—as students and teachers—to analyze situations in which you are confronted with a problem related to movement behavior. It may be a child who has difficulty in learning simple skills, a patient who is learning to use a prosthetic device such as an artificial limb, a skilled performer in an athletic team who, for some reason, is not performing as well as he/she might. Whatever the case, we are assuming some intrinsic benefits to you arising from a fuller understanding of what goes on when people learn skills.

Let me say at the outset that there are not many, if any, *answers* as to how best to acquire or teach skills. This book does not present you with an array of facts that you can immediately use in practical situations. What we are trying to communicate here is the need for you, as students of movement, to develop your own approach to the problem. A key to this is your ability to adopt a *critical thinking* stance on some of the issues. Think about the implications of what the information presented means to you. Try to detect flaws in the logic and suggest alternative viewpoints.

Hopefully, an important stimulus to the development of a critical approach to understanding human movement behavior comes from the perspectives provided by the different theorists contributing to this book. You will find that there are crucial points of departure on how each views the nature of skilled performance. This is all to the good because it forces you to make decisions for yourself. Throughout the following chapters you will hear people tell you a *different* story about the *same* topic—acquiring skill—usually in a plausible and logical manner. It is up to you to take your *own* position on the issues. It matters not at this point whether your position is right or wrong (because there are seldom any right or wrong answers!), only that the stance you take can be logically justified. Enough sermonizing. In this book we have tried to adopt a "spiralistic" approach to knowledge about human motor behavior. We begin with a discussion about component processes in movement and build progressively upon that basis to the learning and control of movements. Ultimately, we discuss how this information may be optimally applied to various skill-learning situations.

My goal in the present chapter is to give you a little background to the area of motor skills, so that the information that follows can be "slotted" into a historical perspective. I wish to recount, somewhat briefly, where the area of motor behavior has been, the changes in approach that have come about, and my own thoughts on why. I also want to give you a feel for my approach to the problems of skill acquisition, which is basically one spanning several disciplines. A full understanding of human movement, in my opinion, can only come about if we integrate behavioral work (which tends to focus on the outcome of performance) with kinesiology (which provides us with information about the kinematics of human movement) and neurophysiology (which tells us the nature of underlying neural mechanisms involved in controlling movement). I return to this point shortly with some specific examples. Firstly, let us review the past for a moment.

BRIEF HISTORICAL PERSPECTIVE

The study of motor behavior has had a continuing, if somewhat phasic, relationship with academic disciplines such as psychology and physiology. Perhaps the relationship has not been as close as it might have been. Certainly, there have been periods during which tight bonds were established. For example, when governments were interested in optimal methods for training military personnel

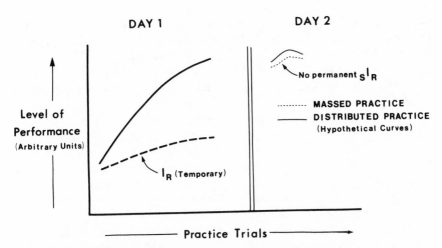

FIG. 1.1.   Hypothetical performance curves illustrating the effects of massed and distributed practice (see text for further explanation).

during World War II, a considerable number of experimental psychologists were involved in funded research. Similarly, when psychological theory (Hull, 1943) was readily testable with motor activity, psychology and motor-performance studies went hand in hand. In general however, motor tasks, such as the pursuit rotor[1], were employed as a means to an end where the ''end'' was exploration of psychological concepts, such as Hull's (1943) reactive inhibition and conditioned inhibition. The explanation of these concepts is not of immediate concern but let me discuss them briefly to illustrate the type of approach taken here; and the resulting outcomes. A short discourse on Hullian theory—if nothing else— affords me the opportunity to make an important distinction between learning and performance. Hull assumed that, whenever an organism makes a response to a particular stimulus, some degree of inhibition toward that response is produced. This is called ''reactive inhibition'' (I_R), which was often assumed to be some type of fatigue. The notion was, therefore, that I_R would dissipate just as long as there was sufficient rest between trials. In contrast, having no rest (massed trials) should lead to a buildup of I_R (i.e., a declining response strength). This prediction is shown in Fig. 1.1, where you can see that massed trials lead to deficits in *performance*.

''Conditioned Inhibition,'' ($_SI_R$) however, is a learned behavior. Because I_R produces a negative response state (poorer performance), the organism is motivated to avoid (reactive inhibition) and through the learned habit of $_SI_R$ is motivated not to respond. In sum, a continued buildup of I_R should lead to a

---

[1]The pursuit rotor is simply a tracking device in which the subject's task is to keep a stylus on a dot or cursor that is attached to a turntable that rotates at various speeds.

permanent effect on performance. Numerous studies showed the presence of a temporary work factor (see Day 1 of figure), but there was negligible support for any permanent work inhibitor. The hypothetical data shown in Fig. 1.1 summarize the results of much of the research on this topic. Massed practice is fatigue inducing and produces inferior *performance*. It has, however, no *permanent* effect on *learning*.

Although this finding is of interest to teachers and coaches, it clearly tells us little about the actual movements involved. In fact, the point that I would like to emphasize is that the study of motor performance per se was not actively pursued by psychologists. Smith (1969) summed up this state of affairs quite nicely: "experimental results on and stimulus–response theoretical ideas about the pursuit rotor seem to have relevance for nothing but the pursuit rotor and even fail to give any really critical suggestions about how people operate and learn this instrument [p. 240]." The key word for us in the foregoing statement is *"how,"* because what we as students of motor behavior are really concerned about are the key processes underlying the acquisition of skill and the control of movement. In the past, however, much of the research carried out using motor tasks was in the behaviorist tradition. Certainly, the work on Hull's theory that extended into the late 1950s was based on stimulus–response accounts of behavior. There was a strong concern for the conditions of reinforcement that established "habit strength" between stimulus and response exemplified by reliable performance of an act. Behaviorists, however, were not particularly concerned with the *manner* in which the act was attained. Implicit in the stimulus–response account was that movements were learned as a result of conditioned stimulus–response elements. Given a cue to start the movement sequence, a response would be generated that in turn would produce the stimulation to elicit a further response. Each response element is conditioned to the stimuli of the prior part of the response, and, when the elements are associatively bonded or somehow tied together, learning is complete and the motor sequence is executed smoothly. To obtain a flavor for the stimulus–response chaining model, consider the model shown in Fig. 1.2. Even the novitiate in the area realizes that this is an unsatisfactory account of human motor learning. Movements are seldom, if ever, executed the same way each time, and the stimulus–response chaining model offers little in terms of understanding the learning and regulation of motor sequences. Yet, it is surprising how long this simple model has been implicitly accepted by a large body of psychology.

Nevertheless, different conceptualizations of motor behavior were available though largely ignored by psychology as a whole. These ideas evolved just prior to World War II and arose out of engineering circles under the name of cybernetics. The basic metaphor of a cybernetic or servotheory approach was that man behaved like a servomechanism or slave system. The common feature of the latter is that they possess a controlling device that can continuously monitor the state of the system for discrepancies between a desired and present state. Otto Mayr (1970) traces the history of such devices ranging from water clocks that

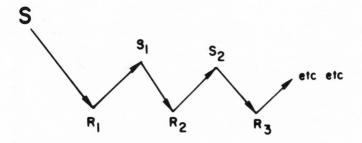

S= Cue to start the motion sequence
R = Response elements of the sequence
s = Response-produced stimulation

FIG. 1.2.   The reflex (stimulus-response) chaining model of movement behavior.

used feedback control in the 3rd century B.C. to James Watt's introduction of a governor for control of the steam engine in 1769.

In terms of the analogy to human motor behavior, the essence of the idea is expressed in a quotation from Norbert Weiner's *Cybernetics* (1948):

> Now suppose that I pick up a lead-pencil. To do this I have to move certain muscles. However, for all of us but a few expert anatomists, we do not know what these muscles are; and even among the anatomists there are few, if any, who can perform the act by a conscious willing in succession of each muscle concerned. On the contrary, what we will is *to pick the pencil up*. Once we have determined on this, our motion proceeds in such a way that we may roughly say that the amount by which the pencil is not yet picked up is decreased at each stage. This part of the action is not in full consciousness. To perform an action in such a manner, there must be a report to the nervous system, conscious or unconscious, of the amount by which we have failed to pick up the pencil at each instant. If we have one eye on the pencil this report may be visual, at least in part, but it is more generally kinaesthetic, or to use the term now in vogue, proprioceptive.

Clearly, motor behavior rather than being constructed by inflexible stimulus-response chains, was viewed as an essentially error-nulling activity. In its simplest form, this basic man–machine analogy is shown in Fig. 1.3. Imagine, for example, the skill of driving a motor car. Information from the environment is provided to the operator that the vehicle has deviated from its desired position on the road. The discrepancy between the *desired* state—"keep to the right of the midline of the road" and the present state of the vehicle—"front and rear

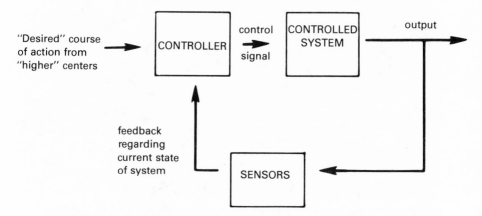

FIG. 1.3.   The basic servomechanism model.

wheels of driver's side to left of midline on the road,'' is detected and a correcting response generated. Feedback from this movement is continually compared to the desired state until the perceived error is nulled.

A more expanded version of this model is shown in Fig. 1.4. Illustrated are some of the key central nervous system operations that are thought to process sensory input and result in coordinated movements. Receptor systems include specialized structures that transform impending mechanical energy. These receptor mechanisms are responsible for picking up information arising from the motor output and transmitting it back to the central nervous system. This activity is referred to as *afferent* which may be visual, auditory, or proprioceptive (information from specialized structures in the joints, muscles, and skin) and is indicated in the figure by the long peripheral feedback loop. The arrow leading from the top suggests that the CNS can modulate afferent input or at least "gate" out irrelevant patterns of sensory feedback. Further sampling and synthesis of incoming information probably occurs so that the main central processing operations—error detection and correction—may function effectively. The error correction unit is then thought to be responsible for programming an appropriate pattern of commands, which, when forwarded to the lower-motor neuron pools, leads to a change in motor output to appropriately correct for the detected error. This we refer to as *efferent* activity, which is the organization of motor commands that are sent from the brain to the muscles. The sequence of information-processing events that I have alluded to is essentially what is meant by closed-loop control. In chapter 4 the concept is developed in more detail.

In Fig. 1.4 you can also see a central processing function referred to as a programming unit. Clearly, this operation bypasses error detection and correction and is included to denote those situations where the CNS is capable of generating quite accurate motor activity without the necessity of utilizing peripheral feedback. It becomes clear in future discussions that processing of input requires *time;* a fact that would necessitate unwanted delays in the production of motor sequences that are often extremely rapid. Clearly, there are occasions when movements are executed so quickly that ongoing error detection and correction based on processing sensory input would be inefficient. Furthermore, the beautifully smooth and coordinated movements of the skilled athlete or ballet dancer have given rise to the notion that, as learning progresses and performance improves, it becomes less and less necessary to sample sensory feedback for error detection and correction operations. There is a famous anecdote in the literature (Lashley, 1951) of the pianist who can strike the keys as fast as 16 times per sec. This is clearly too rapid for movements to be regulated by sensory feedback. Those of us who have spent hot summers in the Midwest of America also have had the experience of swatting flies and mosquitos. Once the action sequence for fly swatting is generated, it runs off unregulated by feedback. Consequently, if the fortunate fly changes its position while the movement is in progress, we miss it. The underlying notion here is that it is possible to conceptualize a system that operates *openloop;* a mode of control that does not require utilization of peripheral feedback.

I have highlighted some of the key issues in the foregoing discussion merely to familiarize you with a theme that pervades the first few chapters; namely,

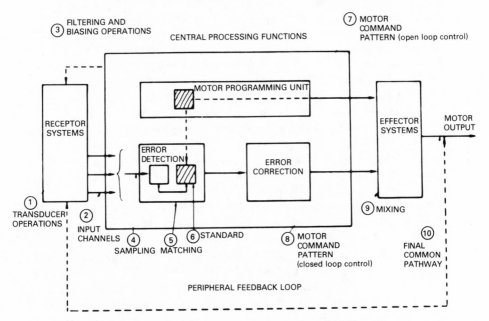

FIG. 1.4. An expanded version of the servomechanism model illustrating some of the hypothetical processes involved in the regulation of movement (modified from Chase, 1965).

human motor behavior involves a complex system of information-processing operations. The details of these operations and their role in understanding human movement behavior is forthcoming in the chapters prepared by Stelmach, Keele, and Schmidt.

Let me backtrack to the historical theme. In terms of the development of motor behavior as an area of academic study in its own right, it seems odd that, given this conceptualization of central nervous system functioning, the S-R behaviorist approach had a continuing influence in psychological thought. Fitts (1964), for example, defined skilled actions as those that involve a high degree of spatial and temporal organization between receptor–effector feedback processes (i.e., a high degree of integration between input and output). When we are skilled, we know that there is a high degree of compatibility between how the muscles are organized and the outcome of our actions. His viewpoint is clearly expressed in the following statement: "Rather than viewing perceptual-motor behavior as a series of responses made to reach some goal, it is possible and I believe considerably more profitable to view such behavior as an information processing activity guided by some general plan or program [p. 248]." Fitts goes on to discuss Woodworth's (1899) work that led to the conclusion that two-phase units of motor activity were patterned in advance of their initiation and remained uninfluenced by peripheral, sensory inputs during their execution. Hitting a golfball might be a example of such a unit where the backswing is the first part of the unit, and the total time for the execution of the act is about half a second. The motor sequence is apparently preprogrammed and run off without movement conditions. We see that Woodworth's conclusions are just as relevant today as they were at the turn of the century. (The programming viewpoint is concep-tualized and expanded by Schmidt and Keele.)

But one might ask—given this high degree of sophistication and awareness of the issues in the motor behavior area that extended back three-quarters of a century to Woodworth—why the motor-skills area did not lead a revolt against stimulus–response accounts of behavior. This question raises important issues that are relevant to the emergence of the process-oriented approach adopted here and more generally in the motor behavior area. Posing it allows us some insight into changes in the area that have come about.

There are several factors that are specially relevant to this discussion of why the motor skills area has had a minor impact in behavioral psychology. Firstly, the motor behavior area has stressed the applied rather than the theoretical. Adams (1971) puts it plainly when he points out that the investigators of skill have approached their topic back to front. He says: "Instead of starting with ideas about the laws and theory of movements and then finding the best situations in which to test them, investigators of skills have often started with tasks that look skillful and, by studying them, hope to arrive at laws and theory (p. 112-113)." Such an approach clearly leads to disconnected pockets of data that are almost impossible to integrate in order to produce general scientific principles. Adams (1971) goes on to point out that the task-centered approach is only justified when specific circumstances of a practical kind require us to understand tasks and the performer's efficiency with them. It is not the way to go about achieving the larger scientific goal of law and theory development.

A second and related factor is that by and large people in the motor-skills area have simply *described* their data and failed to derive general principles from them. The so-called theories that were developed were no more than a paraphrased redescription of the data to be explained (Weimer, 1977). In other words, there was little or no conceptualization of what the data meant. What was clearly needed was a structure within which data could be explained and that would serve to guide experimentation and research. The introduction of this structure did as much as anything to effect a change in approach in the motor-behavior area; an approach that has already been termed *process oriented*. Let us turn now briefly (for the topic is greatly expanded in a later chapter—see Stelmach, Chapter 3) to a discussion of what we mean by the process approach, the factors that brought about its adoption and its broader implications for the study of motor performance, per se.

THE PROCESS APPROACH

Movements are the only means by which we can act and interact with our environment, and to a large degree our movements are defined by environmental constraints. In reaching for a cup, for example, the child must effect a sequence of movements that conforms to the size and shape of the cup and its position in space. At the other extreme, the skilled outfielder in making a catch is constrained in his actions by the spatial and temporal characteristics of the ball. Given the requirement then to meet the environmental demands present in many skill situations, it is not surprising that there has been a good deal of interest in how environmental information is processed and, some would argue, "translated" into a motor response (Welford, 1974). Essentially, the human organism is viewed as a self-regulatory system that is capable of receiving, processing, and transmitting information. This basic information-processing model allows people to ask a number of questions that appear relevant to the acquisition of skill. For example, how is incoming information processed, stored, and retrieved? What information do we ignore and what do we utilize? On what basis do we select the appropriate action? How are movements organized and executed? All these questions (and many more) would seem relevant to understanding the acquisition of skill. If we are to meet the environmental demands imposed upon us, we must be capable of adapting to changing environments. This requires us to detect changes in the environment and regulate our movements accordingly. Error detection and correction would seem to be key mechanisms in achieving this end and feedback regarding movement outcome a crucial learning variable.

But it seems to me that this is only one way of looking at "process," and that in understanding the nature of movement organization and the processes involved in it we should also look at the movement *itself*. In studying the processing of information, motor-behavior researchers are usually interested in manipulating a particular variable—feedback comes easily to mind—and examining its effect on the performance outcome. The principal measure of performance in this case is accuracy, usually expressed as a measure of error from some criterion behavior. It could equally well be speed of reaction and movement. In any case the point is that this score is in itself a product that merely informs us as to the outcome of the movement. If we are to understand the manner in which that outcome was attained, we need to analyze the kinematics of the movement. This is what I would call the "movement process"—an approach that attempts to further understand the underlying organization involved.

At present we have little information on the space-time configuration of movement, or how movement organization changes under various environmental conditions and with learning. One example of the approach that I am trying to convey comes from Brooks' (1974) work with monkeys. Brooks (1974) is a neurophysiologist with a particular interest in understanding how movements are 'programmed' by the brain. This is a very complex problem, as you realize when motor programming is discussed in more detail (see Keele, Chapter 7 and Schmidt, Chapter 8). Brooks' basic question concerned what parameters of the movement, such as extent, intensity, or duration, were preprogrammed in fairly simple movements involving flexing and extending the elbow. Brooks' approach is relatively straightforward. Firstly, he looked at the movements very carefully under different task conditions and came up with criteria for considering a movement programmed. Then, he sought out to record from various brain centers in order to relate their activity to the resulting movements. Using slow elbow movements into target areas specified by visual and auditory cues, but with no visual feedback of the limb, Brooks was able to identify two categories of movement based on their kinematic parameters. Continuous movements (see Fig. 1.5) are classified on the basis that they reach only one velocity peak and, diagnostically, only one zero crossing of the acceleration trace. This type of movement was exhibited by well-trained monkeys in stable task situations. Discontinuous movements (see Fig. 1.5) in contrast were made in successive "steps," which thus created several velocity peaks and crosses of the zero line on the acceleration trace. Monkeys used discontinuous movements when the task situation had just been changed, or when they were unsure of what was expected of them.

Given these subtle changes in the movement output, Brooks asked the following question: To what extent are continuous and discontinuous movements centrally programmed? Try to follow his logic here. If a well-learned movement of a set amplitude or distance is preprogrammed, withdrawal or insertion of the visual and auditory cues signalling the target area should leave the movement unchanged; the same amplitude should be repeated. In contrast, if a movement is not preprogrammed but depends on sensory feedback, such as the target cues, for its regulation, then it should continue beyond the target waiting for the cues to

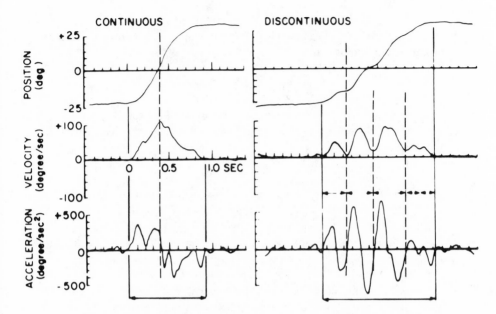

FIG. 1.5. Varieties of self-paced alternating movements made by a Cebus monkey adapted from Brooks (1974) (see text for explanation of continuous and discontinuous movements).

occur, or it should stop short of the target if the cues are inserted earlier than usual. The results were very clear. Animals producing discontinuous movements were "cue" dependent—they overshot or undershot depending on where the cues were inserted—whereas those making continuous movements were impervious to the withdrawal or insertion of visual and auditory input. Brooks went on to examine these different types of movements following cooling of the dentate nucleus in the cerebellum, an important structure involved in motor control.

The message in all this should be apparent: By analyzing the kinematics of the movement—displacement, velocity, and acceleration—Brooks was able to generate logical hypotheses about the underlying movement organization. When he manipulated the variable of target cues, the resultant kinematic analysis informed him of the degree to which the movements were dependent upon that manipulation. He could then infer the relative extent to which the movements were programmed and proceed to the problem of seeking out the responsible brain mechanisms. This analytic and programmatic approach is a common feature of all basic science but has not until recently been the doctrine of motor-behavior research.

The "process" approach then not only involves an understanding of the functional capacities and interactions among receptor, central, and effector mechanisms but also a close analysis of the kinematics of the output. It seems to me that only by employing both "information-process" and "movement-process" approaches are we going to be able to gain fuller insights into the many facets of human motor behavior.

AN EMERGING AREA

Now that we have had a very cursory view of the so-called "process" approach, it might be of some interest—given our historical theme—to consider what the primary stimulants to its adoption were. I must speak in fairly general terms here because not all the motor-behavior area was influenced in the same manner. It can fairly be argued, for example, that some researchers back in the 50s and 60s *were* process oriented, but, in general, compared to the changes that have occurred in the last 8 to 10 years, the impact of their work was small.

Earlier, I indicated that in the past the motor-skills area was devoid of a structure within which experiments could be generated and data interpreted. This state of affairs changed dramatically in 1971 when Adams published his closed-loop theory of motor learning in the *Journal of Motor Behavior*. You will hear much more about the details of this theory, but it is important here to briefly mention its overall importance in bringing about the product to process shift that has occurred in the area. Firstly, Adams' theory was unique to the motor-behavior area in that it dealt with the learning of simple movements and nothing else. Although it had its origins in cybernetic models, such models dealt only with *performance* and failed to incorporate *learning*. Thus, servo theory acted on the hidden assumption that man was at the assymptote or the peak of the performance curve. It did not incorporate basic concepts like learning, transfer, and retention, as attempted in Adams' theory. Secondly, Adams' theory tied hypothetical concepts to experimental data; a feature that was sadly lacking in the past. Thirdly, Adams generated a set of predictions that could be tested and that could lead to the support or rejection of his theoretical premises.

The impact of Adams' theory was considerable and had several implications. As much as anything else, it sent a group of individuals into the laboratory to test the theory. As a result, a solid research effort was initiated that in turn led to refinements and modifications in the theory. In fact, it brought new thinking into the whole issue of how motor skills are acquired, and further and often quite different theoretical viewpoints were the result (Schmidt, 1976; Turvey, 1977).

In addition, Adams' theory served to focus the area on basic issues relevant to information processing. Although experimental psychology had veered toward a cognitive approach and away from behaviorism in the mid 60s (Neisser, 1967), the motor-performance area had not caught up with this trend. With the stimulus provided by Adams' theory and the all-powerful pervasiveness of the feedback concept, investigators began to look much more closely upon models that conceptualized the stages that sensory information passed through on its way to central processing mechanisms, the nature of selective attention, memory, and response programming, etc.

Although Adams' theory was an important factor in the establishment of a process-oriented approach to motor behavior, trends taking place in other disciplines also had an influence. The area of motor control in the domain of neurophysiology had undergone tremendous change as a result of new experimental techniques. In the past, motor control had little to say to those interested in behavior, because much of the work focused on what turned out to be a highly complex unit of analysis: the simple reflex. We, of course, are primarily concerned with voluntary, goal-oriented behavior about which neurophysiology provided virtually no information beyond providing certain types of clinical evidence. However, in the last decade or so, investigators in motor control have been investigating brain mechanisms in normal-behaving animals via techniques that permit single and multiunit recordings from cortical and subcortical areas important in controlling movement. Evarts' work is seminal in this area and his experimental setup is shown in Fig. 1.6 as an example. The monkey is trained to grasp a handle and move it back and forth between two stops. Breaking contact with one stop and contacting the other must be achieved between 400 and 700 grams for the monkey to receive a juice reward. (Monkeys like juice!) Evarts had the monkeys perform this task under different loading conditions that served to oppose the movement. While performing this task, simultaneous recordings from neurons in the monkey's motor cortex were made. The firing of these neurons was tightly coupled to the motor behavior of the animal. Evarts' goal was to find the relationship between the firing of cortical units and the kinetics of the movement. The question was this: When the motor cortex orders a movement, what does it tell the muscles to do? The answer was that cortical activity was most closely related to the amount of force required to produce the movement rather than the displacement of the lever handle. This can be seen in the activity of the motor-cortex unit shown in Fig. 1.6. The tracings show the response to a condition that required a flexion movement against a load of 600 gm. You can see that the unit was almost completely silent when extension against the load was required but highly active in a condition where the load opposed flexion. The bottom trace is an irrelevant movement that shows no relationship to the neurons studied.

Evarts' work is not only important for the findings that he obtained but also because it established a model for many other investigators to use. The experiments by Brooks (1974) on behaving monkeys that I discussed earlier are a case in point. But the implications of Evarts' research extend beyond that, in my opinion. Here at last was a neurophysiological approach that people in motor behavior could relate to. There was no reason whatsoever why similar findings to Evarts' would not be obtained in humans were it possible to do so. In all likelihood the motor cortex of man organizes movements in terms of the forces

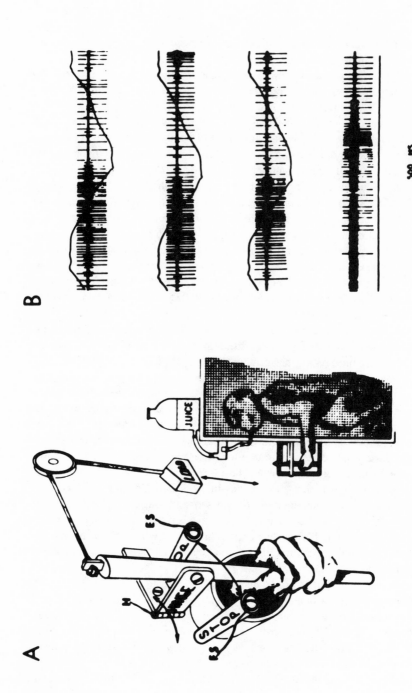

FIG. 1.6. Discharges of a pyramidal cell in the motor cortex in relation to movement (adapted from Evarts, 1967).

required. Evarts' research, then, served to bridge the gap between neurophysiology and motor behavior and helped promote the process approach. The behavior of the normal, unanesthetized animal could be directly related to the functioning of central nervous structures in a quantitative manner.

I have selected emphasized Adams' and Evarts' work because I feel they represent important turning points in the shift toward process. In fact, this assertion—on hindsight—is somewhat insular, for it is evident that investigators elsewhere were already well-attuned to key issues in the control and coordination of movement. In fact, the approach of Nicholai Bernstein in the Soviet Union has stimulated much recent interest in how the motor system regulates its many "degrees of freedom" (muscles, joints). We shall have more to say about this approach—briefly, in the next chapter and in much more depth in the chapters by Turvey and colleagues. But the main message at this point is that cross talk between the disciplines is a crucial element in the advancement of knowledge in human movement.

In the emerging area of motor behavior, as a scientific enterprise by itself, one feature should by now be evident. This is my final point in the present orientation to the following chapters and the topic of motor performance as a whole. I am referring, of course, to the fact that, in the transition from product approach to process approach, the *nature of the questions* has changed dramatically. In an introductory book on human perceptual-motor performance, a natural expectation might have been to obtain information on how best to teach particular athletic skills. Facts on how to select the individuals best suited to particular positions on the team would probably be appreciated also. However, by and large you—as students of motor behavior—have to work out the answers to these problems by yourselves. We are not oblivious to applied questions of this nature, and hopefully some of the information provided here will assist you in decision making. But our major goal in the following chapters is to increase your awareness of the complex issues that make up the study of human motor performance. We are going to discuss some ways in which the issues have been conceptualized and some ways to go about attacking them.

Now let me conclude this introduction with a favorite story of mine. It fills me with a sense of wonderment when I think of the day-to-day skills we employ and take totally for granted. I tell it at this point to make you aware of the tremendous challenge facing those who would attempt to understand the nature of skill acquisition and the development of movement control. The story recounts how, many years ago, a famous scientist to be, Hans–Lukas Teuber, posed a problem in perception to his academic mentor, Karl Lashley. Dr. Lashley was a very important man in his own right and is often regarded as a forerunner in the area of brain research. Lashley was perplexed with the nature of Teuber's problem but offered to supply an answer if his protégé could offer a response to a very simple question: How does man (or woman) flex and extend the index finger? Teuber, in his naiveté, offered to respond with complete assurance at their next meeting in a week's time. As the story goes, Teuber spent many months researching the question—day and night—until he realized that the solution was impossible. There simply was not enough information on how the brain controls movement. He returned, dejected and frustrated, to his mentor, essentially empty-handed for his efforts. Lashley smiled encouragingly and informed him that, just as there was no answer available for such a "simple" motor-control problem, so also was there a lack of knowledge regarding Teuber's problem in perception. There is a message here: We have a long way to go before we can understand even the simplest of motor skills. The following chapters are as much a testimony to this fact as they are a representation of the status of our current thinking.

Postscript. There is a humorous outcome of the Teuber-Lashley dialogue. Throughout the many years that followed this incident, Lashley and Teuber had a secret way of communicating with each other, often in crowded rooms. The sign of recognition from Lashley to Teuber was a "tweak" of the index finger! Teuber was to tell this story many years later to a group of scientists whose main endeavor was to understand the nature of movement control.

ACKNOWLEDGMENT

Preparation of this chapter and this volume was supported by NSF Grant No. SER 77-02986.

REFERENCES

Adams, J. A. A closed-loop theory of motor learning. *Journal of Motor Behavior*, 1971, *3*, 111–149.

Brooks, V. B. Some examples of programmed limb movements. *Brain Research*, 1974, *71*, 299–308.

Chase, R. A. An information-flow model of the organization of motor activity: Part I, Transduction transmission and central control of sensory information. *Journal of Nervous and Mental Disease*, 1965, *140*, 239–251.

Evarts, E. V. Representation of movements and muscles by pyramidal tract neurons of the precentral motor cortex. In M. D. Yahr & D. P. Purpura (Eds.), *Neurophysiological basis of normal and abnormal motor activities*. New York: Raven Press, 1967.

Fitts, P. M. Perceptual-motor skill learning. In A. W. Melton (Ed.), *Categories of human learning*. New York: Academic Press, 1964.

Hull, C. L. *Principles of Psychology*, New York: Appleton, 1943.

Lashley, K. S. The problem of serial order in behavior. In L. A. Jeffries (Ed.), *Cerebral mechanisms in behavior*. New York: Wiley, 1951.

Mayr, O. The origins of feedback control. *Scientific American*, 1970, *223*, 110–118.

Neisser, U. *Cognitive psychology*. New Jersey: Prentice-Hall, 1967.

Schmidt, R. A. The schema as a solution to some persistent problems in motor learning theory. In G. E. Stelmach (Ed.), *Motor control: Issues and trends*, New York: Academic Press, 1976.

Smith, K. U. Feedback mechanisms of athletic skills and learning. In L. E. Smith (Ed.), *Psychology of motor learning*. Chicago: Athletic Institute, 1969.

Turvey, M. T. Preliminaries to a theory of action with reference to vision. In R. Shaw & J. Bransford (Eds.), *Perceiving, acting and knowing*. Hillsdale, N.J.: Lawrence Erlbaum Associates, 1977.

Weimer, W. B. A conceptual framework for cognitive psychology: Motor theories of the mind: In R. Shaw & J. Bransford (Eds.), *Perceiving, acting and knowing*. Hillsdale, N.J.: Lawrence Erlbaum Associates, 1977.

Weiner, N. *Cybernetics: or control and communication in the animal and the machine*. New York: Wiley, 1948.

Welford, A. T. On the sequencing of action. *Brain Research*, 1974, *71*, 381–392.

Woodworth, R. S. The accuracy of voluntary movement. *Psychological Review*, 1899 (Monogr. Suppl. Whole No. 13).

2 Concepts and Issues in Human Motor Behavior: Coming to Grips with the Jargon

J. A. Scott Kelso
Haskins Laboratories and
The University of Connecticut

INTRODUCTION: CHARACTERISTICS OF SKILL

As I mentioned at the beginning of the previous chapter, even the layman has some idea of what the word "skill" means: Most of us are used to observing top-class athletic performance and establishing that as our criterion for skilled behavior. Many of us less-gifted individuals flock to the bookstores to purchase what the star performer has to say about the secrets behind his/her athletic success. The man on the street sees skill—not for what it intrinsically involves—but rather in terms of its results. Thus, athletes are considered highly skilled based on their performance, whether it be a high batting average, a run of victories on the pro golf tour, or a maximum score on the parallel bars in gymnastics.

But I for one am often overwhelmed by the aesthetic qualities of skilled behavior. I can only stare in wonderment at the speed and coordination with which the violinist, Yehudi Menuhin, can move his hands, or the balance and grace displayed by Nadia Comeneche on a beam measuring only 4 inches wide. It's a good idea to keep in mind what we as students of motor behavior are trying to explain, because it forces us to delve deeper into the nature of movement coordination and control. Skill implies spatial precision: The appropriate sets of muscles for a given activity must be ordered correctly. Also, skill has a temporal or timing component; not only do muscles have to function in the proper sequence, but they have to operate at the right time. In reality, however, the spatial and timing components of skill are not really independent, although we may often try to separate them in the laboratory. Actions are performed in a space-time world. David Lee uses examples like intercepting a crossball at soccer or playing a tennis shot as illustrating the fact that skill often involves getting both to the right place *and* at the right time. If the player misses the ball, it makes no sense to attribute his/her error to lack of spatial judgment or to poor timing, as if these could usefully be distinguished. Success in skills can often be achieved by reaching the same place at a different time or a different place at the same time. The errors we make in movement are usually spatiotemporal ones (Lee, 1980).

Moreover, the organization of movements in space and time means nothing if these movements are executed without reference to the environment. The skilled performer can usually accommodate to changing environmental conditions. As a simple example, the wide receiver in football can usually catch the ball under wet and windy as well as dry and sunny conditions. He can, I would argue, adapt his movements—organize them in space and time—to meet the environmental demands of the situation.

Not only is skill characterized by its space–time and adaptability features but also its *consistency* from occasion to occasion. The scratch golfer's swing varies little from shot to shot except to accommodate changes in an essentially static environment. Even then the movement pattern is highly consistent.[1]

These features of skilled movement are familiar to all of us and, of course, are

---

[1]The question arises as to how we might measure some of these components of skill. One way in which motor performance data is unique is that it allows for the quantitative analysis of performance: that is, we can usually determine the accuracy in a task by directly measuring (in cm., say) how far off the target a subject is, since the output is readily observable and measurable. However, one trial performance is usually undesirable, due to unexpected or chance influences on performance; thus, two means of assessing performance have been most commonly used. If we measure accuracy (or conversely the error score) over a number of trials, we can compute the average error (termed constant error or CE) by simply taking the arithmetic average of the signed error scores. If each error is designated x_i, then:

$$CE = \sum_{i=1}^{n} \frac{x_i}{n} \text{ where } n = \text{number of trials}$$

This gives a measure of the average response. For instance a $CE = -2.3$ cm would mean that on the average the subject is 2.3 cm short of the target. However his/her average score does not tell us the consistency (or conversely the variability) of performance. To obtain a measure of this we have to take into account the spread of scores around this average response. The variable error, or VE, which is analogous to the standard deviation of the error scores, is therefore used. If we first compute CE, then VE is simply:

$$VE = \sqrt{\sum_{i=1}^{n} \frac{(x_i - CE)^2}{n}}$$

Thus, knowing both constant and variable error, we now know both how accurate the subject is, on the average, and how consistent, both of which have different interpretations and are normally independent of each other.

far from inclusive. Rather than merely describe what appear to be important elements of skilled movement behavior (although that's an important first step that is often ignored), we seek to understand underlying mechanisms involved in the acquisition of skill and the control of movement. How does skilled performance come about and what does it involve? Let us consider this problem briefly from two basic but interdependent perspectives: One, you might say, has a biomechanical basis where skill and coordination are viewed as a "mastery" by the motor system of the abundant degrees of freedom of the motor apparatus; the other, perhaps, is more in line with the information processing analysis (to be discussed subsequently), where skilled activity is viewed as arising as a result of a complex integration of afferent information—information going to the brain regarding the environment and the consequences of motor activity—and efferent, or outgoing, information, namely what the central nervous system tells the muscles to do. Although this is probably an oversimplistic perspective, I do want you to have some idea of what sensory receptors there are and what they might do, as well as how efferent mechanisms may function. I say "might" and "may" advisedly here, because these are issues that arouse considerable debate among psychologists and neuroscientists. I have called this chapter "coming to grips with the jargon," because that's exactly what you will have to do to follow the chapters that come next.

SKILL FROM A BIOMECHANICAL PERSPECTIVE

As students of motor behavior, perhaps the central problem facing us is how the nervous system comes to regulate the degrees of freedom of the body in the course of a motor act. In later chapters (10 and 11) a more formal definition of degrees of freedom are provided, as well as a more in-depth analysis of this fundamental problem. For now, however, it is sufficient to consider degrees of freedom as the potential variables that must be controlled if we are to function efficiently. It matters not whether we consider these to be muscles, joints, limb segments, or whatever; what is clear is that the brain faces a mammoth problem if it is to control each individual degree of freedom at every point in time during a motor act.[2]

People who study the mechanics or physics of motion have a fairly strict usage of the term *degrees of freedom,* namely, the number of planes of motion possible

---

[2]It is instructive to distinguish between movements and acts, although they are often used interchangeably. Movements are of biological significance in as much as they comprise acts directed at solving problems in the environment. Often we study movements per se independent of their actions. Thus, we may analyze the positioning accuracy of a limb as a movement, but the reaching for a cup (which involves positioning the limb) is an action.

at a joint. For example, the elbow joint involves only one degree of freedom—that on the flexion–extension continuum. The shoulder, in contrast, involves three degrees of freedom for there are three possible modes of motion: flexion–extension, abduction–adduction, and rotation about its own axis. For coordinated movement to occur, these degrees of freedom have to be controlled and regulated. One can readily see that in highly complex movements involving changing posture and transport through the environment, such as the wide receiver catching a ball from the quarterback, the number of degrees of freedom to be controlled is considerable. Furthermore, there is a corresponding increase in the number of kinematic links participating in the activity. (By "kinematic links" we simply mean the rigid moving parts of the body; limbs, fingers, trunk, and so on.)

Clearly, the young child throwing a ball has difficulty not only in regulating muscular forces at the joints but also in sequencing the participating limbs. Yet, with practice the pattern of activity exhibits a smoothness and consistency that suggests the problem has been solved. How might this improvement come about? How are the degrees of freedom managed? One notion, which you will hear much more about later, is that the kinematic links participating in a movement are subdivided into a small number of connected groups or linkages. The idea is that there must be mechanisms capable of reducing degrees of freedom by creating dependencies or linkages among muscular activities at various joints. (Greene, 1972). Turvey and his colleagues (Chapters 10 and 11) refer to these linkages as coordinative structures defined as a functional group of muscles, often spanning many joints that is constrained to act as a single unit.

You recognize the need for this type of postulate when you consider that for any particular movement, such as hitting a golf ball, there is a large number of muscles involved. Moreover, these muscles undergo changes in length continuously. The burden on the brain to directly control each muscle involved would be immense. But if we invoke the coordinative-structure notion, we can see that the problem facing the performer would be reduced to controlling a small number of parameters. Consider locomotion, as an example, which illustrates the coordinative-structure notion rather well. Imagine an animal suspended over a treadmill so that only one limb is in contact with the treadmill belt. This allows the investigators (in this case, Shik & Orlovsky, 1965) to examine the muscular organization of a single limb when it is stepping. Using electromyography, which allows one to measure the electrical activity in muscles, the Russian scientists found that the relative onset times of flexor and extensor muscles in the ankle, knee, and hip joints occurred at the same time regardless of how fast the animal was moving. This same patterning was observed in animals whose spinal cord was sectioned, thus removing the influence of higher brain centers. These findings suggest rather strongly that the stepping pattern of the limbs occurs as a result of systemic relationships among muscles that are established at the spinal cord.

Turvey's (1977) view of coordinative structures is essentially identical to what Russian investigators—who were the first to recognize the importance of the notion—call *synergies,* or, what Peter Greene, who does robotics research, calls *function generators* (Greene, 1972). Gelfand, Gurfinkel, Tsetlin, and Shik (1971) describe the concept as follows:

> In order for the higher levels of the central nervous system to solve effectively the problems of the organization of motor acts it is essential that the number of controlled parameters not be too large and the afferentation required not be too high. The so-called synergies play an important role in the establishment of such conditions of work. It is customary to call synergies those classes of movements which have similar kinematic characteristics, coinciding active muscle groups and conducting types of afferentation [p. 331].

The number of basic coordinative structures or synergies is probably quite small. Nevertheless, they make possible a wide variety of volitional movements. A good example of the coordinative structure style of control in voluntary movements comes from our own work on human interlimb coordination. (Kelso, Southard, & Goodman, 1979). We had subjects, in response to an auditory "go" signal, produce movements of the upper limbs to targets each of which varied in amplitude and precision requirements. Thus, the left limb, for example, would move to an easy target (short amplitude, large target size), whereas the goal of the right limb was to strike a difficult target (long amplitude, small target size). A relationship known as Fitts Law (see chapter by Keele for many more details) predicts that for single-limb movements the easy target should be reached first; that is, movement time should be much shorter for the easy than the difficult target. All I'm saying here is that if a large object is close to the starting position of my hand I should be able to pick it up in a shorter time than a small object that is far away from me. But what happens when I must do both at the same time? The brain has many different muscles to coordinate; how does it accomplish this feat? The main results are shown in Fig. 2.1. The reaction time is simply the time it takes to lift the hand from the home key in response to the auditory bleep. The movement time is the time to hit the target that is sitting on the table in front of the subject. Total response time is the sum of reaction and movement time. Sure enough, in the single-limb case the movement time for the easy target (3 and 4) is much less than the difficult target (1 and 2), regardless of which hand is moving. This effect carries over to the case when both hands are moving to *identical* targets (5 and 6 versus 7 and 8). But look what happens when the two limbs must perform *different* tasks. The hand moving to the easy target slows down, and the hand moving to the difficult target speeds up a little. In fact, the movement times for both limbs are now fairly similar (compare 9 and 12 against 10 and 11). Humans appear to solve this motor problem by responding with both limbs together such that the targets are struck virtually simultaneously. Moreover, when we examine the patterns of displacement, velocity, and acceleration

Total Response Time	Movement Time	Reaction Time	Left Target	Home Keys	Right Target	Reaction Time	Movement Time	Total Response Time
				• •	1 ▯	218	159	377
371	151	220	▯ 2	• •				
287	82	205	4 ▢	• •				
				• •	▢ 3	218	78	296
308	89	219	6 ▢	• •	▢ 5	224	85	309
403	166	237	▯ 8	• •	7 ▯	240	169	409
393	155	238	▯ 10	• •	▢ 9	246	133	379
383	140	243	12 ▢	• •	11 ▯	240	158	398

FIG. 2.1.   Mean reaction time, movement time, and total response times for single-and two-handed movements varying in amplitude and precision requirements (from Kelso, Southard, & Goodman, 1979).

(kinematics) over time for two-handed movements of unequal difficulty, as shown in Fig. 2.2, we see that even though the limbs move to different spatial positions at different speeds (i.e., the height of the curve for the difficult target is greater than for the easy target) they reach peak velocity and acceleration almost in perfect synchrony. Thus, we see in volitional two-handed skill a very nice example of what Gelfand et al. (1971) argue for: The brain solves this rather complex problem by keeping the relative timing between the two limbs constant. Essentially, the number of controlled parameters is kept at a minimum, such that synchronicity between the two limbs is preserved. Note that I am not claiming that the performer cannot break down these types of timing constraints with practice. What I have simply shown is how the brain likes to handle problems that require coordination among many muscles. Presumably, a large number of motor tasks—such as playing the piano—requires the hands to perform in an independent rather than tightly coupled manner. In the broader perspective, therefore, highly skilled performance might be viewed as a release from the type of temporal invariance exhibited in the Kelso et al. (1979) studies.

Nevertheless, these data do suggest that skill acquisition involves the development of functional synergies or coordinative structures that serve to reduce the number of variables requiring individual control. The teacher observing the learning of a new skill, for example, is well aware of the jerky, uncoordinated movements that characterize first attempts. Within the present view of skill learning, the performer is "curtailing" the degrees of freedom via completely immobilizing some joints (which later are used when the skill is performed expertly) and restricting the range of motion of some other joints. This is because he or she lacks the capability of controlling the degrees of freedom in the manner

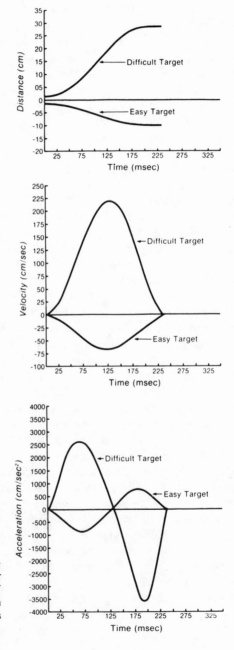

FIG. 2.2. The pattern of displacement, velocity, and acceleration over time for two-handed movements of unequal difficulty obtained from single-frame kinematic analysis (frame rate, 200 frames per second).

demanded by the skill. It follows therefore that increasing skill level involves a lifting of the ban on degrees of freedom (to use Bernstein's 1967 phrase). As Fowler and Turvey (1978) point out, increasing the number of controllable degrees of freedom is synonymous with improvement in skilled performance.

The basic message behind what I've said here is that control of each individual degree of freedom in an activity in which many are involved is not necessary. Nature would not have found this an economic solution for the control of activity. Coordination may be reduced to the problem of marshalling appropriate functional synergies. More precisely, coordination may be thought of as the process of *discovering* how the variables in a very complex system are related for solving particular problems, such as riding a bicycle or learning to speak.

Let me conceptualize the distinction that we can usefully make between terms like *control, coordination,* and *skill*[3] that are often used synonymously. Imagine you have a system in which there are variables whose values can vary along any particular dimension. If you want a concrete example, consider the muscles of the leg. Let's call these muscles, not by their anatomical names, but simply a, b, c, d, and e (there are more than five muscles in the leg, but that's not crucial for the incipient argument). We need to know how a, b, etc. are coordinated in a given action, such as kicking a ball. In other words, *coordination* involves discovering the function that relates these variables in such a way that the act of kicking is possible. Coordination, then, may be defined as the function that constrains the potentially free variables into a behavioral unit, F (a,b,etc.). How is control different from coordination? Even though we've defined a function relating the variables, we have said nothing about which variables to parameterize and which to leave alone in the chosen act of kicking. Control may be thought of as the process by which we assign *values* to the variables in the function. Thus, in the control of the leg movement for kicking, certain variables (e.g., a and b) may have to be contracted with a great deal of force, whereas other variables are not directly regulated. We may view control in notational format as F (a,b,c,d,e), where a and b are the variables that are controlled in a coordinated system. Note that what we have thus far is a function constraining how the variables are linked together (coordination) and a way of parameterizing that function (control). What then do we mean by skill? As I mentioned at the beginning of this chapter, skill is characterized by such things as spatiotemporal precision, adaptability, and consistency. But what principle "sits behind," as it were, these features of skill? Although we can assign values to the variables in the function that we've defined, there is nothing that says these values are the appropriate ones for superior performance. Skill, we can argue, involves exactly that: it requires that the *optimal* value be assigned to the controlled variables. The

---

[3]I thank Peter Kugler for discussions on this issue. A much more detailed account of this conceptual analysis as applied to skill development may be found in Kugler, Kelso, and Turvey (1982) and Kelso, Holt, Kugler, and Turvey (1980).

word "optimal" here is obviously task defined. In the highly skilled long-distance runner, the optimality criterion involves contracting the appropriate muscles such that metabolic demands are kept to a minimum. In weight lifting we attribute the word "skill" to the individual who can assign maximal force to the muscles in a coordinated manner. In the tightrope walker the optimality criterion for skilled behavior surrounds the issue of postural stability, and so on.

Although the foregoing discussion, I believe, is conceptually useful, it may be helpful to think of practical implications. One that immediately fits in with this perspective comes from the field of physical therapy or rehabilitation. The use of a prosthetic arm requires that we rediscover the function relating the muscles of the limb, something that we acquired at a very young age when we first reached and grasped for objects. The act of grasping itself requires not only that we activate the appropriate muscles (control) but also that we assign to them the *correct* contraction values (skill). Otherwise, like the "bionic man" whose arm has been maltreated, we could crush the object that is grasped or drop it on the floor. The task of the rehabilitator—if this analysis is useful—follows the logical progression of coordination—control—skill. Clearly, control subsumes coordination and skill subsumes both.

SKILL: THE ROLE OF INFORMATION

The organization of skill involves more than the use of functional synergies, at least as I have developed the concept thus far (Chapters 10, 11, and 12 go into many more of the details). I have yet to say anything about what role *information* plays in motor activity. Much of what we do is regulated in terms of the visual context of the movement (e.g., whether there is an obstruction in our path as we locomote through the environment), and by how we "feel" the movement itself. Moreover, in some psychological and neurophysiological circles, there is a notion that we use not only *feedback* but also *feedforward* information; that is, there are methods that the nervous system employs to prepare the system for the impending consequences of activity—ways in which the system is set up or "tuned." This last idea is still somewhat speculative, but you should be aware of its potential importance and the fact that a good deal of research has been generated in search for the central nervous structures involved, as well as how feedforward mechanism(s) work. I shall discuss these various sources of potential information for the performer in what follows, but, firstly, I want to tell you something about how it is thought muscles are controlled, and how the sensors in muscle—proprioceptors—seem to function.

Proprioception—Muscle Receptors.   As you have already realized, the essential property of a feedback control system is that there is a flow of information from the thing controlled to the device that controls it. This flow of information allows for continuous adjustment of the control system to accommodate the changing conditions of the control task. Receptors in the muscle, called muscle spindles, seem well-suited for this type of control function and play an important role in the control of muscle length.

In Fig. 2.3 you can see a diagram of the muscle spindle and its relationship to the main muscle. For simplicity, you can see only one motoneuron (called an alphamotoneuron because of its size and because it innervates the main muscle), one extrafusal fiber (the main muscle), and one intrafusal fiber. In reality, of course, whole populations of these elements are involved in each muscle and, in all honesty, we have little idea about their combinatorial properties. Note however, that the intrafusal fiber runs parallel to the main muscle and contains the proprioceptive organ that we're interested in—the muscle spindle. Because of this parallel feature between the two fibers, the muscle spindle is very sensitive to changes in length of the main "workhorse" muscle. A feel for how the spindle seems to work can be gained by imagining a load being placed on the main muscle. It's as if my arm were outstretched and someone hung a bucket of water on it. Because the muscle spindles are attached in parallel, they, like the main muscle, are also stretched. Little sensory endings in the middle of the intrafusal fibers (the equatorial region) are highly responsive to stretch, and they send out an afferent feedback signal to the spinal cord via a large sensory nerve (called the 1A afferent). These sensory neurons synapse or connect in the spinal cord with alphamotoneurons, which carry an outgoing, efferent signal to the main muscle leading to an increase in the force of contraction. The larger muscle force will counteract the extra weight, tending to move the mass back to its former position by restoring the muscle to its original length. If I'm lucky—and by virtue of the fact that this type of special mechanism exists—I shall not drop the bucket and its contents.

The example is intended to show how the length-control system functions as an automatic regulator that quickly compensates for disturbances.[4] But the sensory endings in the spindle are not merely sensitive to passive muscle stretch. The efferent output of the spinal cord also consists of nerve axons of much smaller diameter, called gammamotoneurons. These neurons are influenced by higher brain centers and supply efferent signals to small bundles of contractile muscle fibers inside the spindle. Their contration results in stretching of the central portion of the spindle where the primary endings are located and causes the receptor to discharge more rapidly. Thus, the muscle spindle is under efferent, gamma control as well as being a sensor. What advantages might such a system have? Imagine we wanted to change the length of the muscle to some desired

---

[4]More recent evidence suggests that it is not just muscle length alone that is regulated by the neuromuscular system. Rather, it is the *ratio* of muscle length to the tension produced by the muscle or stiffness. The arguments for this notion are a little more complicated than the simple length-control system I have discussed here. The student interested in pursuing this issue, namely, "what are the regulated variables of the neuromuscular system?," could make a useful start by referring to Houk (1978).

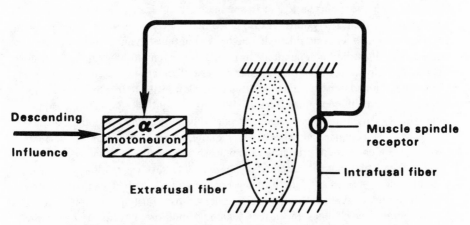

FIG. 2.3. A simplistic diagram for the control of muscle length (see text for explanation).

state (see Fig. 2.4). The alphamotoneurons can be activated to yield appropriate muscle contraction under minimal loading. At the same time, for alpha and gammamotoneurons are activated simultaneously (called $\alpha\ \gamma$ coactivation), the gamma motoneurons are excited causing the spindle to fire more rapidly at the *same* muscle length. This results in a large feedback signal (via the 1A afferent), which reflexly increases the output of the alphamotoneurons. As a

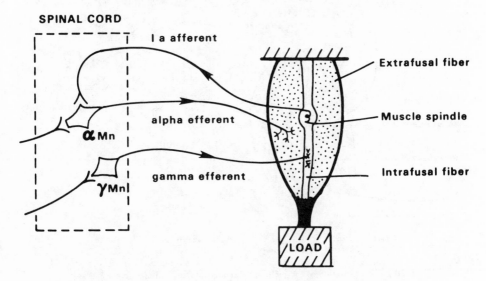

FIG. 2.4. A more expanded version for the control of muscle length illustrating alpha–gamma coactivation.

result, the muscle shortens and its spindle decreases its frequency of firing, until eventually the new muscle length is obtained.

There are, then, two pathways through which the central nervous system may bring a muscle to its desired length: one by way of the alphamotoneurons and the other by way of the gammamotoneurons. Each happens to have unique advantages. The alpha system is much faster because there are fewer delays between motor neuron and muscle. Gamma outputs are slower due to transmission delays in slowly conducting gamma efferents. Why, you might ask, has nature designed the two systems to be coactivated, but one to be slower than the other?

We might speculate that when we're required to make very rapid movements we use the alpha system primarily, and that where smooth, continuous control is required gamma inputs are employed. Some people have argued that alpha activation quickly brings the length of the muscle "into the right ballpark," after which gamma activation "fine tunes" the length by adjusting the alpha activity to accommodate changes in current loading conditions (Arbib, 1972). More broadly, the alpha system seems to get the muscle close to its desired length, but the gamma system is responsible for the fine and very precise control that we

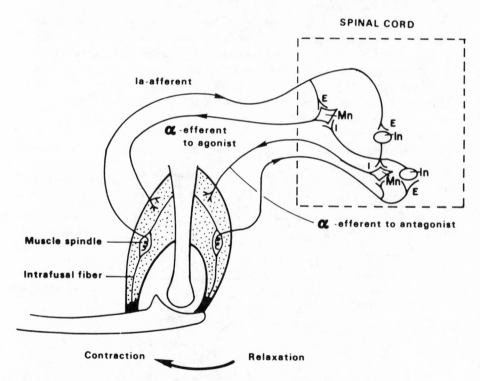

FIG. 2.5. Illustration of the reciprocal relationship between an agonist and antagonist muscle pair (see text for explanation).

know is typical of skilled movement. Let me give you a brief example that appears to corroborate this viewpoint. One of the classical tests neurologists use in patients with suspected brain damage (particularly of the cerebellum) is the finger-to-nose test. The task is to bring your index finger to your nose as rapidly as possible. If our analysis is correct, the alpha system would be used to bring the finger close, whereas the gamma system would perform the fine tuning near the end of the movement. In fact, when a drug is injected that selectively impairs the small gammamotoneurons, the subject hits himself on the nose (Smith, Roberts, & Atkins, 1972)! All this suggests that the dual-control notion, alpha-gamma coactivation, is the way the system works in skills that require fine control.

It's important to recognize however that joint action is controlled by at least one *pair* of muscles. Consider the flexor–extensor pair shown in Fig. 2.5. The angle of the joint obviously depends on how much flexor contraction exceeds extensor contraction and vice versa. It would not be very efficient to have both muscles contract to obtain that difference. For example, if we wanted to reduce joint angle, it would be desirable not only to increase flexor contraction but also decrease extensor contraction. In the figure you see the circuits that automatically effect this joint action. The spindle activity of the flexor muscle not only is responsible for activating alphamotoneuronal activity in its own muscle but also, via inhibitory neurons, decreases the activity of the alphamotoneurons of the antagonist muscle. What we have, then, is a very nice cophasic relationship between pairs of muscles such that when the agonist muscle contracts the antagonist, by virtue of the process of reciprocal inhibition, relaxes. As you can see, receptors in muscles are an intrinsic part of an automatic feedback system that plays an important role in controlling movement.[5] We don't even have to know in any conscious way what such systems are doing. The benefit of having available automatic regulation is that higher brain mechanisms are released from "on-line" monitoring. Thus, they are not burdened with the problem of telling what muscle to contract and at what time. I think you'll agree that performing motor skills would be very difficult indeed if that was the way the system worked.

A question that has interested many investigators and is germane to the issue of the role of proprioception concerns whether muscle spindles provide us with any conscious information about limb position and movement. How do we know where our limbs are in space? Are muscle spindles involved in this function? The old answer to that question seemed to be "no." Muscle spindles are used in the automatic regulation of movement but are not involved in telling us about where our limbs are or how fast they are moving (see Kelso & Stelmach, 1976, for the data relevant to this position). More recent evidence however seems to indicate

---

[5]I have not discussed, by any means, all the details regarding muscle receptors and their neural functions. To those interested in finding out more, I suggest Matthews (1972) as representing one of the most rigorous analysis of muscle receptors and their functional significance.

that muscle spindles can perform this function at least under certain experimental conditions. (Whether they do in normal movement is another issue that has yet to be satisfactorily demonstrated.) For example, Matthews and Simmonds (1974) examined motion perception in five subjects who had an ailment called carpal-tunnel syndrome. This debilitation arises because the carpal tunnel at the wrist compresses the nerves going into the hand, and thus the patient loses both sensory and motor function. Anyone lifting heavy weights on a regular basis tends to be prone to carpal-tunnel syndrome. It's an occupational hazard of coal miners in Wales. What Matthews and Simmonds did was this: They opened the carpal tunnel at the wrist under local anesthesia and then pulled on the relevant muscle tendons. The hand was stabilized while the tendon was pulled to and fro with fine forceps, so as to stretch the muscle without moving the finger. As we have already discussed, stretch on the muscle activates muscle spindles, and, if such information accesses consciousness, people should feel it. This is precisely what happened: All subjects perceived that their finger moved when the muscle tendon was pulled. Matthews and Simmonds interpreted this finding as revealing that muscle spindles are potentially capable of providing information about limb movement.

There are other experiments that seem to show the same thing. For example, placing a vibrator on the biceps tendon at a frequency of 100 cycles per sec elicits an involuntary reflex contraction of the muscle. Physiologists have shown that this occurs as a direct result of the stimulation of the large 1A sensory afferent fibers from muscle spindles that are very sensitive to vibration. Imagine that the subject is asked to track the position of the vibrated arm. He/she will not be able to do so very accurately; in fact, the subject typically perceives the arm as more extended than it actually is. Obviously, this does not happen in the absence of vibration. Moreover, when the experimenter prevents the vibrated arm from flexing, subjects experience a feeling of extension even though none could actually occur. These illusory effects seem to illustrate that muscle spindles can be a source of information about the position and movement of limbs (see Craske, 1977, for further demonstrations of vibratory effects).

Proprioception—Joint Receptors. Nevertheless, the classical view regarding how we sense position and movement of our limbs is that there are receptors in the joint itself that perform this function. As we shall see, the evidence is no longer convincing for this position, and this fact, coupled with new findings on muscle receptors, has led to revised thinking on the functional role of joint receptors. Joint receptors are mechanoreceptors that respond to mechanical forces like tension, pressure, torque, and so on that are exerted at the joint capsule. Depending on their mechanical properties, joint receptors may be classified as slowly or rapidly adapting. Rapidly adapting receptors fail to respond after their initial response to a stimulus, whereas stimulation of a slowly adapting receptor in the cat's knee joint, on the other hand, leads to a discharge of impulses that persists for some time. In Fig. 2.6 you see three curves from such a receptor illustrating the neuronal response to three different movements all of the same velocity. Each curve has three distinctive stages: When stimulation—twist on the joint, for example—exceeds some threshold value, a large discharge, called the dynamic frequency, occurs that is directly related to the movement phase. The second stage portrays a decline in the frequency of firing—called the decay state—that is unaffected by the magnitude of the movement. The third stage is the steady-state phase that lasts for a long time and appears to be a function of limb position, because different positions lead to different steady-state frequencies.

Figure 2.6 does not tell us anything precise about how steady-state values relate to limb position. The most popular model illustrating this relationship is

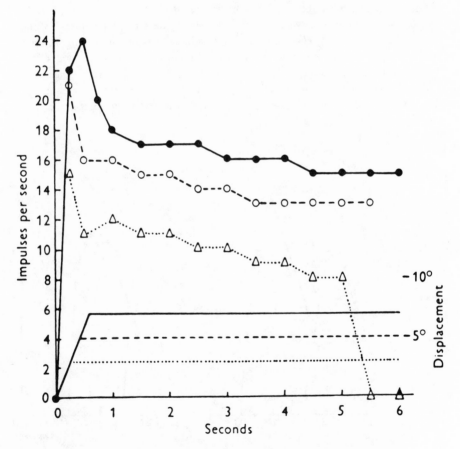

FIG. 2.6. Neuron discharge from a slowly adapting receptor in the knee joint of the cat (adapted from Boyd & Roberts (1953). See text for further explanation.

shown in Fig. 2.7. I call it the "angular specificity" model, and it's based on Skoglund's (1956) data showing that joint receptors can have a narrow range of sensitivity of around 15 to 30 degrees. Thus, as the limbs move through particular joint angles, particular joint neurons fire. The peaks in activity that can be observed in Fig. 2.7 are the maximum response of a specific slowly adapting receptor in the cat's knee joint. This evidence leads one to a "bionic-man" view of the regulation of limb position and movement. Impulses discharging at certain rates for certain angles are continually returning to the central computer in the brain providing information about the movement and position of the limb.

But the story is not quite that simple. A model stands or falls on the basis of the data that support or negate it. The recent work on joint receptors completely refutes the angular specificity model that I have presented previously (see Kelso, 1978, for a more thorough review). In fairness, it is not that Skoglund's data are totally incorrect, but rather that they misrepresent the broader picture of limb-movement sensitivity that we seek. The most likely reason for the demise of the angular specificity view is that it was based on inferior sampling of joint afferent neurons. The first to question the original findings were Burgess and Clark (1969), who found that the majority of joint afferent neurons in the cat knee joint (and they sampled 209) were activated only at "marked flexion" or "marked extension." Only a very small proportion fired at intermediate joint angles.

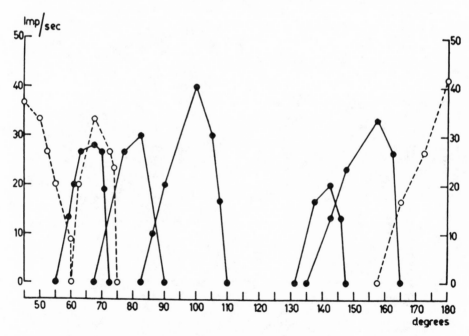

FIG. 2.7.   Neuronal response of eight slowly adapting receptors in the knee joint of the cat from Skoglund (1956) (See text for further explanation).

In an even more thorough study, Clark and Burgess (1975) used a method that allowed them to study in detail a large sample of unmyelinated fibers in an articular nerve, and hence every slowly adapting receptor activated in the midrange of movement was examined. It turned out that all these midrange fibers were very sensitive to a drug—succinylcholine choride—that is selectively excitable to muscle spindles. When the same drug was injected into those fibers that fired at the extremes of the movement range (i.e., possible joint receptors), there was no response. Moreover, when the muscle inserting on the cat's knee (the popliteus muscle) was carefully removed, bit by bit, the response to stretch and the drug were completely eliminated. Thus, it transpires that with improved research techniques the midrange responses were actually due to muscular and not joint receptors.

In fact, a more recent study by Grigg (1976) supports the foregoing perspective rather well, in showing that joint afferent neurons in the cat's hindlimb respond to activation of the quadriceps (thigh) muscle. Figure 2.8 shows this relationship beautifully. The joint is held steady in a fixed position, yet the

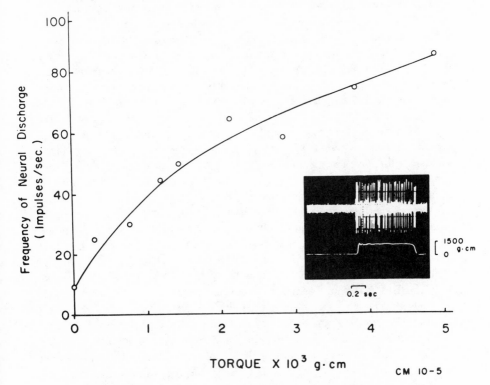

FIG. 2.8.   Neuronal response of a slowly adapting receptor in the knee joint of the cat to a torque developed by activating quadricep muscles. Inset depicts the response of the neuron at one level of torque (from Grigg, 1976).

response in the medial articular nerve is tightly coupled to the force of muscular contraction. Again, these results are not consistent with the simpler view, that there is a population of receptors located at some strategic point in the joint that is capable of providing a signal that varies only as a function of joint angle and that does not change with the changing motor output that is required for different loading conditions.

All the evidence I have discussed thus far is physiological; no one has yet recorded from *human* joint afferents, and it is often tenuous to extrapolate from animal data to human behavior. Fortunately, all that I have said thus far regarding the inability of joint receptors to signal limb position and movement can be supported by human findings. It is unfortunate in another sense, in that the data are obtained from individuals suffering from chronic arthritis who have had to have their finger joints replaced. The interesting aspect of this surgical procedure is that the joint capsule—the hypothesized "seat" of joint receptors for position and movement—is completely removed and the joint surfaces replaced. The patient therefore provides a unique opportunity to examine motor performance in the absence of the joint capsule. How well do they locate their fingers in space? The data that you can see in Fig. 2.9, obtained shortly after the operation in 13 patients indicates that they perform very well indeed. Patients were asked to make a movement of the index finger to a certain position and then to reproduce either the movement to the same position (location) or to reproduce the actual amplitude of the original movement from a different starting position (distance). As you can see in the figure, it is clear that the location condition is superior to distance, and that the effect is even greater at the extreme starting position (the original starting position was 20 deg. flexion of the index finger, and the starting position for the reproduction was either 5 deg. $[SP_1]$ or 15 deg. $[SP_2]$ beyond the original starting position, i.e., 15 deg. or 5 deg. flexion). The location condition, then, makes smaller errors than the amplitude condition (see Footnote 1 for an explanation of how errors are computed), but, more importantly, a comparison with normal performance (not shown in Fig. 2.9) reveals that they perform equally well; that is, the mean absolute error for unoperated individuals in the same task was 4.44 deg. in a condition where starting position was not altered from trial to trial (see Kelso, Holt, & Flatt, 1980 for details).

That such accurate performance can obtain in patients who lack slowly adapting joint afferents certainly supports the physiological data that I have reviewed, indicating that joint receptors are not suitable candidates for coding limb position. But what are the alternatives to joint receptors? It seems unlikely that tactile information is sufficient to account for the performance of joint replacement patients. Experiments performed many years ago that examined the positioning of limbs showed no disturbing effects of removing touch information by anesthetization. Other possible candidates are muscle receptors that are largely unaffected by joint replacement in the finger. Certainly, the evidence that I discussed in the previous section, though not entirely conclusive, supports that view.

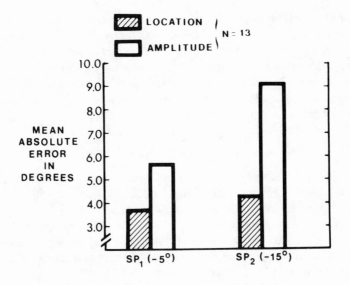

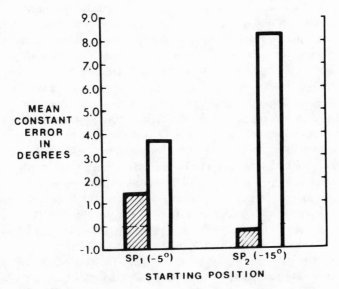

Fig. 2.9. Mean absolute (unsigned) and constant (signed) error for location and amplitude conditions in joint replacement patients as a function of changing starting position (from Kelso, Holt, & Flatt, 1980. See text for further explanation).

In summary, as far as proprioception is concerned, we know that: (1) Muscle receptors seem to be important in the control of movement based on the gamma efferent–muscle spindle linkage; (2) muscle receptors also seem to be capable of providing, at least under certain conditions, conscious information about limb movement; and (3) joint receptors, as revealed by recent physiological and behavioral work, seem unsuited for the task of relaying position and movement information to the central nervous system.

A Dynamic Alternative to "On-Line" Proprioception

The evidence that I have discussed thus far certainly indicates that proprioception plays an important role in the control of movement and hence figures prominently in skilled behavior. But do we have to monitor it all the time? Some of the notions you will hear about later (e.g. in Chapter 5) suggest that during the production of movement we continually compare proprioceptive information about limb position to an internalized memory for the movement (which may be at different stages of development depending on how skilled we are). When we have a match between the two, instructions are sent to the limb to tell it to stop. Now the "angular specificity" view of joint receptor function—which I have refuted here—was very compatible with this conceptualization of how we get the limb to a desired position. I want to briefly introduce an alternative notion of this process, one that is much more economical in terms of the amount of neural computation involved, and one that is much more congruent with recent data, including the joint replacement work discussed earlier. The idea is simply to use a physical system—the mass-spring—to model how limbs reach specified positions even when important sources of feedback are not available and even when the initial conditions change continually. The original proponent of this view was Bernstein, but it was Fel'dman (1966) who developed it into a viable theoretical viewpoint. Fel'dman argued that the nervous system "sets" the desired position by adjusting the length-tension relationships of the muscles involved. This notion is illustrated in Fig. 2.10 for a pair of muscles that normally work together, namely, an agonist and an antagonist (Hollerbach, 1980). Imagine wanting to change the desired position of the arm by changing the angle of the elbow joint. When the arm is in a static position, a state of equilibrium exists between the forces acting about the joint. At length L_0, for example, the innervation rate (the amount of activity in the alphamotoneurons) is x_1 for the biceps and y_1 for the triceps. If the innervation rate of the biceps is changed to x_2, a different length-tension curve is selected, and the desired position changes to L_1. Assuming that the amount of delay in developing tension in the muscle is negligible, the arrow in Fig. 2.10 indicates the tension course. There is an isometric development of tension from P_0 to P_2 followed by a reduction in tension to P_1, where the balance between the tensions in agonist and antagonist occurs. The curves shown in Fig. 2.10 lead to a model of localization as the outcome of parameterizing the resting

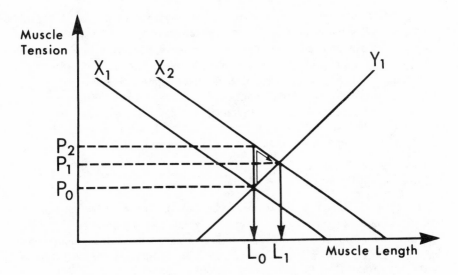

FIG. 2.10. The control of limb position seen as an equilibrium point of intersecting length-tension curves of agonist (X_1 and X_2) and antagonist (Y_1). The equilibrium position shifts from L_0 to L_1 when the rate of alphamotoneuronal activity in the agonist is raised from X_1 to X_2 and the rate remains the same in the antagonist (Y_1). See text for further details.

length of a mass-spring system. The slope of the curves represents the spring constant or stiffness of the spring, and the variable resting length corresponds to the selection of firing rate.

The important point to grasp from the foregoing discussion may not really rest with the details of agonist-antagonist muscle contractions, specification of stiffness values for each individual muscle, and so on. Rather it is that a number of characteristics of movement share behaviors qualitatively like a mass-spring system. For example, a major characteristic of a mass-spring system is its *equifinality;* that is, you can stretch the spring to whatever length you wish (within limits), but it will *always* return to its resting length. Thus, despite changes in initial conditions—as occurred in the joint replacement experiment when we changed the starting position of the finger—a mass-spring system will always reach an invariant final position or equilibrium point, depending on the *system's* dynamic parameters of mass, stiffness, and damping. The beauty of such a system is that there is no need for ongoing detection and comparison of feedback to some desired state; a collective of muscles viewed as a mass-spring system, has only to be parameterized or "tuned," and the desired behavior, including the trajectory of the limb, is closely approximated by mechanical principles (cf. Kelso, Holt, Kugler, & Turvey, 1980).

Clearly, this type of dynamically oriented approach has many implications not least for the design of robots. Thus, one might try—as many have—to control the position of a robot arm by continually comparing its current state, based on feedback with some desired state coded in the robot's central computer. The "dynamic" approach—of which the mass-spring model is an example—argues that we should model the robot arm after the biological arm and exploit its constraints using mechanical principles. This latter approach promises to reduce the burdensome computational requirements of the former style of control. Moreover, it is based on principled grounds, namely, the intrinsic properties of joint-muscle linkages, and hence is a more likely candidate for a viable approach to the control of movement and a broader understanding of skill.

Some Examples of the Role of Vision

Propriception is obviously not the only type of information important for controlling and coordinating movement. Most of us would have little trouble in believing that vision supplies an important source of information for the learning of motor skills. For example, in learning a free-throw shot in basketball we have vision to inform us of the success of our attempts. Or in ten-pin bowling the adjustments to our planned activity are obviously based on the number of pins still standing. Visual information then can provide us with knowledge of movement outcome—we missed the basket or scored—and it can also tell us something about how we are to prepare future actions—knock pins 7, 4, and 2 down to complete the frame. All this is intuitive; research doesn't have to tell us these things; we know them from everyday experience. But there are many questions about the nature of visual information processing and its relationship to the organization of skilled activity that we know a good deal less about. For example, what are the critical features of the optic array that we use for the control of activity? How does visual information specify particular action sequences? How is vision integrated with the other perceptual systems? Efforts to answer each of these questions and many others relevant to skilled activity would require much more than can be said here. Some of these issues are addressed in more detail in the following chapters, particularly the crucial relationship between vision and action (Chapter 12). For present purposes, however, and to familiarize you more fully with the role of visual information in the control of activity, I shall discuss three issues that have directed research. I have chosen these particular issues as much for their innovative and interesting approach to problems of vision, as well as the fact that they have important implications for those of us involved in understanding movement.

The first issue concerns the role of vision in the ongoing guidance and regulation of an extended motor sequence. The second addresses the importance of vision in the development of a very basic skill: standing in infants. The third issue involves understanding the relationship between vision and the other important modality for movement: proprioception. This discussion allows me to speculate briefly on why it is that vision seems to be a dominant source of information for skilled movement and at the same time allows me to introduce the concept of *feedforward*.

Example 1: Visual Guidance in Skilled Long Jumpers

A skilled long jumper can strike the takeoff board extremely accurately. After a 40 m. run, for example, to take off 10 cm. from the board represents an accuracy of 0.25%. How is this accuracy achieved? Many coaches stress the importance of developing a stereotyped run-up that usually consists of an acceleration phase, a "coasting" phase, and concludes with the "gather," a procedure designed to get the athlete into a good posture for the jump, whereas at the same time maintaining speed. This stereotypical pattern may be thought of loosely as a "program" for the activity; that is, a rough prescription of the sequence of actions involved. This is not say that feedback is not also used, for clearly the athlete has to adjust to varying environmental conditions as well as maintain balance and keep on a straight run. Nevertheless, one might argue that given the development of a good consistent run-up or well-learned motor program, little adjustment needs to be made to strike the board on or near the target.

In the following study, however, it is shown quite clearly that vision is intimately involved in the extremely difficult task of striking the take-off board at the highest possible speed and in the correct posture (Lee, Lishman, & Thomson, 1977). This was a somewhat surprising result, for the coaches of the three international-class long jumpers who participated in the study had not observed them making visual adjustments in stride pattern when approaching the board. Indeed, Lee et al. note that both the coaches and the athletes themselves were somewhat skeptical about the possibility that visual adjustments were being made. Figure 2.11 shows the mean stride pattern of one of the athletes obtained by single-frame film analysis. The strides are numbered backwards from the board with stride number 1 being the stride to the board. The points represent the mean stride lengths over six jumps and the vertical bars the variation of the stride lengths. You can see that during the accelerative phase of the run-up the stride lengths are reasonably consistent across runs and progressively increase in magnitude as the athlete progresses down the track. At about stride 10 the athlete appears to enter the coast phase (i.e., there is no further increase in stride length). She seems to have started her gather phase at stride 6, which tends to be slightly longer than those preceding it. Moreover, the gather stride pattern becomes most pronounced as she approaches the board, with alternating long and short strides. It is apparent that visual adjustments are made over the last three strides with about 50% of the total adjustment made on the last stride. (The number printed over each stride is an estimate of the percentage of the total adjustment that was

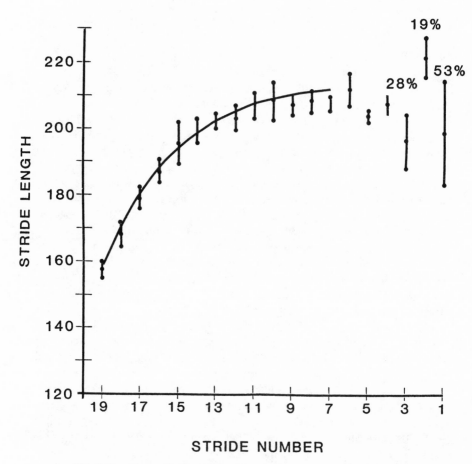

FIG. 2.11. Mean stride length of an Olympic-class long jumper in approaching
the board. The strides are numbered backwards from the board with stride number
1 being the stride to the board (adapted from Lee, Lishman, & Thompson, 1977).
See text for further details.

made on that stride.) This finding is supported strongly by the data on footfall
position that show a steady increase as the athlete runs down the track until she is
a few strides from the board, when there is a rapid decrease. It seems reasonable
to conclude with Lee et al. that athletes visually adjust their final strides to
coincide with the take-off board.

Two other important practical implications emerged from this research.
Firstly, it was shown that the motor pattern of the "run-through" was quite

different than the motor pattern of the jumps themselves. The goal of the run-through is to practice the approach to the board for the actual jump situation and to also enable adjustments to be made on the starting position to suit external conditions. The coaching assumption here is that the run-through mimics the real thing. But this turned out not to be the case, for the patterns of adjustment in the gather phase of the run-throughs and jumps were often dissimilar. Clearly, then, this is the phase that coaches should pay close attention to if they want to achieve full benefits from the run-through procedure. The second implication is that it would seem appropriate to adjust the start mark for the jump not on the basis of the error at the board but rather on the basis of the error soon before the gather phase. It is this error that the athlete has to compensate for during the final strides of the run-up. If the error is too large, then it may not be easy to adjust it without totally disrupting the gather pattern. This in turn would have an ultimate effect on the jump itself. Lee et al., for example, reported that the athletes in their study reported having to ''reach'' for the board or ''squeeze'' to prevent overrunning it.

The Lee et al. study, then, is a nice example of how research in the field, using real-life nonlaboratory skills, can provide important insights into the informational support for activity. Not only is this research of applied value to coaches and athletes alike, but it also has theoretical significance demonstrating the important role of vision, even in highly practiced situations that at first blush do not seem to require it.

Example 2: The Role of Vision in Learning to Stand

In any discussion of receptor systems—within an information-processing model, for example—we tend to assume that each system serves a unique role. But some theorists, such as J. J. Gibson (1966, 1979), correctly point out that this is not necessarily the case. If exteroception involves the pickup of information of external events in the environment and proprioception the pickup of internal information regarding one's own actions, then vision not only has an exteroceptive but also a proprioceptive role. Does vision function proprioceptively in the control of very basic activities, such as standing?

At first glance we might answer no to this question. It would seem more obvious that the most sensitive feedback for standing would derive from mechanoreceptors in the joints and muscles and those in the soles of the feet. Our intuitions would probably be wrong, however, as the following study by Lee and Aronson (1974) so clearly reveals. Infants were chosen to investigate this problem because they have only limited experience in standing and walking, and thus their standing posture should be sensitive to manipulations of visual information if it is indeed important. The procedure that Lee and Aronson used was an innovative one based on the following logic. Imagine a child standing in a room whose walls and ceilings can be moved by a suspension system, but whose floor is perfectly stable. Movement of the room toward the child will produce an optical-flow pattern specifying the same type of information as the child moving forward (see Fig. 2.12). Similarly, moving the room away from the child specifies backward movement. From this we can reason, that if the child used vision to maintain posture and the room is moved away from the child, the consequent visual information signalling backward movement should induce compensatory muscle action in the *forward* direction; that is, in order for the child to maintain his/her relationship to the room, forward motion must occur as the room is moved away from the child. Now what, we may ask, is proprioception doing in this situation? Surely, children can use this information to inform them that they are standing still. As we shall see, however, proprioception provides insufficient information for this function.

Seven infants (ranging in age from 13 to 16 months) experienced both forward and backward moving-room conditions, each receiving up to 20 trials. "Positive" responses (that is, if vision is dominant) were those in which the child swayed, staggered, or fell in the direction the room was moved, thus indicating a compensatory adjustment based on the optic-flow pattern arising from the motion of the room. By far the majority of the responses were of this nature, and on a third of the trials the child actually fell over. Furthermore, three of the seven subjects became very distressed, and as a result the experiment had to be curtailed.

What do these results mean? One argument might be that backward positive responses are simply an avoidance behavior in response to the "looming" of the room; that is, the room is coming toward the subject, and there is a natural tendency to fall backwards. But this account does not seem feasible, for there is no reason whatsoever to believe that a similar effect is occurring in forward positive responses where the room is moving *away* from the subject (unless the subject has eyes on the back of his head!). No, the data suggest rather strongly that vision is very important in the development of learning to stand. Remember that veridical ("true") information was available from proprioceptors; yet, in the conflict situation proprioceptive information was overcome by the more potent visual modality.

In retrospect, this interpretation seems quite reasonable. The proprioceptors in joints and muscles of a developing infant must be sensitive to growth changes in body parts, weight gains, and so on to provide precisely calibrated information to the performer. It seems likely that our sensitivity to this information would increase via continual activities that employ these proprioceptors. The young infant has had little opportunity in this regard, and the proprioceptive system is likely to afford only crude information. In contrast, the infant's visual system is more highly developed and consequently more reliable. Furthermore, it is less likely to be influenced by changes in skeletal structure. There seems no reason therefore why vision should not provide the more potent information for the acquisition of basic activities such as standing. One might logically argue, then, that early activities designed to enhance the utilization of proprioceptive informa-

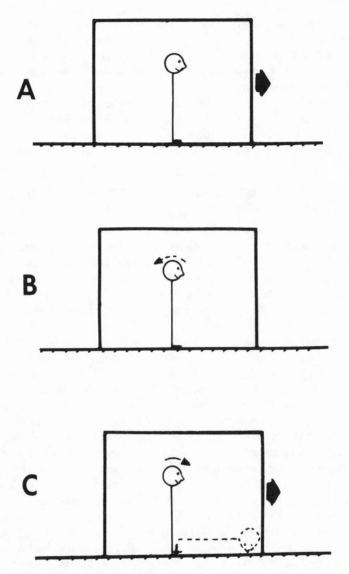

FIG. 2.12.   The moving-room experiment. See text for explanation.

tion would reduce the dependence on vision. For example, Zelazo, Zelazo and Kolb (1972) have found that continuous practice of the stepping reflex in very young infants increases the likelihood of early walking. Furthermore, later studies by Lee and his colleagues using adults as subjects in the moving-room experiment have found similar, but much less pronounced, effects on body sway (Lee & Lishman, 1975). Thus, the adult seems more attuned to the proprioceptive information than the infant. To use a pun, the adult is not as easily swayed by vision as the child.

This finding has interesting implications for it suggests a relative shift as skill develops, from relying on purely exteroceptive information to guide movement, to an increased reliance on proprioceptive information. Indeed, some coaches have attempted to "speed up" this shift in basketball players, for example, by placing goggles that prevent vision of the lower limbs and the ball. The idea, of course, is to dribble the basketball via "feel" and leave the visual system free to specify the positions of other players and direct what tactics are appropriate.

Example 3. When Vision and Proprioception are Available, Which Predominates and Why?

In the Lee and Aronson (1974) standing study, there were strong indications that vision was capable of dominating proprioceptive information. Indeed, there is good reason to believe that in situations where vision and proprioception are both available, we spontaneously attended to vision. For example, Jordan (1972) had novice fencers initiate a fencing move when the foil they were holding was deflected by a mechanical foil, thus giving rise to proprioceptive information. He measured reaction time to initiation of response under: (1) a blindfolded condition where only proprioceptive feedback was available; (2) a bimodal condition where the subject could both see and feel the mechanical foil; and (3) a visual condition in which the subject only watched the mechanical foil. Reaction time to initiation of response was slower in the visual than in the proprioceptive condition (a typical finding), but more interesting was the finding that reaction time in the bimodal condition was 27 milliseconds slower than reaction time in the proprioception only condition. In other words, in a condition where both visual and proprioceptive inputs were available, the subject was biased toward the visual response. The net effect of this was detrimental, of course, for the speed of reaction was decreased. I think the immediate implication of this finding is apparent. If somehow we were capable of ignoring vision and attending strongly to the "feel" of the mechanical foil, we should be able to respond faster. Although this might be a useful strategy in this particular laboratory task, obviously, I am not saying it would be a useful strategy in the skill of fencing. Indeed, we can assume that our ability to pick up visual information from an opponent's movements is crucial to how skilled we are as fencers. But the issue I am trying to address is why vision predominates when one can both see and feel the consequences of one's movements. Proprioception is the "faster" modality, as it were, at least when we have to react to some stimulus. Thus, it might be argued that we are predisposed to attend to vision because it is inherently slower than the other modalities, including audition, for example, But there is a flaw in this viewpoint (Posner, Nissen, & Klein, 1976); vision may indeed be slower when we have to respond to it as a source of *feedback*. As we've seen, however, from Lee's work, vision seldom operates as a feedback modality in the *ongoing regulation of* activity. Rather, it provides information about what activity we should plan in the future; that is, it is more appropriate to talk of vision as a source of *feedforward* to the central nervous system—"tuning" the motor system in an adaptive way so that the environmental demands of the skill can be met. Chapter 12 develops this notion in much more detail. Suffice to emphasize here that vision is the most reliable source of information for the control of activity, and we attend to it naturally because it allows us to plan our activities more effectively. It thus acts as a potent source of feedforward in addition to telling us the results of our actions in its more typical feedback role. The advantage of using vision as a source of feedforward information is probably quite obvious. By using information prior to actually effecting the activity, we can eliminate in large part some of the delays that are inherent in feedback systems. More precisely, feedback operates only after an output has been produced. If this output is faulty, the feedback system may actually be compensating for disturbances that are no longer present! For this reason, it seems desirable for nature to have designed a system that samples information at an earlier stage.

Feedforward Information at Central Levels

As I have intimated previously, the organization of skill requires more than a knowledge of traditional feedback mechanisms. Rather, I have emphasized here the *information support* for activity that is not peculiar to feedback alone. A key role for vision, for example, is to feedforward information for the control system so that the performer can avoid obstacles in the world before bumping into them. But the concept of feedforward may be extended beyond information as it is extrinsic to the performer.[6] Earlier, I emphasized that skill involves a complementarity between efference and afference. Does feedforward play an "efferent" as well as an "afferent" role? More precisely, are there internal signals generated within the CNS that obviate the need for reliance on feedback, and if so what is their relationship to skilled behavior?

According to Evarts (1971), there are indeed well-established circuits in the CNS that involve different neural centers interacting with each other before the occurrence of overt action in the muscles themselves. These internal, feedforward signals have often been viewed collectively as a single concept. For example, notions like "efferent copy," "corollary discharge," and "central efferent monitoring" have often been viewed synonymously, despite the fact that in my

---

[6]I use the word "extrinsic" not in the sense that the information is separate from the actor and the activity. The example from the studies of vision that I reviewed illustrate that visual information is *specific* to the activity being performed. "Extrinsic" is used here merely to draw the comparison between feedforward as it is provided by an exteroceptive modality and feedforward as intrinsic or within the CNS itself.

view they play different theoretical functions. In what follows, I briefly illustrate the hypothetical role of these mechanisms in movement control. I emphasize the word "hypothetical" here; neuroscience has yet to provide hard evidence for these notions and some might question the need for them in any case. Debate and argument, however, are just the stimulants that research requires. The following discussion is as much an attestment to this statement as anything else.

The Efference-Copy Concept. In Fig. 2.13 we can see, in diagrammatic form, the "copy of command," or efference-copy notion. The idea is that when we prepare to move, a copy of the command is sent to some comparison center, where it can be briefly stored and used as a "checking device" for the feedback returning to the system ("reafferent" or response-produced feedback). Theoretically, the utility of efference copy is that it serves as a basis for detection and correction of errors in the motor output. Efference copy may also have a perceptual function. Because the feedforward signal is necessarily tied to movement production, we know that an active rather than passive movement is taking place. So efference copy is a potential mechanism that distinguishes active and passive activity of the system.

Two sources of indirect evidence speak to the efference-copy notion. The first comes from an analysis—done many years ago by von Helmholtz—of eye

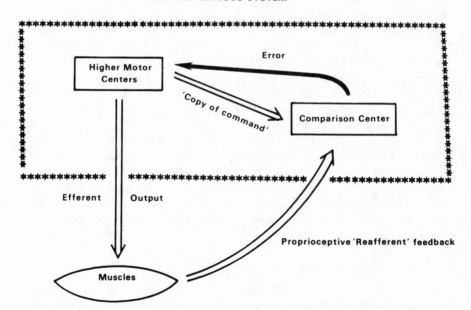

FIG. 2.13. A diagram of the efference copy or copy of command notion of feedforward information.

movement. It's an experiment that you can try yourself. Place your finger on the edge of one eye and move the eyeball gently. What Helmholtz observed was a shift in the visual field brought about by the passive movement. But we know that when we actively move our eyes the visual field does not jump; without stability in the visual world, life would be difficult indeed. The reason why the voluntary and passive conditions are different—so the theory goes—is that an efferent copy is available in the active condition to cancel out the visual information arising from eye movement. The visual world remains stable under normal conditions, because there is a perfect correlation between what the eye muscles were told to do (command information) and what they actually did. The visual world jumps under passive conditions because there is no efference copy to correlate with the retinal input. The corollary experiment (which I do not recommend you try) is to paralyze the eyeball with curare. Now if a subject is told to look to one side or the other, the visual field again appears to jump in that direction. In this case, von Helmholtz argued that the efferent command had been sent out, but because of the paralysis, no return information correlated with the command was available. Thus, perception suffers because the normal relationship between the feedforward copy of command and its associated feedback is decoupled.

A second type of evidence for the efference-copy concept—again indirect—comes from a clever experiment by Held (1965) that has been called the Kitten Carousel study. Held placed one kitten in a harness and had it pull another kitten that simply sat passively in a basket around a large circular drum in carousel-like fashion. The active kitten, so it was argued, could correlate her active movements with the visual environment, whereas the "passive" kitten having only visual input was deprived of the normal coupling relationship. In a series of visuomotor tasks, only the active kitten showed normal development. The argument is similar to the eye-movement work; without the orchestration of efferent copy and afferent input, learning is severely retarded.

An important implication from this work—independent of whether efference copy is a viable notion or not—is that active practice in acquiring skills is absolutely crucial. Few of us would want to argue with such a tenet; mental practice—contemplating the activity to be performed—is not likely to be much good to us unless we combine it with actual coordinated activity.

Like all concepts that at first seem plausible, the efference-copy notion has a major flaw. Because the efferent copy is a copy of the command for movement, it can only be useful in checking whether *that particular movement* was executed correctly, not whether the plan itself was correct for achieving the desired goal. There are ways around this problem, but unfortunately they require additional assumptions, as we see later (Chapter 8).

The Corollary-Discharge Concept.   Efference copy and corollary discharge are usually thought to be one and the same (Evarts, 1971), but in fact the two notions may well be conceptually distinct. Efference copy is a copy of command;

its so-called "code" is in motor language. Corollary discharge as shown in Fig. 2.14 is a feedforward signal from motor to sensory systems in the CNS that hypothetically *prepares* the sensory systems for the consequences of movement. Corollary discharge, then, is a predictive set of signals that carries the expected *sensory* consequences of the movement planned. The idea is that when I produce a well-learned movement such as reaching for a cup, there are, at the same time as signals are sent to the muscle groups involved, a set of signals "warning" information pick-up systems what the expected results of the movement will be. The advantage of such a mechanism is that incoming information is subject to facilitated processing. By virtue of the corollary discharge, the sensorimotor system is "tuned" for impending actions. Clearly, and as Fig. 2.14 shows, corollary discharge also carries the advantages of the efference-copy concept; namely, it may provide an error-correction function as well as signalling active movement.

Some behavioral evidence—again of an indirect nature—suggests that this type of central tuning occurs prior to movement. The experimental paradigm was quite simple. Blindfolded subjects either made active positioning movements to desired locations and then reproduced them, or they produced passive movements to desired locations prior to reproduction. In the latter condition, the muscle activity of the subjects was monitored electromyographically while the limb was moved passively by the experimenter until the subject issued a signal to

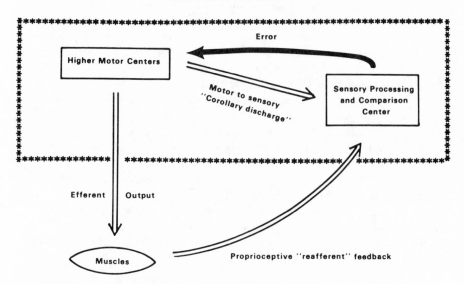

FIG. 2.14. A diagram of the motor-to-sensory corollary discharge notion of feedforward information.

stop. Both groups of subjects knew where the limb was going to end up, but only the active group made self-produced movements.

In several experiments (Kelso, 1975 , 1977) the results were identical; the active group was much more accurate. Moreover, when compared to a group of subjects who moved actively to a mechanical stop (i.e., that could not preplan the movement), the active preselection group maintained its superiority. Taken together, these results favor a central tuning notion: Subjects who move actively to selected positions in space may be sensitized to incoming information. In contrast, feedforward signals are not available during passive movements and are not effective when a subject moves in an exploratory manner. Again, we can envision the functional significance of such central, corollary discharge signals. When we enter a dark room whose layout is known to us, our movements are quite effective in comparison to entering a strange dark room.

Planning ahead allows us to process incoming information more effectively perhaps because internal, central tuning signals are available to us.

The Central Efferent Monitoring Concept.   The third notion of central feedforward is illustrated in Fig. 2.15. It is almost the same as Fig. 2.13 (the efference-copy notion), with the single exception that there is no returning feedback to the central monitoring system. The main claim of proponents of central efferent monitoring (Jones, 1974; Taub, 1977) is that proprioceptive feedback is not a *necessary* condition for the control of movement. The idea is that a human or an animal has a set of stored efference copies that constitute an internal monitoring system, whose role is to check the outgoing efferent signals before they can exert their effects at the periphery. In contrast to the ''inflow'' model shown in Fig. 2.13, the central monitoring—detection, comparison, and ultimate correction—is of the *efference,* not of the afference. Control of movement is thought to be purely internal to the CNS with no reliance on proprioceptive information to check the accuracy of command signals.

The evidence for central monitoring of efference comes from work on deafferented animals who can learn movements, it is claimed, without any afferent information available (see Chapters 7 and 8 for more details of these studies); that is, all the sensory information returning to the brain is surgically eliminated by cutting the dorsal roots entering the spinal cord (refer to Fig. 2.5). Yet in spite of the deafferentation and often the removal of vision as well, monkeys can learn to grasp objects, climb cages, locomote, and so on (Taub, 1977).

These studies have not been without their critics (Adams, 1971). It remains somewhat mysterious, for example, how the proposed internal monitoring system originates in the first place. However, exposure to the idea is important for it suggests the possibility that, just as vision and proprioception are sources of information that support activity, so also is the information generated within the CNS itself. Whether the efference is monitored in the manner suggested by the model or whether there is a progressive refinement of the efferent information per

CENTRAL NERVOUS SYSTEM

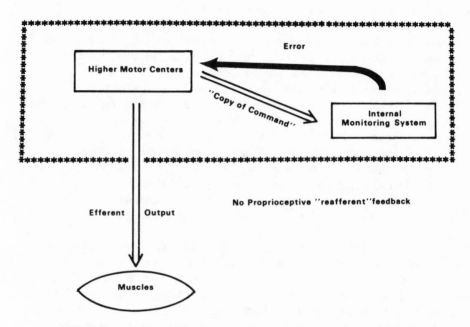

FIG. 2.15.   A diagram of the central monitoring of efference notion of feedforward information. Note in contrast to Fig. 2.13 that no returning proprioceptive information is required in this model.

se is open to question. Certainly, it must be reemphasized that the central feedforward models I have discussed here are necessarily simplistic in terms of the neurophysiology involved. Information, whether it be defined traditionally as efferent or afferent, is modulated throughout the CNS. Thus, feedforward may be thought of playing a role at peripheral as well as central levels of the nervous system, a topic to which I now turn briefly.

Feedforward Information at Peripheral Levels

Prior to the onset of simple motor activities such as lifting an arm or raising a foot, widespread changes may be observed in muscular organization. These changes are postural adjustments and seem to have a feedforward role, in that they prepare the individual to perform a restricted class of activities. The Soviet investigators, Belen'kii, Gurfinkel, and Pal'tsev (1967), examined a task in which the subject was asked to raise his left arm as rapidly as possible following an auditory signal. Electromyographical (muscular) recordings were taken from a variety of muscles including those not directly involved in the activity. It was found that during the latent period between signal and response, electromyographical activity occurred in the musculature of the trunk and lower limbs. These feedforward adjustments in the postural or equilibrium state of the performer apparently function to prepare the subject for the total complex of forces that will arise as a result of raising the arm. In Belen'kii et al's (1967) terms, feedforward of this kind is necessary: "to 'set' in advance, the mechanical parameters for the kinematic limbs of the body in such a way as to minimize the perturbation of the whole kinematic chain [p. 157]."

The function of the feedforward adjustments is not only to prepare the performer for a particular activity but also to *preclude* other activities. The sequence of muscular changes that occur therefore are specific in the case of Belen'kii et al. (1967) to the activity of left arm raising. They are entirely incompatible with other types of actions such as right leg raising. The message is this: The performer in a feedforward state is constrained to produce one of a limited set of acts (Fowler, 1977). The advantage of this mechanism, then, is economy of control: The number of decisions by the central executive is reduced.

Summary and Conclusions

In this chapter I have attempted to provide you with a flavor of some of the issues that are addressed in more detail in upcoming chapters. I have discussed some of the projected roles for the various types of information that are involved in skilled activity. I do not wish to convey the idea that feedforward and feedback are separate entities in skilled performance. Classically, these two notions have been dichotomized, but it is my belief that the control and coordination of movement involves a subtle interaction between the two. Arbib (1972) gives a nice example of how this interactive system may function. In the normal mode of walking in a familiar environment, the style of control may be predominantly feedforward in nature; that is, we are confident of our footing without explicitly testing where our feet are in space. In a seeking or exploratory mode, however, we need information about the "spot" (the nature of the surface, potential obstacles, and so on) on which the foot will land. The reality of this situation is apparent when we misjudge the number of steps on a staircase. The work to which I previously referred on preselected and constrained movements dovetails with Arbib's example. Preselected movements may be under predominantly feedforward control; the subject may be optimally tuned to incoming information in this case. Constrained, exploratory movements on the other hand seem more dependent on continuous processing of feedback information. Attention must be directed to detecting the locus of the experimenter-defined stop.

To understand skilled performance we need to have some idea, not whether control is via feedforward or feedback alone, but rather the relative contributions of each source of information. If an unexpected event occurs in the environment, peripheral information is necessary to inform us of this situation. Highly skilled individuals on the other hand are primed or tuned not only to the consequences of their actions but the information in the environment that enables them to set up the parameters for the motor system in the first place. This tuning effect may take place at different levels in the system, for example, in cortical, spinal, and even receptor systems such as the muscle spindle.

Speculating further, early skill development, according to this notion, might be characterized by an inability to take advantage of feedforward control; that is, the beginner is not sensitive to what the effects of his/her movements will be and hence must rely on continually monitoring peripheral information. Higher levels of skill, on the other hand, are characterized by an apparent improvement in processing peripheral information; the capacity to process incoming information is, in a sense, less limited than before. According to the "tuning" hypothesis, this improvement is due at least in part to enhanced feedforward control that enables the performer to attend to other regulatory details in the environment.

In conclusion, it is quite apparent that many of the details of the relationship between feedforward and feedback in contributing to skilled performance have yet to be worked out. In the following chapters you will perceive differing biases on their relative roles. I think it is fair to say that the whole notion of feedforward and its operation has not received the theoretical attention that feedback has. Yet, even though feedforward is an elusive issue to examine experimentally, it may play a significant role in skilled movement. Time and the burden of scientific evidence will prove me right or wrong.

ACKNOWLEDGMENT

Preparation of this chapter and this volume was supported by NSF Grant No. SER 77-02986.

REFERENCES

Adams, J. A. A closed-loop theory of motor learning. *Journal of Motor Behavior*, 1971, *3*, 111–149.

Arbib, M. A. *The metaphorical brain*. New York: Wiley, 1972.

Belen'kii, V. Y., Gurfinkel, V. S., & Pal'tsev, Y. I. Elements of control of voluntary movements. *Biophysics*, 1967, *12*, 154–161.

Bernstein, N. *The coordination and regulation of movement*. New York: Pergamon, 1967.

Boyd, I. A. & Roberts, T. D. M. Proprioceptive discharges from stretch receptors in the knee-joint of the cat. *Journal of Physiology*, 1953, *122*, 38–58.

Burgess, P. R., & Clark, F. S. Dorsal column projection of fibers from the cat knee joint. *Journal of Physiology*, 1969, *203*, 301–315.

Clark, F. J., & Burgess, P. R. Slowly adapting receptors in cat knee joint: Can they signal joint angle? *Journal of Neurophysicology*, 1975, *38*, 1448–1463.

Craske, B. Perception of impossible limb positions induced by tendon vibration. *Science*, 1977, *196*, 71–73.

Evarts, E. V. Feedback and corollary discharge: A merging of the concepts. *Neurosciences Research Program Bulletin,* 1971, *9,* 86–112.

Fel'dman, A. G. Functional tuning of the nervous system with control of movement or maintenance of a steady posture—III. Mechanographic analysis of the execution by man of the simplest motor tasks. *Biophysics,* 1966, *11,* 766–775.

Fowler, C. A. *Timing control in speech production.* Indiana University Linguistics Club, Bloomington, Ind., 1977.

Fowler, C. A., & Turvey, M. T. Skill acquisition: An event approach for the optimum of a function of several variables. In G. E. Stelmach (Ed.), *Information processing in motor control and learning.* New York: Academic Press, 1978.

Gelfand, I. M., Gurfinkel, V. S., Fomin, S. V., & Tsetlin, M. L. (Eds.). *Models of the structural–functional organization of certain biological systems.* Cambridge: M.I.T. Press, 1971.

Gelfand, I. M., Gurfinkel, V. S., Tsetlin, M. L., & Shik, M. L. Some problems in the analysis of movements. In: Gelfand, I. M., Gurfinkel, V. S., Fomin, S. V., & Tsetlin, M. L. (Eds.). *Models of the structural–functional organization of certain biological systems.* Cambridge: M.I.T. Press, 1971.

Gibson, J. J. *The senses considered as perceptual systems.* Boston: Houghton Mifflin, 1966.

Gibson, J. J. *The ecological approach to visual perception.* Boston: Houghton Mifflin, 1979.

Greene, P. H. Problems of organization of motor systems. In R. Rosen & F. Snell (Eds.), *Progress in theoretical biology* (Vol. 2). New York: Academic Press, 1972.

Grigg, P. Response of joint afferent neurons in cat medial articular nerve to active and passive movements of the knee. *Brain Research,* 1976, *118,* 482–485.

Held, R. Plasticity in sensory–motor systems. *Scientific American,* 1965, *213,* 84–95.

Hollerbach, J. M. *An oscillation theory of handwriting.* M.I.T.: Artificial Intelligence Laboratory, 1980.

Houk, J. C. Participation of reflex mechanisms and reaction time processes in the compensatory adjustments to mechanical disturbance. *In Cerebral motor control in man: Long loop mechanisms,* J. E. Desmedt, (Ed.), *Progress in Clinical Neurophysiology* (Vol. 4). Basel: Karger, 1978.

Jones, B. The role of central monitoring of efference in motor short-term memory (for movements). *Journal of Experimental Psychology,* 1974, *120,* 37–43.

Jordan, T. C. Characteristics of visual and proprioceptive response times in the learning of a motor skill. *Quarterly Journal of Experimental Psychology,* 1972, *24,* 536–543.

Kelso, J. A. S. *Planning, efferent and receptor components in movement coding.* Doctoral dissertation, University of Wisconsin, 1975. University of Michigan Microfilms, Ann Arbor.

Kelso, J. A. S. Planning and efferent components in the coding of movement. *Journal of Motor Behavior,* 1977, *9,* 33–47.

Kelso, J. A. S. Joint receptors do not provide a satisfactory basis for motor timing and positioning. *Psychological Review,* 1978, *85,* 474–481.

Kelso, J. A. S., Holt, K. G., & Flatt, A. E. The role of proprioception in the perception and control of human movement: Toward a theoretical reassessment. *Perception & Psychophysics,* 1980, *28,* 45–52.

Kelso, J. A. S., Holt, K. G., Kugler, P. N. & Turvey, M. T. On coordinative structures as dissipative structures. II. Empirical lines of convergence. In G. E. Stelmach & J. Requin (Eds.), *Tutorials in motor behavior,* Amsterdam: North Holland, 1980.

Kelso, J. A. S., & Stelmach, G. E. Central and peripheral mechanisms in motor control. In G. E. Stelmach (Ed.), *Motor control: Issues and trends.* New York: Academic Press, 1976.

Kelso, J. A. S., Southard, D., & Goodman, D. On the nature of human interlimb coordination. *Science,* 1979, *203,* 1029–1031.

Kugler, P. N., Kelso, J. A. S., & Turvey, M. T. On the control and coordination of naturally developing systems. *The development of movement coordination and control,* Wiley, New York, 1982.

Lee, D. N.   Visuomotor coordination in space-time. In G. E. Stelmach & J. Requin (Eds.), *Tutorials in motor behavior,* Amsterdam: North-Holland, 1980.

Lee, D. N., & Aronson, E.   Visual proprioceptive control of standing in human infants. *Perception & Psychophysics,* 1974, *15,* 529-532.

Lee, D. N., & Lishman, J. R.   Visual proprioceptive control of stance. *Journal of Human Movement Studies,* 1975, *1,* 87-95.

Lee, D. N., Lishman, J. R., & Thomson, J.   Visual guidance in the long jump. *Athletics Coach,* 1977, *11,* 26-30 and *12,* 17-23.

Matthews, P. B. C.   *Mammalian muscle receptors and their central actions.* Baltimore: Williams & Williams, 1972.

Matthews, P. B. C., & Simmonds, A.   Sensations of finger movement elicited by pulling upon flexor tendons in man. *Journal of Physiology,* 1974, *239,* 27-28P.

Posner, M. I., Nissen, M. J., & Klein, R. M.   Visual dominance: An information-processing account of its origins and significance. *Psychological Review,* 1976, *83,* 157-171.

Shik, M. L., & Orlovskii, G. N.   Coordination of the limbs during running of the dog. *Biophysics,* 1965, *10,* 1148-1159.

Skoglund, S.   Anatomical and physiological studies of knee joint innervation in the cat. *Acta Physiologica Scandinavia,* 1956, *124,* 1-99. (Monograph Supplement).

Smith, J. L., Roberts, E. M., & Atkins, E.   Fusimotor neuron block and voluntary arm movement in man. *American Journal of Physical Medicine,* 1972, *51,* 225-239.

Taub, E.   Movement in nonhuman primates deprived of somatosensory feedback. In J. Keogh, *Exercise and sports sciences reviews* (Vol. 4). Santa Barbara: Journal Publishing Affiliates, 1977.

Turvey, M. T.   Preliminaries to a theory of action with reference to vision. In R. Shaw & J. Bransford (Eds.), *Perceiving, acting and knowing,* Hillsdale, N. J.: Lawrence Erlbaum Associates, 1977.

Zelazo, P. R., Zelazo, N. A., & Kolb, S.   "Walking" in the newborn. *Science,* 1972, *196,* 314-315.

INFORMATION PROCESSING, MOTOR LEARNING AND MEMORY

Editor's Remarks (Chapters 3, 4, and 5)

In the next three chapters, George Stelmach builds upon many of the ideas introduced in Chapters 1 and 2 and develops them into a broader theoretical framework that incorporates both information processing and cybernetical notions. In contrast to earlier views in which the individual was viewed as a passive receiver of information (the stimulus–response model), Stelmach emphasizes the learner as an active explorer of his/her environment. Via the latter "information-processing" approach, the teacher and the student of movement can potentially analyze the capacities and limitations of the learner in terms of the tasks that are performed. "Information" (one of the favorite buzz words of the area) is thought to proceed through a set of identifiable states (e.g., detection, recognition, response selection, and so on), before any overt action occurs. The main thrust of the information processing (IP) approach is to analyze the various mental operations—not directly observable—that precede action, rather than the real-time action itself. Stelmach treats us to a detailed account of the dominant methodology used to evaluate mental operations—reaction time. He presents a selected body of data showing how various experimental manipulations appear to selectively influence the activation of stages and provides possible applications of the approach to sports skills. Whether the IP approach captures the essential ingredients of the latter is a moot point. By far the greatest emphasis of the information-processing framework has been on the role of stimulus variables, with only limited concern for the processes underlying movement organization. In spite of these and other criticisms, the IP approach does offer one, albeit limited, way of thinking about human movement behavior.

By and large however, as Stelmach points out, the IP approach does not address the problems of motor learning and control—topics that the author takes up in some detail in Chapter 4. Although aware of other, contrasting views on this problem (to be considered in later chapters), Stelmach focuses on the closed-loop cybernetic view of human motor learning that originated in the engineering sciences. We already have some idea of what the underlying notions of closed-loop theory are: Essentially, feedback is used as the primary agent of movement regulation. Stelmach documents for us some of the many experiments on distorted feedback and augmented feedback, showing that performance can be degraded or enhanced accordingly. But the bulk of Chapter 4 is devoted to articulating one of the most dominant and highly investigated theories of motor learning—developed in 1971 by Professor Jack Adams. Adams' theory restricted itself to "simple" unidirectional movement tasks like line drawing and lever positioning; as a consequence, it may have very little to say about complex day-to-day activities, or even other types of laboratory skills that scientists are interested in. But, as mentioned before, Adams' theory was an important event in giving the field of motor behavior a much-needed kick, and it sent many people into the laboratory to test its predictions. As Stelmach points out, some of these have not stood the test of time, and some of the assumptions behind the theory are questionable at best, but that should not detract from Adams' contribution—it was a significant one indeed.

Learning is one thing—it focuses on acquisition processes, but what does it mean to "remember" a motor act? In the final chapter of this section, Stelmach reviews for us much of his own work on the retention of simple motor skills. Perhaps it is here that Stelmach's personal contribution to the area has been greatest, for he had a seminal role in attracting attention to the problem of motor memory (especially its short-term aspects). From its initial parallels with verbal memory, the area of short-term motor memory has developed its own set of concepts. Nevertheless, the paradigmatic issues are the same: Do verbal and motor "items" have similar retention characteristics, and what are the critical variables that affect retention?

One may well ask what the parallels are between "items" of verbal material (e.g., words and nonsense syllables) and "items" of motor acts. Indeed, how would one go about itemizing a motor activity? One way is to attempt to break up the movement into its constituent elements. Separating the "codes" for the distance moved by a limb and the end location of the limb following movement is one approach to the problem. But is it realistic to draw parallels between movements (and aspects of movement) and verbal material and expect that they should follow the same retention patterns? More important, is it realistic to assume that aspects of movement are "coded" in the first place? This is a question that the reader and movement science in general has to grapple with. It may be, for example, that elements of movement are not coded in a storage system at all. Imagine, for example, that instead of the human motor system we inquired how a motor car registers or "codes" its velocity. If I accept the conventional viewpoint and define velocity as distance covered per unit time, I could imagine a system that continually senses the distance that is covered as well as the time that elapses and, by some continuous computational process, derives the velocity of the vehicle. But, as we all know, this is not the way that a complex variable, velocity, is registered in a motor car. Instead, velocity is the *direct* analog of a voltage provided by an electric generator that is driven by the wheels. Distance and time, then, are not coded or represented anywhere. Is it possible that the motor system is characterized by smart, "special purpose" devices, rather than by rote, general purpose computational devices? (Runeson, 1977). If it is, then it may be possible to reduce the number of explanatory constructs that are required in the sorts of models that Stelmach discusses. And that is one of the major goals of movement science.

REFERENCE

Runeson, S. On the possibility of 'smart' perceptual mechanisms. *Scandinavian Journal of Psychology*, 1977, *18*, 172–179.

3 Information-Processing Framework for Understanding Human Motor Behavior

George E. Stelmach
University of Wisconsin

INTRODUCTION

As you observe a tennis player execute a perfect forehand, you wonder how the motor skill was accomplished. If you focus your attention on the motor response itself and limit your inquiry to only movement execution, you will miss many important aspects of skilled performance. Often what happens before the response, on the perceptual side, determines the success or failure of the motor act. A performer continually processes information from the surrounding environment. The performer perceives stimuli, uses memory, makes decisions, and then executes responses. In this chapter I introduce an approach to skill learning that examines the mental operations that intervene between the stimulus and response. The appealing aspect of this approach is that it focuses attention on the cognitive activities that precede action. I try to examine the origins of the information-processing approach to look at how it has developed through the years, illustrating its strengths and weaknesses.

Before going further it is important to delimit the term skill as I use it here. When most people use the term *motor skill,* they probably think of it in a sport context like a spike in volleyball or a forehand volley in tennis. However, I use the term skill in a much broader context, namely, to refer to the types of activities we perform in daily life such as hand movements, typing skills, or precision acts.

Process-Oriented Approach

The information-processing approach provides a framework for understanding many problems that might otherwise remain unclear and provides an alternative to the black-box model. We can use an information-processing approach to model the contents of the impenetrable black box, such as viewing the transformation of information as a continuum, linked by a series of complex but researchable processes. Adopting the information-processing approach enables us to view the perceiver as an active processor, not just a passive recipient of information. Also, employment of the information-processing approach allows us to compare the ways in which different aspects of perception are established in memory so that common properties can be discussed. Finally, we use this approach because it provides a means to describe as precisely as possible the many separate steps, stages, and processes that an active processor goes through (Haber, 1969).

It is logical that, if physical educators are to become better teachers and coaches, they need a better understanding of the numerous and complex problems associated with motor performance. Teachers need to know the capacities and limitations of the learner along with the behavioral demands of the motor tasks. Because the teacher must mediate between the learner and the task when providing learning experiences, it is important that knowledge about both components is available. In other words, if the teacher is to begin to understand how certain complex tasks are learned, it is vital to consider how information is processed and behavior regulated. It is this knowledge that will allow the teacher to make sound and useful statements about human performance and to prescribe rational, meaningful activities.

Moreover, information processing provides a unified framework that allows investigators to study systematically many aspects of motor skill. Unlike the black-box approach, which deals with only a small part of total behavior, the cognitive approach to skill learning stresses a complete conceptualization of behavior through the description of the mental operations that characterize skill.

BASIC CONCEPTS OF INFORMATION PROCESSING

According to information-processing theory the human is a processor of information, comparable to a computer. The organism is viewed as consisting of receptors, effectors, and an intervening control system, with information processing concerned primarily with the operations of the control system. Information processing attempts to examine the role of the control system in sensing, attending to, transforming, retaining, and transmitting information.

This approach is one that is certainly not new and has not been developed specifically for motor behavior, but it is one that I believe contributes to the conceptual understanding of motor skill. Recall that the individual is viewed as an active processor of stimulus information rather than a passive recipient, as in the previous research era in motor behavior. The central tenet of the approach is that when we perform an activity there are a number of mental operations that are performed by the learner to solve a particular problem or perform a task. Neisser (1976) describes the task of understanding human behavior from a psychological perspective as analogous to a person trying to discover the sequential operations a computer executes in arriving at a solution, whereas at the same time being unconcerned with the "hardware" required.

Processing Stages

Humans, like other animals, are constantly interacting with their environment. When changes occur individuals react to these changes by processing information from the environment. As you read this text, you might hear someone speak or feel something touching you. Or, on your way to class, as you are walking, perhaps you were thinking about what you would be doing that night. Similarly, you might be playing basketball and as you were shooting you were reacting to your opponent, or, if you were on defense, you might have attempted to block a shot while thinking about what you would do next. The point I am trying to make is that an individual is continually processing information from all modalities and actively operating on it to transform it for a particular use. We continuously register, process, and respond to a variety of stimuli such as images, movements, or sounds. With a little reflection it is easy to realize that a great deal must go on between the act of sensing and the act of responding to stimuli. What goes on during this interval is actually a complex series of events which take very little time. Information processing may be thought of as the transformation of raw data gathered by sensory receptors into interpretable percepts (Haber, 1969).

The implication from the foregoing is that behavior can be partitioned into stages. It is not the final act that is so important but the mental operations that precede the motor act. An analogous example of this approach can be found in the creative processes of scientists, teachers, or artists. According to Massaro (1975) they go through identifiable stages or mental operations before they solve a problem. They first become aware of a problem; they typically gather information about it, reshape it, manipulate it, and ponder over it for some time. When the idea emerges again, it is transformed into a completely different type of concept, usually a solution. Adapting this analytical framework allows us to make statements about human-performance processing and problem solving.

There are certain stages of processing such as detection, recognition, and memory that are quite important. A fire-alarm scenario is useful to illustrate the mental operations that we go through in deciding what to do upon hearing an alarm sound. Let us assume that we decided to leave the room. We can now analyze the processes that have taken place (see Fig. 3.2). First of all, we become aware that some new stimulation was present: Something registered on our sensory receptors. The first stage of information processing is usually referred to as detection. Sensation or detection is the process through which the flow of information enters our bodies. Before we can act appropriately on this information, however, we must be able to properly identify it. If we did not know what a fire alarm sounded like, it would have no meaning for us (with perhaps fatal consequences). Therefore, we must be able to recognize its importance. The assignment of meaning or importance to the signal implies that we make contact with some type of knowledge. We are really tapping memory at this point. Next, we must decide what we are going to do—a decision dependent on whether we recognize it as a danger signal or as a meaningless sound. At this point we decide what action to take and we make a response. We have just gone through the various stages of motor behavior from detection through recognition to response selection. From the foregoing scenario, the mental operations that precede action are obvious. Extending this concept to movement situations should be a straightforward exercise. The point is that the information-processing approach allows you to distinguish and compare the processes of detection, recognition, response selection, and response execution.

Let me specify the assumptions of the information-processing approach from the previous example (see Fig. 3.1). First, the stages of processing exist and are identifiable. Second, these stages are operations that require time. The importance of time as a variable becomes crucial as we develop methods for examining the various processes. Third, each stage operates only on the information available to it. Fourth, each stage transforms the information in some way and makes it available to the next stage of processing (Massaro, 1975). Note that as informa-

The Central Assumptions Underlying Information Processing

1. Numerous processing stages occur between stimulus and response.

2. The sequence of processing stages is initiated by stimulus presentation.

3. Each stage operates only on information available to it.

4. Each stage transforms in some way the information supplied to it, an event which requires time for accomplishment.

5. Upon completion of processing performed at one stage, the transformed information is made available to the next stage of processing.

FIG. 3.1.   Five assumptions we make in utilizing the information-processing approach.

tion first passes through the system, the order of processing stages is invariant. For example, it would not be possible to recognize a fire alarm unless you had first detected its presence. These assumptions outline a continuous system. A definite flow of information from detection to execution is established, making the approach one that lends itself to flow charting. Figure 3.2 is a very simple flow chart illustrating that information starts as a stimulus and advances through the mental processing stages of detection, recognition, decision making, and response execution. This type of representation yields a descriptively simple view of behavior, the many decisions and complexities are not represented.

To extend our discussion and show how the information-processing model can be used to analyze the mental operations that precede action, let us return to the fire-alarm scenario (Fig. 3.3). The alarm sounds and we begin to process the information. We first detect the alarm. Next, depending on our past experience, we either recognize it as a fire alarm or we do not. Also dependent on our past experience is our decision as to whether the alarm is a hoax, a drill, or the real thing. Based on this decision, we may choose to respond by remaining in the room and perhaps calling the fire department. If we decide it is a drill, we may respond by leaving or, perhaps, by staying. If we decide it is the real thing, we respond by leaving immediately. Note that in the course of the stages we have already described the original information—an auditory sound—has undergone successive transformations. From a auditory event, it has changed to a recognized category (fire alarm), then changed again to a condition for applying a rule (leaving the room). This illustrates a general point: Isolating a stage of processing generally corresponds to some representation of the stimulus information. As the information is transmitted from one stage to another, its representation changes accordingly.

We can see how flow charts are a helpful way of modeling behavior allowing clarification and distinction of the various mental operations. Information processing consists of a series of stages with each stage characterized by a different

Three psychological operations or stages of information processing that occur between stimulus and response.

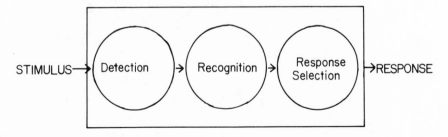

FIG. 3.2.   A simple flow chart of the course of information processing.

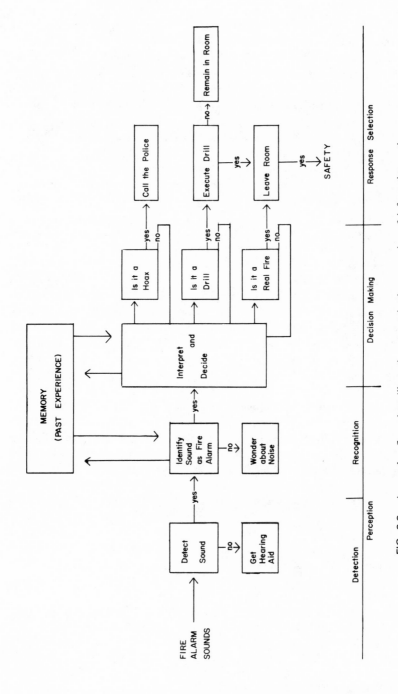

FIG. 3.3. A complex flow chart illustrating stages in the processing of information on the fire-alarm scenario.

operation. Blocks are drawn and labeled to represent specific processes and are connected by lines in order to represent the sequence in which operations are believed to occur.

ORIGINS OF THE INFORMATION-PROCESSING APPROACH

A number of developments in related disciplines provided the impetus for the developing science of information processing. One of the major theoretical events contributing to information processing was the development of mathematical models for communication, in which information was quantified in unambiguous terms (Shannon & Weaver, 1949). It became possible to measure information content, in and of itself, without reference to the specific event or mode of communication.

All information, regardless of type, can be defined in terms of uncertainty. For example, the statement "the sun came up today" conveys information about an event with little uncertainty associated with it and, therefore, less information that the statement "there was an eclipse today." Measuring information in this way provides researchers with the capacity to reliably quantify the inputs to the system, permitting more confident conclusions about the output. This particular development encouraged the application of the information-processing approach by providing reasonable control on its primary independent variable, information.

The legacy of other disciplines consisted of evidence for the presence of intervening operations between stimulus and response. At a time when behaviorists believed that the physical properties of the stimulus completely defined the response, signal-detection theory (Green & Swets, 1966) demonstrated that through decision theory intervening processes could alter that relationship, making the physical properties of the stimulus unreliable. Similarly, attention was drawn to underlying operations in psycholinguistics when Chomsky (1957) began to investigate the "deep structure" of linguistics as opposed to "surface structure." The sentence "the shooting of the hunters was terrible" is grammatically correct but ambiguous in its interpretation, providing an example of different levels of processing.

The last development leading to the information-processing approach comes from the widespread use of digital computers. This was not just because computers allow one to conduct experiments more easily or analyze data more thoroughly. Rather, it was because the activities of the computer itself seemed in some ways akin to cognitive processes. Computers accept information, manipulate symbols, store items in memory and retrieve them again, classify inputs, recognize movements, and so on (Neisser, 1976). Suddenly psychologists became aware that the tasks computers were doing were very similar to human operations. Psychologists began to draw parallels between how a computer operated and how humans perform mental operations, a metaphor that led to new models of human behavior based on computer operation. The coming of the computer provided a much needed reassurance that cognitive processes were real and that they could be studied and perhaps understood. It also provided a new vocabulary and a new set of concepts for dealing with cognition; terms like information, input, processing, coding, and subroutines became commonplace.

Now that you have become acquainted with the various stages of processing and have been exposed to the origins of these ideas, it is appropriate to examine the early work in psychology that attempted to unravel the mental operations that occur between stimulus and response.

INFORMATION-PROCESSING METHODOLOGY

Reaction Time

Perhaps the most basic assumption of the information-processing framework is that all mental operations take time. It is assumed that the total time from the onset of a stimulus to the occurrence of a response can be divided into separate time intervals of definite duration. When a stimulus is presented, it takes a certain amount of time before a response is initiated. This interval from the stimulus presentation to the beginning of the response is referred to as reaction time. Reaction time reflects the time that is required for a stimulated receptor nerve (visual, auditory, or kinesthetic) to carry its message to the brain, and for the brain to activate the appropriate muscles to initiate a response. The duration of the reaction time is thought to be proportional to the number of mental operations that takes place between the stimulus and the response. The concept of using reaction time to infer the nature of processes comes from Donders, as long ago as 1868. Because reaction time is very frequently employed in information-processing studies, it is important to know how it is measured and what factors influence it.

One variable influencing reaction time is the type of modality stimulated. For example, reaction to a visual stimulus is approximately 180 msec, for an auditory stimulus it is 160 msec, and for a tactile stimulus it is approximately 140 msec. Further, Chernikoff and Taylor (1952) have reported that kinesthetic reaction time is approximately 120 msec. Reaction time is dependent on many factors other than modality or presentation. It is affected by stimulus intensity, the amount of information in the stimulus, the number of choices that have to be made in decision and response stages, etc. Reaction time is a volatile measure that is sensitive to many variables. Therefore, a good understanding of it is necessary to appreciate the information-processing framework. It is important not to confuse reaction time with movement time. A good rule for distinguishing the two is that reaction time ends when the movement begins. If the time measured involves part of the duration of a movement, reaction time and movement are confounded (see also Chapter 6).

Subtractive Method

Perhaps the first experimenter to study mental functions in terms of stages of processing was F. C. Donders (1869). He extended the earlier work of others (Helmholtz, 1866), who were measuring "nerve time" and "muscle time" with involuntary reflexes. In these earlier studies, various points of the body were stimulated, and the time differences between the points were subtracted to obtain an estimate of nerve-conduction time. For example, if I were to stimulate my wrist and then stimulate my shoulder and obtain reaction times to each, I could then infer the difference between the two reaction times to be due to nerve-conduction time. With the information about time and distance, it is possible to compute the rate or speed of nerve conduction through the central nervous system.

Donders, who was not interested in nerve conduction, per se, saw the utility of the procedure for studying mental operations. Donders placed electrodes under each foot of a subject and generated two experimental conditions. In the first condition, the subject was told which foot was going to be stimulated and was asked to react as fast as possible with the hand on the same side. Because the stimulation was applied to one foot and the subject knew which foot in advance, the task was one of detection. In the second condition, the subject was told that it could be either foot, and that he was to respond with the hand on the same side as the foot that was stimulated.

Let us compare the two situations. In the latter condition there are additional mental operations because the subject must detect the stimulation, identify which foot was stimulated, and select the appropriate hand with which to respond. This adds the operations of identification and response selection. As you might predict, Donders found that when the subject had to respond in the choice situation, reaction time was 67 msec slower than the simple condition. Donders concluded that the additional 67 msec was the time required for deciding which side had been stimulated and for selecting the appropriate response. The inference from Donders' results is that the additional stages of processing have been isolated and measured with a duration of 67 msec. The logic underlying Donders' approach was that a task requiring additional operations will require additional time to respond. It follows that this additional time may be attributed directly to additional mental operations.

Donders repeated these experiments in the visual modality to ascertain whether his evidence was modality specific. In the simple condition, subjects made one response to the illumination of a single light. In the choice condition, subjects were required to determine which of two lights came on and respond with the response appropriate to that light. Donders found that the choice condition was 154 msec longer than the simple condition. The finding that additional operations increase processing time in both the tactile and visual modalities lends generality to the subtractive method.

Donders performed a third set of experiments in which the nature of both the stimulus and the response were changed. Subjects reacted to and responded with letters. The subject's task was to say the name of one of two letters, A or F, as fast as possible. In the first condition, the subject knew in advance which letter would be presented and could prepare his response. In the second condition, one of the two letters was presented randomly, precluding any advance-response preparation. Note that between each condition the stimuli and responses are identical, making the paradigm useful for comparison. The only differences between the two conditions were the probability of stimulus occurrence (100% versus 50%) and the number of operations required to respond correctly. In the first condition, the subject was not required to recognize the stimuli or choose a response, making the task one of detection only. In the second condition, all three operations were required. The difference in reaction times between the two conditions was 166 msec; thus the results were similar to the previous studies.

In an effort to "tease" apart all three stages, Donders developed three tasks, each of which would require one more operation than the one before. The rationale was that he would then be able to subtract their respective reaction times and obtain time quantities for each stage. The first task (A) required only detection (Fig. 3.4). In this situation the subject was informed that a certain letter would appear on every trial. His task was to name it as soon as he saw it. Thus, as before, recognition and response selection are not required operations. The second task (B) was a two-choice situation in which either of two letters could be presented. The subject responded by naming the letter that was presented. The operations required to perform this task included detection, recognition, and response selection. The third task (C) was similar to task B in that either of the two letters would be presented. However, the subject was instructed to respond only to one of the letters, and not to the other. This third task required the subject to detect and recognize the stimulus. However, only one response was required, effectively allowing the subject to prepare it in advance. According to Donders, this manipulation eliminated response selection from the third task. In order to isolate the time required for stages of processing, a series of subtractions was made, a simple procedure permitted by the assumption that the stages of processing are additive in nature (Fig. 3.5). Detection was the only stage that could not be separated from the other events contributing to reaction time. This is the origin of how researchers came to isolate and separate stages of mental processing.

Donders' ideas were stated many years ago, allowing plenty of time for scrutiny and criticism from psychologists. One of the main criticisms of Donders' work referred to his simplistic view of stages of processing. For example, in the third condition, Donders assumed there was no response selection because

DONDER'S A,B,C REACTIONS

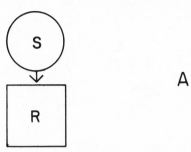

A

1. The Donder's A-reaction time situation (Simple RT). A stimulus light goes on and you respond by pressing a button.

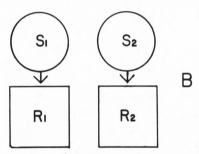

B

2. The Donder's B-reaction time situation (choice RT). There are now two stimuli (S₁ & S₂) each has its own response (R₁ or R₂). Since you do not know which of the two lights will come on, you must be prepared to make either of the two responses.

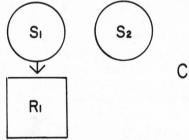

C

3. The Donder's C-reaction time situation. Only one stimulus S₁ calls for a response. If the S₂ light goes on, the observer must be careful not to press R₁.

FIG. 3.4.   A graphic representation of Donder's A, B, and C reaction tasks.

TASK	REACTION TIME IN MSEC	STAGES OF PROCESSING REQUIRED
A	201	DETECTION
B	284	DETECTION, RECOGNITION, RESPONSE SELECTION
C	237	DETECTION, RECOGNITION

DURATION OF RECOGNITION = TASK C − TASK A

= 237 msec − 201 msec

= 36 msec

DURATION OF RESPONSE SELECTION = TASK B − TASK C

= 284 msec − 237 msec

= 47 msec

FIG. 3.5. Application of the subtractive method to the A, B, and C reaction times and the resulting processing stage durations.

the subject had to make only one kind of response. From a different perspective, the task may be viewed as possessing two alternative responses: (1) The subject chooses to respond to the specified letter; or (2) he or she chooses not to repond to the other letter. In the latter situation, the subject is inhibiting a response dependent on stimulation, which is very much the same as making a response. Thus, via this perspective it appears that task C requires the same operations as task B. Further criticism, stemming from the simplistic framework, was generated by Donders' lack of consideration for the possible consequences of inserting and deleting stages. Apparently, Donders considered the stages to be discrete and consequently uninfluenced by situational circumstances. However, in comparing task B with task C, we decided that the same stages were present. The finding that the reaction time differed between the two conditions indicates that the processes themselves were changed. If this is indeed the case, Donders' method has some limitations as a means of separating stages. However, the analytical thought and methodology initiated by Donders is still with us today.

Additive Factor Method

The central assumption of Donders' subtractive method, the additivity of the times for mental events, was criticized over the years. The major criticism was that processing stages cannot be added in a task without affecting the time to complete other stages. Consequently, investigative interest in Donders' substractive method as a tool for studying mental processes was reduced.

One hundred years later, Sternberg (1969a,b) proposed some modifications to Donders' methods. Sternberg's argument was that, when we add or delete stages, we selectively affect other stages. The result is a confounding of stages. Instead, he proposed a modification to the original Donderian idea, in which the study of information processing was in terms of the amounts and levels of processing rather than the insertion or deletion of stages of processing. Sternberg's modification consisted of the manipulation of the amount of processing or the number of transformations required within a single stage. The researcher chooses an independent variable that is capable of varying the processing within a specific stage. For example, if we wish to study identification, we need to choose a variable that alters the amount of processing required for identification.

Suppose we wish to determine the accuracy and speed of identification of a specific pitch as a strike. The balls used are either pure white or a mottled black and white. If the background is of neutral color, which ball color should be accurately perceived with the faster reaction time? The mottling on the black and white ball will interfere with normal visual cues, requiring more time for processing and identification. The modification we are making on the Donderian method is to work within stages of processing and not across or between the stages. The tasks are the same in that they affect the same stages of processing. The only variable that could affect the results is the color of the ball. There are many manipulable variables available for application of this approach, and in most cases, the dependent variable is reaction time.

Combining different levels of processing in more than one stage allows a factorial design in which interactions between stages may be studied. If processing of one stage does not affect another stage, the effects of levels of processing on reaction time would be additive. If interactions are present between stages, the effects on reaction time would not be additive. Hence, the method has been dubbed the "additive" method.

The following example illustrates this method more clearly. We manipulate the processing of two stages, detection and response selection. The variable manipulated for detection is stimulus intensity. It is known that a more intense stimulus is responded to faster than one of low intensity. The variable manipulated under response selection is stimulus–response compatibility. This variable is generated by the complexity of the relationship between the stimulus and response. Consider the situation in which a subject is confronted with two lights capable of two intensities, high and low. One light is located on the subject's left and one on the right. Under each hand is a key with which the subject responds to the stimulus light. In a compatible condition, the subject would respond with the hand on the same side as the stimulus light. In an incompatible situation, the subject would respond with the hand on the opposite side to the stimulus light. In this example, we are manipulating two stages of processing: Stimulus intensity affects the time required for detection, whereas compatibility affects the time required for response selection.

For a clearer picture of the experimental situation, Fig. 3.6 provides some hypothetical results. The possible outcomes are limited to two types, simple additive effects and an interaction. If the processing difficulty in one stage does not affect the processing in another stage, a simple additive-effects model is supported. In such a model, more difficult processing results in uniform increases in reaction time. The graph in Fig. 3.6 illustrates an additive-effects model with two parallel lines. The stages of processing appear discrete, with the manipulated variables affecting only their respective stages. In the interaction model, processing in one stage differentially influences processing in another stage, producing an interaction between stages. In Fig. 3.6 you can see that when low compatibility and low intensity were combined the deficit exhibited is much greater than a simple addition of the individual deficits. The graph of the interaction depicts two nonparallel lines that diverge sharply. It appears that processing difficulty in the detection stage is adversely affecting the response-selection stage.

The value of Sternberg's method lies in its utility for examining the operations of various stages, a benefit not derived from the use of Donders' approach. Donders sought simply to establish the presence and duration of various stages of processing. Had he been successful in his objective, our knowledge about processing stages would be very limited. With Sternberg's method we can answer specific questions about *how* the mental operations function.

CONTEMPORARY INFORMATION PROCESSING

Since the advent of Sternberg's additive-factor method, the information-processing approach has gained momentum and prestige. The increasing popularity of the information-processing framework has resulted in expanded research efforts in several directions. The rapid development of new techniques devised by Broadbent (1958), Sperling (1960), Sternberg (1967), and others has created much enthusiasm and appreciation for scientifically respectable methods that seem to avoid the pitfalls associated with the previous "black-box" approach. As the concept of information processing developed, the attempt to trace the flow of information through the system became the paramount goal. The following section illustrates some of the major research efforts motivated by an information-processing conceptualization.

Attention

It has been argued since the early beginnings of psychology that man is limited in the amount of information he can process at any given time (James, 1890). Such

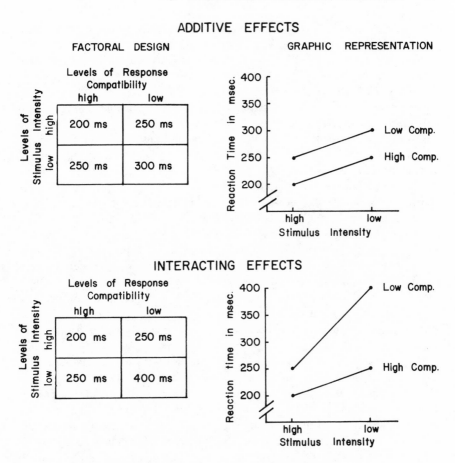

FIG. 3.6. Hypothetical results comparing conditions in which effects are additive or interacting.

an assertion has been the foundation upon which psychological research has sought to determine the nature and quantitative bounds of attention. By examining the limitations of processing capacity, an attempt has been made to define factors involved in limiting, controlling, and directing attention. To appreciate the role of attention one must recognize that each stage of information processing is severely limited, and, if the system is overloaded, information may be lost. At any given time, an incredible amount of information from the environment impinges on our sense organs. Objects, surfaces, colors, sounds, and movements exist in great abundance and variety in everyday life. We cannot process information from all possible sources in a meaningful way. Consequently, we are forced to pick and choose, according to the meaning and importance that particular stimuli may hold for us as individuals. Selective attention makes it possible for the performer to focus on or "tune in" on the relevant information, while filtering out the rest. Thus, attention ensures that it is only the important information that occupies the processing system.

Over the years, research efforts have focused on two distinct views of attention allocation: capacity and structure. Capacity models (Kahneman, 1973; Moray, 1970) are based on a processing system containing a limited capacity or pool of attention. All mental processes are assumed to require attention. Processing capacity can be flexibly allocated to any number of input channels or processing operations, provided the summated attention demands remain within the limitations of the system. When the demands of two or more simultaneous operations exceed the system's capacity, decrements in performance ensue. Capacity interference is nonspecific and depends solely on the sum of the demands that simultaneous operations levy on the limited capacity system.

In contrast, structural models (Broadbent, 1958; Keele, 1973) have a more rigid view of attention allocation. These models maintain that early processing stages (i.e., detection and recognition) can operate without attention, whereas later processing stages (i.e., decision, response selection, etc.) require attentional capacity. In addition, only one operation at a time can demand attention. Interference results when two or more mental operations compete for attention, regardless of their summated demands. Finally, it is possible for a process that does not require attention to operate while attention is allocated to another process.

Regardless of the model adopted, attention research has asked some very interesting questions. The major questions that have perplexed investigators in this area concern the upper bounds of attention capacity, and whether capacity is dependent on the nature of the task to be performed. For example, one research question frequently asked is whether we are capable of performing two tasks at once with the same precision and efficiency (i.e., without delays and/or loss of accuracy) as is possible if the tasks were performed independently. In football, the wide receiver is charged with the complex task of eluding his opponents while attempting to catch the quarterback's pass. If his attentional capacity is strained by these two actions, the result may be an incomplete pass, an interception, or an unexpected tackle.

The ability to selectively focus or allocate attentional capacity to relevant aspects of the environment lessens the handicap of processing with a limited capacity. Selective attention is analogous to the focusing of a spotlight to illuminate only relevant parts of the scenery. Over the years, two methods have emerged to study this elusive construct—the secondary-task technique and the probe technique (Keele, 1973; Posner & Keele, 1969; Salmoni, Sullivan, & Starkes, 1976). The secondary-task technique was developed to measure attention demands of mental activity and has since been adapted to the study of attention demands in motor activity. Subjects perform two different tasks independently and then simultaneously. If performance on either task suffers when performed simultaneously in comparison with when the task is performed alone, it is assumed that the limit of attentional capacity has been exceeded. The probe technique is basically a derivation of the secondary-task technique. Instead of performing two ongoing tasks simultaneously, the subject performs one movement task during which a discrete signal (probe) is introduced. The subject is required to respond to the probe concurrent with the movement task. The probe onset occurs at different points in the temporal course of the movement, so that it occurs during different stages of processing. If the reaction time to the probe alone is shorter than to the probe during a particular stage of processing, that stage is said to be attention demanding. Results from probe-technique studies indicate that the following processes and conditions are attention demanding: movement initiation (Ells, 1973; Posner & Keele, 1969); movement termination (Posner & Keele, 1969); movement corrections (Ells, 1969); more precise movements (Ells, 1969); and instances of stimulus uncertainty (Kerr, 1975). Further, some contemporary theorists have advocated that attentional capacity is not restricted to any one stage of processing, nor is it modality specific, but rather that it can be flexibly allocated depending on the nature of the task.

Perception

On the input side of the information flow, it has been shown that detection and recognition are important stages in the perceptual processing of information. Typical questions addressed in the study of perception include: How sensitive is the system in responding to different stimulus intensities?; what are the elements of stimulus information that make it more or less discriminable?; is the information that is detected stored in some way or immediately passed on?; and, of course, what is the temporal duration of perception? One assumption of the information-processing model is that, during the detection stage stimulus information is preserved in sensory storage. Such a storage would provide a comparison of the stimulus information preserved there with descriptive information in memory and would lead to recognition. An experimental procedure known as "backward masking" has been employed to determine the duration of sensory storage. A stimulus is presented and at some later time a second stimulus is presented. If the second stimulus interferes with recognition of the first stimulus (backward masking), the time between the stimuli is presumed to be insufficient for recognition. In general, evidence has indicated that the sensory storage persists for approximately 200 to 300 msec (Averbach & Coriell, 1961; Haber & Standing, 1969). Of course, the duration of persistence is dependent on the modality utilized and is affected by variables in the experimental environment. It is during this interval that the recognition process via memory search compares the features in sensory storage with features in memory for the purpose of identification. Thus, information-processing research has supplied evidence for the presence of a brief storage of sensory information prior to perception. We are left with the knowledge that perception is not instantaneous and can be disrupted.

This finding also highlights one limitation of the processing capacities of the individual; namely, time. The time limitation manifests itself in two restrictions on performance. As mentioned previously, each stage of processing requires time and if the time provided is insufficient the result is partial or incorrect processing for the following stages, eventually resulting in poor performance. The second restriction places a limitation on the speed with which a task may be accomplished. For example, even a well-trained track performer with many years of practice cannot reduce reaction time to the starting gun below a minimum time. It is beyond the scope of this discourse to even marginally summarize research in perception. Suffice to say, the information-processing approach has been instrumental in determining the effect of numerous variables on perception (Eriksen & Eriksen, 1971; Kristofferson, 1972; Lindsay, 1970; Massaro, 1974; Murdock, 1971; Reicher, 1969). As a result, the body of knowledge surrounding perceptual behavior has been broadened and has achieved a more comprehensible status.

 ## Memory

In the latter phase of perception, information must make contact with memory for the purpose of identification and recognition. Thus, memory is the hypothesized mechanism that acts to retain the information sent to it by the perceptual system. As such, it plays a critical role in the information-processing model. Its importance has made it the focal point of voluminous amounts of research. Memory research addresses specific questions about how we mentally represent our knowledge about the world, how we get access to that knowledge when we need it, why we fail to get access to it, and how we integrate new information with our existing knowledge. As such, some of the specific research questions addressed have been: Are there qualitatively and quantitatively different memory stores?; how does information get into memory (encoding)?; what factors determine whether information remains in memory (retained) or is lost (forgotten)?; how does memory search take place?

Commonly, there are three functions associated with memory: encoding, storage, and retrieval. Encoding is the process of transforming information received from the perceptual apparatus into some form suitable for storage. At least four types of memory codes have been proposed: image codes, verbal codes, symbolic codes, and motor codes (Ellis, 1979). Storage refers to the process of maintaining information over time. For many years, the popular conceptualization of memory involved three stages of storage, each with a greater degree of permanence associated with it: sensory storage (see previous section), short-term memory, and long-term memory. However, I along with others (Crowder, 1976; Murdock, 1962) prefer to conceptualize memory along a continuum of permanence determined by two restrictive elements, time and space. Research findings have shown that information that has entered memory decays with time and is subject to interference from intervening stimuli (Posner & Konick, 1966; Stelmach, 1974; see also Chapter 4). A limit of approximately seven items has been established (Miller, 1956) for number of items retainable upon first presentation. The key to retention of information is rehearsal. Rehearsal reduces the time and space limitations and moves the to-be-remembered item further along the permanency continuum toward a permanent, limitless store.

Retrieval is the process of searching, locating, and extracting information from memory. Retrieval strategies occupy much of the literature, because retrieval must also reflect encoding and storage for the researcher. Memory searches basically fall into two categories: serial search and content-addressable search. A serial search, as its name suggests, takes place when memory is examined in a linear fashion (Sternberg, Monsell, Knoll, & Wright, 1978). Some examples of serial memory searches would be: How many traffic signals are there on your way to school?; or in what innings were runs scored in your baseball game?. Theios (1973) has proposed a "push-down stack" model for memory in which the most recently presented item to be stored is placed on top of a memory stack, the other items being pushed down in order of their recency. Therefore, retrieval time of any item is a linear function of its position in the stack. In a motoric situation, commands for similar motor responses are stored in the stack, the highest one possessing the shortest initiation time. In a search characterized as content addressable, the list item itself designates the memory address to be checked and does not require an item by item search. For example, is there a signal at the intersection of State Street and University Avenue, or in what inning did you make a home run? Shiffrin and Schneider (1977) suggest a special case of this type of memory search when they postulate that perceptual learning can result in the automatic processing of information such that automated movement skills are directly accessible. Strategies for retrieval may also shed light on memory processes, some of which are mentioned in the following chapter.

Response

On the output side we have a response that, given that it is voluntary, is goal directed; that is, the individual attempts to achieve specific patterns of limb motion, correct in time and space to meet a particular movement goal. The goal itself is determined by the intentions of the performer and the nature of the environment in a problem-solving manner and can be manifested in a number of ways; for example, the individual's interaction with the environment, as in a foot race; the individual's manipulation of objects in the environment, as in archery; or of both, as in racquetball or tennis.

The components of the response have occupied considerable attention in motor behavior, and rightly so. However, dissection of movement execution per se has been largely avoided due to the unknown effects of each preceding state, yielding a cumulative-effects problem. Examination and manipulation of various input features and the resulting effects on reaction time and/or accuracy constitute the majority of work in this area. Topics of interest have revolved around the following questions: What distinctions can be made between errors in response selection and in response execution?; what effect does response complexity have on response latencies?; does the selection of response parameters take place in a serial or parallel fashion?; what effect does stimulus–response compatibility have on reaction time?

Certainly one benefit of the conceptual division of response components is the distinction between different types of errors and the realization that there are several sources of error for the response. Schmidt (1976) identified, specifically, two kinds of error: errors in response selection and errors in response execution (see also Chapter 8). Errors in response selection may arise in basically two ways. The performer may misperceive the environment and select the incorrect response based on that misperception; or the performer perceives initial conditions correctly and chooses the appropriate response, but the environment fluctuates after response selection making the response incorrect.

Errors of response execution may occur even when response selection was correct but for some reason the performer does not execute the pattern as it was chosen. Schmidt (1976) suggests that unexpected variations in the environment, fatigue, or "neural noise" may all be sources of deviation from the desired goal. Examples of these types of error are provided later in this chapter.

The reduction of response-programming time into its component parts was a logical step in the information-processing framework. Antecedent to much of the current response-programming literature is the work of Franklin M. Henry (Henry & Rogers, 1960) on response complexity. Henry studied the effect of varying the complexity of a movement on reaction time. He found that as the complexity of the movement increased so also did the reaction time. The increase in reaction time was ascribed to the additional "programming time" needed for the upcoming response. Similarly, Klapp and Erwin (1976), using positioning responses, and Sternberg et al. (1978), using typewriting tasks, have found that reaction time increased as movement complexity increased. Within the information-processing framework, the additional reaction time is typically attributed to extra processing at the stages of response selection and execution.

An alternative method for examining response programming is to vary the amount of movement preparation prior to initiation. Rosenbaum (1980), in his quest to understand response initiation, developed such a paradigm. He was interested in the amount of time required to program response variables such as limb, direction, and extent. The tack taken was to fractionate the task in terms of its dimensions and then manipulate the uncertainty (number of choices) on each. Rosenbaum (1980) used precuing to control the amount of preprogramming in each response. He chose extent (long or short) and direction (up or down) as bipolar features to manipulate the number of choices in any one dimension. Simply

stated, the assumption is   ogram'' precued information in
advance and thus exhibit a re   ...un in reaction time. As more information was
available to allow preprogramming, reaction time was found to decrease. For
example, when no decision was required in the condition where all choices were
specified, reaction times were approximately 300 msec. When one or two dimensions were allowed to vary, reaction times increased by around 150 and 300
msec, respectively. When no precues were provided, reaction times lengthened

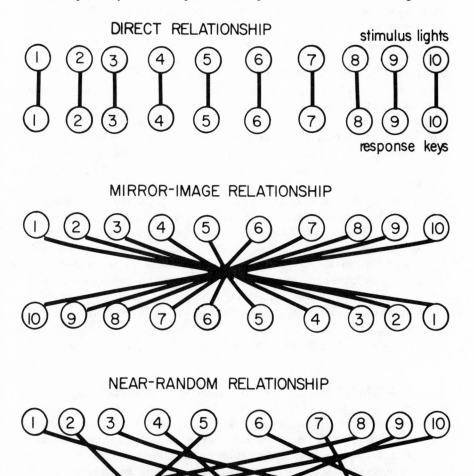

FIG. 3.7.   Possible relationships between stimuli and the required responses in a
stimulus–response compatibility paradigm.

by approximately 400 msec. Rosenbaum saw this procedure as an opportunity to distinguish between serial and parallel processing of the task parameters. His results indicated that the selection of response parameters proceeds in a serial fashion, in contrast to other research supporting parallel processing (Goodman & Kelso, 1980; see also Zelaznik, submitted for publication).

Earlier in this chapter an example of stimulus–response compatibility was presented in reference to the additive-factors method. The compatibility between the stimulus presented and the response desired is a function of the degree of correspondence between the two, relative to the entire display. Inspection of Fig. 3.7 reveals a typical manner of manipulating stimulation–response compatibility. It should be kept in mind that compatibility may be placed on a continuum from a direct stimulus–response mapping to a completely random relationship. Thus, the degree of compatibility can be seen to reflect a dimension of complexity in response selection. The benefit of a highly compatible response is seen in a reduction in reaction time (Morin & Grant, 1955). The deficit encountered in less-compatible combinations is due to the additional complexity in the selection of a response. Note that this paradigm alters the relationship between stimulus and response without altering the response and examines the resulting changes in reaction time.

In reviewing the preceding section, you may have wondered what value may be derived from studying processes in isolation. It appears that experimental procedures have been designed to examine the representation of stimulus information at almost every stage in the sequence of processes we perform. Although we have established that stages of processing interact, the predictability of that interaction is directly related to the knowledge of the behavior of single stages. If we are to apply the information-processing approach in a practical sense, knowledge of the variables affecting capacities and limitations of the learner are logically the tools for this application. With such information, pinpointing problems in the transformation of information may be simplified.

A SIMPLE MODEL OF INFORMATION PROCESSING

As you can see, the information-processing framework has provided guidance and a subtle theme for research concerned with understanding the human behaving system. Perhaps its broadest application lies in its orderly form for studying cognitive processes. Massaro (1975) states that: "the information processing methodology can be thought of as a microscope: It allows us to see what is not directly observable [p. 599]." In a heuristic manner, the approach permits the integration of experimental results in some coherent manner from many different studies. Thus, it functions as an organizational medium for the area of motor-behavior research and imposes consistency in methodology, interpretations, and conclusions.

of statement about why it is successful or not. Making such a diagnostic declaration requires much more information (for a parallel example, see Marteniuk, 1976).

How might a teacher or coach apply this information? It is possible to classify or characterize activities as being "loaded" in any or all of these stages. The components that determine the success of the task may fall under one stage's influence more than another. For example, archery would be classified as a skill containing a heavy perceptual component, requiring very little in the way of decision processes. Although execution is important, it is completely determined by the perceptual mechanism. On the other hand, weight lifting could be considered to emphasize the effector aspect.

How would you capitalize on these findings? As a teacher or coach, you might emphasize those components of a skill that contribute most to its success. For example, batting contains a heavy perceptual component. It is important that your batters be able to correctly identify the pitch. In order for the players to learn the critical perceptual cues associated with each type of pitch, you may set a camera in the batter box and film different kinds of pitches. Your players may view the films and make a simple response when they have identified the pitch, providing a simple check on accuracy. With this information you may be able to identify players as potentially good batters. You may also be able to train those with poor perceptual performance. You should begin to see how it is possible to dissect a task by knowing where its demands are heaviest.

CRITIQUE OF THE INFORMATION-PROCESSING APPROACH

A realistic view of information processing must also include its inadequacies and negative facets. Perhaps the original optimism for the approach was premature and the positive flavor of this discourse should be tempered with some criticism. Neisser (1976) states that: "the study of information processing has momentum and prestige but it has not yet committed itself to any conception of human nature that could apply beyond the confines of the laboratory [p. 6]." The approach has lavished much attention on hypothetical models of the mind and has neglected the details of the real world in which humans perceive and act. Any theoretical orientation taking such a tack for too long will find itself close to a state of irrelevancy. In the same vein, information-processing theorists have not devoted much effort toward understanding cognition as it occurs in the ordinary environment and in the context of natural, purposeful activity. Neisser (1976) warns that the approach must come to terms with the sophistication and complexity of the cognitive skill of which performers are really capable.

Two aspects of the information-processing approach that also add to its possible sterility are its dependence on time and its neglect of the response itself.

Reaction times are the most common dependent measures used in information-processing research. Although reaction times are an important tool in understanding mental processes, they have been found to be quite sensitive to extraneous variables that are not of interest. The use of reaction times as the sole dependent measure detracts from the power and generality the approach might otherwise possess. From an applied standpoint, the use of reaction times are most impractical for the practitioner, which hinders easy transfer to the everyday world. A preoccupation with reaction times may have contributed to the neglect the processing approach has demonstrated for response variables. In practice, information-processing researchers have effectively inserted another "black box" in the model. In any case, the lack of knowledge about system output has only contributed to the preceding criticisms.

The approach has been shown to provide an impressively flexible model of performance but sheds little understanding on the changes in performance that characterize learning. We in physical education are most concerned with the circumstances surrounding learning, as evident in the quantity of research examining it. Unfortunately, the concept of skill acquisition through repeated practice has not been stressed in the model. Certainly organizational structures and mechanisms must exist in memory to account for learning when physical storage is limited and potential input is infinite. Attention to learning and the variables affecting it would increase the appeal the information-processing framework may hold for the practitioner.

The information-processing approach has also been criticized for an imbalance in the relative emphasis placed on certain aspects of performance. Recall the historical part of this discourse that characterized early research efforts as product or output oriented. In a pendular fashion, the emphasis appears to have swung toward the mental processes preceding the response. The paucity of recent research directed toward problems intrinsic to the motor system suggests that our future efforts should aim at balancing this emphasis. To understand the motor system, we must study motor issues. Thus, I feel that future research should attack performance problems with emphasis on both the preparatory processes and the effector products. Such a direction, I feel, would stress the complexity of the motor system (for example, its specification of nondiscrete parameters such as force, velocity, and acceleration), which the present information-processing framework does not communicate.

CONCLUDING COMMENTS

One of the most common observations of educators is the difficulty that individuals have in gaining insight about their own mental structures and information-processing activities. The information-processing model advanced in this chapter presents a nice way to conceptualize mental functions, partitioning them into separate stages. It is concerned with how individuals gain knowledge about the world, and how they use that language to make decisions and perform effective actions. In essence, it allows students of motor behavior to infer and measure mental processes that they cannot see. In this way it provides the player, teacher, and coach with information about the cognitive aspects of skilled acts that are often neglected. Nevertheless, despite the broad appeal of the information-processing framework, its contribution has been somewhat narrow, focusing primarily on the analysis of specific experimental situations. If the trend continues, the danger is that the information-processing framework will be fragmented into pockets of isolated and competitive subdisciplines, where research ideas or situations become ends in themselves. If the information-processing model is to contribute to our understanding of the functioning of the learner outside the experimental situation, it must attempt to place cumulative findings in a broader perspective that stresses biological and psychological determinants.

As emphasized also in Chapter 1, students of motor behavior must resist the temptation of extreme reductionism and move toward a multidisciplinary course of study. The basic reason for such a reorientation is that the human organism presents a highly complex, multilayered system. Unless we use diverse approaches that encompass a variety of concepts and methods, our own insights will not go beyond some narrow province in the area. It is perhaps too early to evaluate the theoretical advances achieved by information-processing models— the scientific community will do that in time—but at least these models have exerted a potent energizing influence in the field. They have generated new research techniques for the exploring of cognitive activities that are much more complex than had been considered possible by investigators within the framework of earlier "black-box" theories.

ACKNOWLEDGMENT

Appreciation and a sincere thanks to Virginia Diggles for her background work and editorial assistance in preparing this chapter.

REFERENCES

Averbach, E., & Coriell, A. S. Short-term memory in vision. *Bell System Technical Journal,* 1961, *40,* 309-328.

Broadbent, D. E. *Perception and communication.* London: Pergamon Press, 1958.

Chernikoff, R., & Taylor, F. V. Reaction time to kinesthetic stimulation resulting from sudden arm displacement. *Journal of Experimental Psychology,* 1952, *43,* 1-8.

Chomsky, N. *Syntactic structure.* The Hague: Mounton, 1957.

Crowder, R. G. The organization of memory in free recall. In R. G. Crowder (Ed.), *Principles of learning and memory.* Hillsdale, N. J.: Lawrence Erlbaum Associates, 1976.

Donders, F. C. On the speed of mental processes. 1868–1869. *Attention and Performance II: Acta Psychologica*, 1969, *30*, 412–431.

Ebbinghaus, H. Uber das Gedacht vs. Leipzig, Duneker, 1885. Translation by H. A. Reiger & C. E. Bussenius, in *Memory*. New York: Teacher's College, Columbia University, 1913.

Ellis, H. C. *Fundamentals of human learning, memory and cognition.* Dubuque, Iowa: Wm. C. Brown, 1979.

Ells, J. G. Analysis of temporal and attentional aspects of movement control. *Journal of Experimental Psychology*, 1973, *99*, 10–21.

Eriksen, C. W., & Eriksen, B. A. Visual perceptual processing rates and backward and forward masking. *Journal of Experimental Psychology*, 1971, *89*, 306–313.

Goodman, D., & Kelso, J. A. S. Are movements prepared in parts? Not under compatible (naturalized) conditions. *Journal of Experimental Psychology: General*, 1980, *109*, 475–495.

Green, D. M., & Swets, J. A. *Signal detection theory and psychophysics.* New York: Wiley, 1966.

Haber, R. N. Information processing. In R. N. Haber (Ed.), *Information-processing approaches to visual perception.* New York: Holt, 1969.

Haber, R. N., & Standing, L. G. Direct measures of short-term visual storage. *Quarterly Journal of Experimental Psychology*, 1969, *21*, 43–54.

Helmholtz, H. von. *Treatise on physiological optics. 1856–1866.* Translated from the 3rd ed. by J. P. C. Southall (Ed.). New York: Dover, 1962.

Henry, F. M., & Rogers, D. E. Increased response latency for complicated movements and a "Memory Drum" theory of neuromotor reaction. *Research Quarterly*, 1960, *31*, 448–458.

James, W. *The principles of psychology* (Vol. 1). New York: Holt, 1890.

Kahneman, D. *Attention and effort.* Englewood Cliffs, N. J.: Prentice–Hall, 1973.

Keele, S. W. *Attention and human performance.* Pacific Palisades: Goodyear, 1973.

Kerr, B. Processing demands during movement. *Journal of Motor Behavior*, 1975, *7*, 15–27.

Klapp, S. T., & Erwin, C. I. Relation between programming time and duration of the response being programmed. *Journal of Experimental Psychology*, 1976, *2*, 591–598.

Kristofferson, M. W. Types and frequency of errors in visual search. *Perception and Psychophysics*, 1972, *11*, 325–328.

Lindsay, P. H. Multichannel processing in perception. In D. I. Mostofsky (Ed.), *Attention: Contemporary theory and analysis.* New York: Appleton–Century–Crofts, 1970.

Marteniuk, R. G. *Information processing in motor skills.* New York: Holt, Rinehart, & Winston, 1976.

Massaro, D. W. Perceptual units of speech recognition. *Journal of Experimental Psychology*, 1974, *102*, 199–208.

Massaro, D. *Experimental psychology and information processing.* Chicago: Rand McNally College Processing, 1975.

Miller, G. A. The magical number seven, plus or minus two: Some limits on our capacity for processing information. *Psychological Review*, 1956, *63*, 81–97.

Moray, N. *Listening and attention.* London: Penguin Press, 1970.

Morin, R. E., & Grant, D. A. Learning and performance of a key-pressing task as a function of the degree of spatial stimulus response correspondence. *Journal of Experimental Psychology*, 1955, *49*, 39–47.

Murdock, B. B. The serial position effect in free recall. *Journal of Experimental Psychology*, 1962, *64*, 482–488.

Murdock, B. B. A parallel processing model for scanning. *Perception and Psychophysics*, 1971, *10*, 289–291.

Neisser, U. *Cognition and reality.* San Francisco: W. H. Freeman, 1976.

Norman, D. A. Introduction: Models of human memory. In D. A. Norman (Ed.), *Models of human memory.* New York: Academic Press, 1970.

Posner, M. I., & Keele, S. W. Attention demands of movement. In *Proceedings of the 16th International Conference of Applied Psychology.* Amsterdam: Swets & Zeitlinger, 1969.

Posner, M. I., & Konick, A. F. On the role of interference in short-term retention. *Journal of Experimental Psychology*, 1966, *72*, 221-231.

Reicher, G. M. Perceptual recognition as a function of meaningfulness of stimulus material. *Journal of Experimental Psychology*, 1969, *81*, 275-281.

Rosenbaum, D. A. Human movement initiation: Specification of arm direction and extent. *Journal of Experimental Psychology: General*, 1980, *109*, 444-474.

Salmoni, A. W., Sullivan, S. J., & Starkes, J. L. The attention demands of movements: A critique of the probe technique. *Journal of Motor Behavior*, 1976, *8*, 161-169.

Schmidt, R. A. Control processes in motor skills. In J. Keogh & R. S. Hutton (Eds.), *Exercise and sport sciences reviews*. Santa Barbara: Journal Publishing Affiliates, 1976.

Shannon, C. E., & Weaver, W. *The mathematical theory of communication*. Urbana: University of Illinois Press, 1949.

Shiffrin, R. M. Capacity limitations in information processing, attention, and memory. In W. K. Estes (Ed.), *Handbook of learning and cognitive processes: Attention and memory* (Vol. 4). Hillsdale, N. J.: Lawrence Erlbaum Associates, 1977.

Shiffrin, R. M., & Schneider, W. Controlled and automatic human information processing: II. Perceptual learning, automatic attending, and a general theory. *Psychological Review*, 1977, *84*, 127-190.

Sperling, G. The information available in brief visual presentations. *Psychological Monographs*, *1960*, *74* (Whole No. 498).

Stelmach, G. E. Retention of motor skills. In J. A. Wilmore (Ed.), *Exercise and sport sciences reviews* (Vol. 2). New York: Academic Press, 1974.

Sternberg, S. Two operations in character recognition: Some evidence from RT measurement. *Perception and Psychophysics*, 1967, *2*, 45-53.

Sternberg, S. Memory scanning: Mental processes revealed by reaction-time experiments. *American Scientist*, 1969, *57*, 421-457. (a)

Sternberg, S. The discovery of processing stages: Extensions of Donder's method. *Acta Psychologica*, 1969, *30*, 276-315. (b)

Sternberg, S., Monsell, S., Knoll, R. L., & Wright, C. E. The latency and duration of rapid movement sequences: Comparisons of speech and typewriting. In G. E. Stelmach (Ed.), *Information processing in motor control and learning*. New York: Academic Press, 1978.

Theios, J. Reaction-time measurements in the study of memory processes: Theory and data. In G. H. Bower (Ed.), *The psychology of learning and motivation* (Vol. 7). New York: Academic Press, 1973.

Zelaznik, H. N. *Response execution in rapid force generation: Evidence for a parallel motor programming process*. Submitted for publication.

4

Motor Control and Motor Learning: The Closed-Loop Perspective

George E. Stelmach
University of Wisconsin

INTRODUCTION

The information-processing approach to motor control and learning discussed in Chapter 3 provides a conceptual framework in which to study and understand human performance but does not adequately account for the coordination and regulation of movement. Superficially, the coordination of appropriate muscular commands for a specified movement appears to be a relatively simple task, yet the successful completion of a refined motor act requires a high degree of temporal precision among the motor commands for the agonist and antagonist muscle groups. Questions and controversies concerning how we control our limbs during movement execution have stimulated neurophysiological and psychological inquiry for many years. Perhaps it is helpful to begin our discussion by defining the various theoretical views in which motor control has been characterized or explained. The first—and until recently—favored position claimed the reporting and updating of information about the present state of the organism via peripheral receptors (feedback) to be necessary for the control of intentional, coordinated movement. With such information the organism is operating in a closed-loop fashion and thus is capable of detecting errors and correcting them. The opposing position contends that movement is regulated by central rather than peripheral sources, operating in an open-loop mode, as it were. In such a framework the information generated from central sources to specify movement is purportedly sufficient for the control of movement. The controversy existing between open- and closed-loop modes of control has dominated the motor behavior literature for many years (see Kelso & Stelmach, 1976, for review).

In the present chapter I only briefly consider open-loop systems of control (see Chapters 7 and 9 for many more details). My primary emphasis is on closed-loop systems; in particular I present a detailed overview of one specific closed-loop theory, postulated by Jack Adams in 1971. The closed-loop theory of Adams is examined in detail, not because I believe it to be the most veracious, but because it represents one way to conceptualize how skill acquisition may take place, and it posits many testable predictions. Since its introduction, it has served as a catalyst for numerous research efforts and theory development in motor behavior. Moreover, it has been a driving force that inspired many of the investigations reviewed in Chapters 6 through 9, in their conceptualizing of motor behavior.

OPEN-LOOP AND CLOSED-LOOP MODELS

It is helpful to begin our discussion by outlining two ways in which motor control has been characterized or, if you will, dichotomized: open-loop models and closed-loop models. In any open-loop system, not limited to humans, peripheral sensing mechanisms detect conditions in the environment. This information is recorded, evaluated, and aids in determining a response appropriate for those conditions. The response is specified and executed, presumably to institute some change in the environment. There is no mechanism for detecting the changes that may occur due to the system's generated response. Thus, in its purest form this mode of control has no feedback mechanisms for checking the correctness of the response, allowing errors to go unnoticed and uncorrected. See Fig. 4.1, part A, for a graphic representation of an open-loop system. Some examples of open-loop control systems include: an unattended bathtub and a running faucet that will result in a water overflow; a gas station air pump without a pressure gauge that will burst a tire if the user is not cautious; and traffic signals at an intersection with fixed timing that will not adjust for traffic loads, therefore causing traffic jams in heavy traffic and slowing the flow of light traffic.

When our attention is turned to human movement, the open-loop view proposes that information from peripheral sources enters the higher centers of the central nervous system (CNS), where it is operated on and transformed into information necessary for movement patterning. These higher centers dictate the characteristics of the desired movement (i.e., the exact motor commands for each muscle group and their exact temporal sequence). This centrally stored and generated movement plan has been termed a motor program (Keele, 1968, and Chapters 7, 8, and 9) after a computer analogy. Neorophysiologically, this outflowing signal from the CNS is termed efference, as opposed to afference, which is the inflowing signal from the peripheral sensory receptors. Open-loop theorists propose that the efferent command is all that is necessary to control coordinated movement. Consequently, open-loop control does not utilize feed-

MOTOR CONTROL MODELS

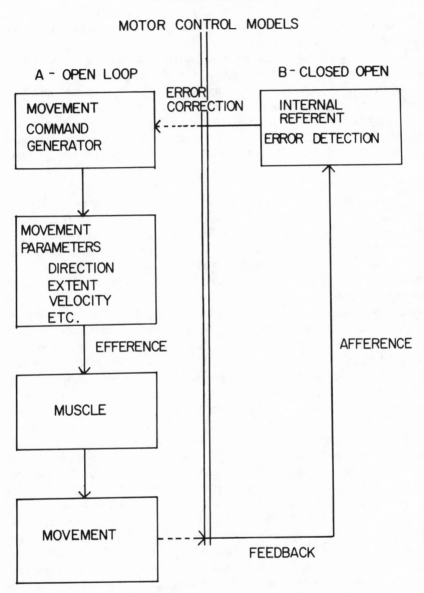

FIG. 4.1. A graphic representation of open- and closed-loop models. Part A depicts an open-loop system and parts A and B depict a closed-loop system. It should be noted that the addition of the dotted lines to the open-loop system provide the capability of error detection and correction.

back as a mechanism for movement regulation, implying that feedback is unnecessary for the coordinated movement.

In movement controlled in an open-loop fashion, all parameters of the movement are specified in the motor command and the movement is carried out to completion without alteration. Typically, fast movements are under open-loop control: for example, any rapid movement sequences found in skills like typing, piano playing, and throwing. This central control position had been out of the mainstream for many years. However, evidence that motor responses are often programmed in advance is becoming more common, attracting a strong following among motor-behavior theorists (Keele, 1968; Kelso & Stelmach, 1976; Schmidt, 1976; Stelmach, 1978).

The contrasting point of view, closed-loop theory, has been dominant in motor behavior for many years. The theory originated in the engineering sciences from servotheory and cybernetics and has seen many variations in motor behavior (Anokhin, 1969; Chase, 1965; Fairbanks, 1954; Sokolov, 1969). The model itself differs from the open-loop view in basically two features. First, mechanisms for communicating information of the response outcome to the executive control system are required. Second, an internal reference against which this information may be compared and measured is needed to modify the system's response. The addition of these two features closes the information loop of the control model (Fig. 4.1, A *and* B). Some examples of closed-loop systems in operation are: a home heating system that relies on a thermostat for temperature regulation; street lights that are turned on and off by light sensors; and stop lights that are regulated by traffic-flow meters.

The closed-loop view in the human environment proposes that feedback, error detection, and error correction are necessary requirements for movement regulation. The *motor command* that specifies the response to be generated is executed, and, depending on the duration of the movement, sensory information produced from the movement via proprioceptive receptors (e.g., muscle spindles and joint receptors) is *fed back* to the central nervous system (see Chapter 2). The feedback is compared to the internal referent to check for discrepancies between the output specified initially and the movement actually produced (error detection). The errors are evaluated and the organism attempts to minimize the size of the error (error correction) to achieve the desired movement. Thus, it is clear that the closed-loop system is self-regulating and uses the error detection and correction processes to continually minimize movement deviations from those specified. In movement under closed-loop control, the parameters of the movement are specified but are subject to modification during and after movement completion. Typically, slower-movement sequences that take some time for completion are under closed-loop control (i.e., any of the slow-movement sequences found in skills such as handwriting, canoeing, sailing, swimming, tightrope walking, etc.).

It should be clear now that motor behavior can be catagorized into two distinct control modes. To help you conceptualize how these positions have evolved and to establish the credibility of each, it is helpful to examine the kinds of data that support each position. In the review to follow, however, I focus on closed-loop behavior. In particular, I want to give you a feel for the various methods of manipulating the parameters of motor control to illustrate the methods by which motor behaviorists draw inference about human movement. Later chapters delve more deeply into the open-loop, motor-programming view.

EVIDENCE SUPPORTING A CLOSED-LOOP SYSTEM OF MOTOR CONTROL

In the following section it is clear that support for a closed-loop system is rather well-documented. To begin, examinations of whether the behaving system is regulated in a closed-loop mode typically involve quantification of the contribution feedback makes to movement precision and timing accuracy. In other words, to what extent does error information generated from feedback actually influence the motor response? The major test of feedback utilization is to determine whether feedback can produce either facilitating or interfering changes in some observable aspect of the response.

Delayed and Disrupted Feedback

A number of published studies suggest that auditory feedback plays a role in the perception of movement requiring temporal regulation. If the acoustic signals associated with a movement sequence lag behind each of the responses that caused them, by approximately 200 msec, it is often observed that performance is slowed and/or disrupted (for review, see Glencross, 1977). This finding has been reported for a wide variety of motor skills, such as handclapping (Kalmus, Denes, & Fry, 1955), tapping (Chase, Harvey, Standfast, Rapin, & Sutton, 1961), and speech (Fairbanks, 1955). Given the effect of delay on performance, it is reasonable to infer that subjects do monitor auditory feedback associated with movement. The principal changes in speech that occur include a lengthening of phrase utterances, repetition of syllables, omissions, substitutions, and mispronunciation. These findings have been attributed to increased jaw-opening excursions, overshooting, and increased jaw velocity (for review, see Stelmach, 1978). Similarly, the normal relation between vision and hand motion can also be distorted temporarily by delaying the sight of one's moving hand. This technique of delaying visual feedback, as developed by Smith (1972), induces movement-regulation disturbances similar in some respects to those found with prism displacement (Bowen & Smith, 1976).

Perturbations in visual feedback have also been shown to affect the speed and accuracy of movements (Held, 1967; Kohler, 1947). The well-studied effect of visual distortion by prismatic displacement is an excellent example. A hand movement from the left to a target on the right, while wearing right-displacing prisms, will induce an error of overshooting to the right of the target due to the distortion of visual information. If the hand, however, is moved slowly enough, the induced error can be detected visually, and corrections can be made in order to compensate for the initially incorrect command to the motor system. With practice under prism displacement, movement accuracy can be regained, a change well-known as adaptation (Craske, 1975). The fact that disrupting and delaying normal feedback affects the speed and accuracy of movement is evidence of the prominent role feedback plays in motor control.

Mechanical vibration is another method utilized in research to seek evidence in support of a closed-loop position. Goodwin, McCloskey, and Matthews (1972) found that when vibration was applied to the arm over a tendon or muscle belly it produced an illusion of limb movement. Specifically, applying vibration to the biceps–brachii produced a sensation of extension, and, contrastingly, vibrations of the triceps produced the sensation of flexion. Additionally, when the movements were resisted, the subject reported a strong sensation that the arm was being moved in the opposite direction. This type of research suggests that muscle receptors are biased via vibrations and are capable of inducing the perception of movement where none exists. In other words, the higher centers of the CNS were overridden by stimulation of a peripheral receptor, a finding that provides strong support for closed-loop control.

Augmented Feedback

In studies involving feedback augmentation, the response-produced feedback is enhanced or amplified. The rationale for such feedback manipulations follows the logic that an increase in the amount of feedback will lead to an increase in performance. Adams and Creamer (1962) found that subjects in a discrete visual tracking task performed their task more accurately when their manual controls were loaded with spring tension than when they were not. Similarly, the experiments of Burke and Gibbs (1965) and Holland and Noble (1953) have shown that increased tension improved movement accuracy in tracking tasks. Ellis, Schmidt, and Wade (1968) believed that increasing position and force cues would provide more discriminable information for the reproduction of a motor response. A coincident positioning task was used in which the resistance of a carriage along a track was either minimal or equal to 18.9 kg. Performance under the augmented conditions was found to be better than that in the minimal feedback conditions.

We have seen that there is substantial evidence for the closed-loop position, and in later chapters you will find equally strong support for the open-loop notion. In

light of the voluminous research in support of both positions, the rational observer cannot reduce the matter of motor control to an "either-or" decision.
Accepting that both modes exert influence, one is prompted to ask under what
conditions each mode of control prevails. However, when the human organism is
viewed mechanically, a multisegmented system is perceived whereby movement
of one segment can influence the motion of an adjacent segment in a variety of
ways. The plasticity, flexibility, and intricate organization of a skilled individual
presents researchers with a complex, multilayered puzzle possessing countless
pieces and limitless combinations. In such a system, the dichotomy of open- and
closed-loop modes of control is surely a limited way of conceptualizing movement control. These topics are and will remain prominent in the study of motor
control, but will no doubt be integrated into a more complex and comprehensive
approach to modeling control.

A theory that recognized the importance of both kinds of control was posited
by Jack Adams in 1971 in his closed-loop theory for positioning responses. In
this theory, an open-loop structure is used to generate movements, whereas a
closed-loop structure is used to regulate movements. The use of both structures
allows the theory flexibility to account for a variety of types of behavior. For
example, such an integrated theory was thought to be able to account for rapid,
ballistic movements, where there is insufficient time to correct or modify the
movement, as well as for slow movements in which feedback is available for
modification.

ADAMS' CLOSED-LOOP THEORY OF MOTOR LEARNING

Genesis and Development

The process of movement control and regulation has intrigued psychologists for
many years, but it is apparent that the understanding of motor control is still at an
elementary level. The controversy between open- and closed-loop systems of
performance has dominated much of the research literature in motor control.
Although there are a number of closed-loop theories that stress feedback and
error correction (Adams, 1971, 1976; Anokhin, 1969; Bernstein, 1967; Smith,
1969; Sokolov, 1969), I think it best that we examine one theoretical position in
detail so that the reader will more fully understand the strengths and weaknesses
of a closed-loop model. For demonstration purposes, Adams' closed-loop theory
is examined as one way of viewing motor learning that has developed from a
large quantity of empirical evidence. After it first appeared in print, the theory
progressed and gained momentum, generating questions that served only to
generate more questions. The theory was reduced in scope in that it concentrated
on learning specifically and not performance in general. This reduction in scope

resulted in a clarity and focus in explaining for students of movement those parameters that determine skill acquisition. As a result, clear and definitive expectations for many learning situations could be derived from the theory, resulting in testable predictions that have over the years spurred investigations and inquiry that might otherwise have not occurred. Adams' theory forced investigators to attend to the processes underlying coordinated movement by examining the neurological substrates of action. Along these lines emphasis on the physiological functioning of specific receptors and effectors became prominent in the literature, providing some impetus for the shift toward strictly control processes. In yet another instance, schema theory for movement (Schmidt, 1975; see Chapter 9) was developed to answer some of the problems plaguing Adams' theory. Although its precursor elements had existed for some time, schema theory would never have crystallized had it not been for Adams' theory. For a number of reasons discussed later in this chapter, Adams' theory has been found less than satisfactory as an explanatory model of motor learning and memory. However, from a theory–development perspective I think it is enlightening to examine some of the factors that prompted Adams to develop his theory.

To fully appreciate why a closed-loop theory for motor learning was proposed by Adams (1971), it is necessary to place the thinking of the time in a historical perspective. Prior to 1970, behaviorism was an influential power in psychology; its laws were applied to all aspects of learning, using positive and negative reinforcement to explain and control behavior. For example, open-loop theories assumed that, if the stimuli were adequate and if the internal states of the organism such as habit and motivation were sufficient, a response would occur. If an error occurred in performance, then the stimuli or the transformation imposed by the internal states of the organism were inadequate. The stimulus–response approach to learning appeared adequate in explaining animal behavior but was not entirely applicable to human behavior. Underlying processes between stimulus and response were ignored, resulting in a simple descriptive relationship.

In rejecting the laws of behaviorism, Adams adopted a more intuitive, logical approach to motor behavior that possessed constructs subject to empirical tests. By surveying past trends in psychology and anticipating new ones, he concluded that open-loop control could not answer some of the pressing questions learning theorists were asking. The subject of these questions revolved around the issues of error, its detection and correction. Adams drew on a large body of data, generated through the years, on simple arm movements (e.g., reproducing the length of a line with a pencil), to develop an error-centered theory, in which error detection, error correction, and knowledge of results play a major role. The learner was no longer considered a passive organism, as behaviorists proposed, but was seen as an active participant, controlling, manipulating, and generating behavior. This analytic aspect of motor behavior was promoted to the extent that learning a skill was considered analogous to problem solving. The learner's problem is to perform a particular motor skill accurately, but how the learner goes about using stimulus information and feedback determines success. Keep in mind throughout this discussion that when the theory was first proposed the frame of reference for movement was the learning of simple, self-paced, graded movements, like line drawing and lever positioning. Over the years, many attempts have been made to generalize the theory to a variety of movements with varying degrees of success (Schmidt & White, 1972; Williams & Roy, 1972).

The Nature of Knowledge of Results

Motor learning presents the individual with a problem to be solved and knowledge of results is the information used to develop the solution. I want to emphasize the role assigned to knowledge of results primarily as a source of information contributing to the functions of error correction and detection early in learning. It assists the learner in building a strong internal referent, an image of the movement as it were, as a function of practice. Knowledge of results is a function of error and can be given in varying degrees of precision. For example, qualitative knowledge of results is a gross description of error, like the statement "too long" or "too short." Quantitative knowledge of results is an exact, precise description of error usually given in stated numerical information, like "you're 27 centimeters too far." The learner uses knowledge of results to formulate strategies to eliminate errors in responding. Thus, the perceptual, motor, and verbal systems interact to "solve a problem." One premise of this view is that the learner must comprehend the form of the knowledge of results presented. For example, knowledge of results given in nanoseconds would be of little use to a sprinter struggling to improve his or her time in the 100-yard dash. Knowledge of results is primarily a source of information that leads to movement corrections, resulting in execution of a correct response.

Memory Structures

One major difference between Adams' closed-loop theory and the traditional open-loop view is the proposition that learning is dependent on *two* memory structures, the *memory trace* and the *perceptual trace*. The role of the memory trace is to select and initiate the desired response and is cued to action by the volition of the learner. The memory trace, the learned capability for a response, is implicit in most of the traditional theories of learning (Hull's "habit," Henry's "motor program," etc.). Because the contiguity between the response and the memory trace determines the exact parameters of the memory trace, its strength increases as a function of practice and rehearsal. The memory trace, in effect, acts in an open-loop fashion as a "modest" motor program to initiate a response operating without feedback. Necessarily, its use precedes the second memory structure, the perceptual trace.

The perceptual trace is a construct for evaluating the correctness of the response as executed by the memory trace. It determines not the choice of movement but the extent of movement. The subject uses the perceptual trace as the reference to adjust the next movement on the basis of knowledge of results that has been received. The perceptual trace is not a single state but a complex distribution of traces that has been produced over many practice trials. The strength of the perceptual trace grows as a function of practice and feedback; feedback as used here is not to be limited to proprioception but should include visual, auditory, tactile, vestibular, and similar information. Important to the development of the perceptual trace is the labeling of errors related to a specific response. In the initial stages of learning, the learner must use knowledge of results to identify and amend errors detected in the previous response before executing a subsequent response.

There are three reasons to postulate the existence of two memory states. First, if the mechanism that initiates the response is also the reference against which the same response is tested for correctness, the response must be judged correct because no discrepancy exists between the command and the execution, indicating that response activation and evaluation require independent mechanisms. Second, use of the perceptual trace requires feedback occurring after the response is in progress, which means some other construct is needed to initiate the movement. Third, recall and recognition are "allegedly" independent functions, such that the starting of a response is motor recall based on the memory trace, and realizing whether the movement is proceeding correctly is response recognition as governed by the perceptual trace and feedback. The strength of both traces is a function of practice. They are distinguished by their independent functions, the memory trace being responsible for selection and initiation of the movement, and the perceptual trace governing movement regulation.

Stages of Learning

Learning of motor skills seldom occurs in a uniform, stepwise fashion as a function of practice. We are all aware from past experience that definite qualitative changes occur in learning, usually a result of refinements in precision and form. Adams proposed two stages of learning that are differentiated by the strength of the perceptual trace and, consequently, the locus of control. The first stage is characterized by conscious verbal control and is designated as the Verbal-Motor Stage. Control in the second stage, termed the Motor Stage, becomes more automated, requiring less cognitive manipulation. The characteristics of each stage are described in the following sections.

Verbal-Motor Stage.   In the initial stages of learning, the individual typically performs with large errors. At this point in learning, the perceptual trace is comprised of information from erroneous attempts at correct performance and is therefore weak and poorly defined.

Attempts by the learner to adjust the response relative to an uncertain referent results in confusion and uncertainty about the correctness of the performance. The individual has had little experience with the specific sensory consequences of his or her actions; thus, there is a dependence on external knowledge of results to equate the feedback associated with movement and the outcome of that movement. It is the continual linking of movement feedback and movement outcome that develops the perceptual trace. With practice this translation process progresses to the point where response-produced feedback is directly interpretable by the learner. Errors are typically small and knowledge of results becomes superfluous, marking the termination of the Verbal–Motor stage.

Motor Stage.   After the individual has developed a strong internal standard and has consistently performed with little error, the distribution of perceptual traces develops a prominent modal value that defines the parameters of the correct response. The perceptual trace is now robust and comprised of feedback representations of nearly correct responses. The learner can compare feedback from a given response to this modal trace and determine the correctness of that response; in fact, the individual may continue to improve performance and learn without knowledge of results (Bilodeau & Bilodeau, 1958; Newell, 1974; Schmidt & White, 1972). One consequence of a strong perceptual trace is an increase in the individual's confidence in the evaluation of his or her performance. The learner knows when errors have occurred and their magnitude and is aware when the "right" moves have been executed. At this point in time, the perceptual trace is very resistant to forgetting.

EXPERIMENTAL EVIDENCE IN SUPPORT OF ADAMS' THEORY

The first section reviews research substantiating the importance of feedback. The next section addresses the theory as it applies to the acquisition of a motor skill in the *Verbal–Motor Stage*. The third section covers the literature on the delay of knowledge of results. In the fourth section the withdrawal of knowledge of results at different points in time is discussed in relation to both stages of learning. Finally, the distinction between memory states is reviewed where efforts have been made to discriminate recall from recognition.

Feedback

The importance of sensory feedback acts as a cornerstone of support for Adams' theory, essentially closing the information loop hypothesized. Examining performance in the absence of feedback or learning under conditions of minimal or impaired feedback are common methods for determining its contribution to performance. Fairbanks (1955) required subjects to read prose aloud and delayed the speech output delivered to the speaker via earphones. Speech was badly disturbed in timing, pitch, and number of errors. Kelso, Stelmach, and Wanamaker (1974) found rapid tapping tasks to be severely impaired when a pressure cuff was applied to the upper arm preventing kinesthetic sensation (although motor impairment was also a source of impaired performance). Stelmach (1973) found evidence that augmented feedback (visual, auditory, and proprioceptive) resulted in increased retention when compared to performance with these modalities minimized.

Feedback should also play a role in one's ability to detect and correct errors in performance. Testing this notion directly, Adams and Goetz (1973) required subjects in one experiment to detect errors (i.e., move from a discrepant location to the one learned earlier). Learning phases were conducted under two levels of feedback (minimal and augmented) and two levels of practice (high and low). They found that the accuracy of error detection and correction was positively related to amount of feedback and amount of practice.

In a learning paradigm, Adams, Goetz, and Marshall (1972) examined the effect of response-produced feedback during acquisition trials with knowledge of results available and later trials with knowledge of results withdrawn. Feedback (visual, auditory, or proprioceptive) was augmented or minimized in a lever-positioning task under conditions of high practice and low practice with knowledge of results. After the acquisition trials an additional set of trials without knowledge of results was administered to all groups. Feedback proved to be a determiner of acquisition for both high- and low-practice groups, and when knowledge of results was withdrawn only those high-practice groups with augmented feedback continued performance unchanged.

Acquisition

One of the major principles Adams emphasized was the dependence of performance improvement on knowledge of results. There are scores of studies in support of this principle, which is not unique to Adams (see Newell, 1974, for a review). Of interest here are those aspects of knowledge of results that modify its use and usefulness in a variety of settings. The potential impact is evident when you note that the rate of improvement is dependent on the precision of the knowledge of results. In Fig. 4.2 we see results from a study of Trowbridge and Cason (1932) designed to test the effects of different types of knowledge of results on performance. Knowledge of results was manipulated in four ways. In the irrelevant condition, knowledge of results that had no correspondence to actual performance was administered. In the qualitative condition, inexact, qualitative knowledge of results was administered. Exact, precise knowledge of results was administered to a third group, whereas the fourth group received no knowledge of results at all. Irrelevant knowledge of results resulted in the worst performance, because it was not helpful in correcting errors and indeed caused

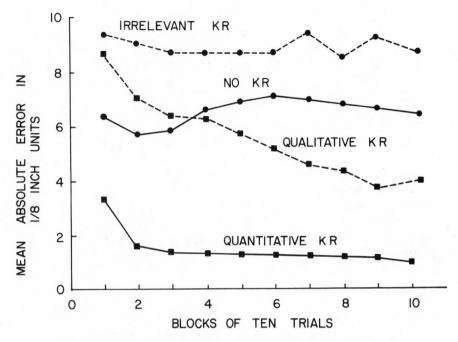

FIG. 4.2.   Taken from Trowbridge and Cason (1932). Absolute error for the knowledge of results conditions plotted as a function of trials.

larger errors, whereas the lack of knowledge of results was not as disruptive to performance. Qualitative knowledge of results reduced error considerably, but not as effectively as quantitative knowledge or results.

Delay of Knowledge of Results

The theory predicts that delaying knowledge of results has little or no effect on acquisition. It appears that this rule may not be as crucial as we once believed. Boulter (1964) required subjects to learn to draw a 3-inch line and subjects received knowledge of results; but in one condition knowledge of results was immediate and in the other knowledge of results was delayed 20 sec. Performance for the two groups in acquisition was the same. Because the subject uses knowledge of results cognitively, the delay interval, prior to the presentation of knowledge of results, is simply an unfilled interval. The emphasis in administration of knowledge of results is the ability to interpret knowledge of results and assign a corrective response prior to the next trial. Accordingly, a delay in the administration of knowledge of results is inconsequential, providing adequate time is allowed for processing prior to the next response (Bilodeau & Bilodeau, 1958).

The post-knowledge of results delay interval (Fig. 4.3), that period between the presentation of knowledge of results and the next response, is of greater importance early in learning where cognitive processing is required to plan and adjust the next response. If the interval is too brief, there will not be sufficient time for complete processing and planning. As a result learning will proceed at a retarded rate because decision making is interfered with.

A natural extension of the foregoing stage interpretation is that interfering activities in the post-knowledge of results interval should affect learning. If the activities are sufficiently interfering to disrupt cognitive processing, deficits will result. However, this result should only manifest itself in the *Verbal–Motor* stage of learning. During the *Motor Stage* cognitive activity is minimal, so interfering activity will have a lessened impact on performance. Boucher (1974) tested this hypothesis by examining the accuracy of an arm displacement task with knowledge of results. In the post-knowledge of results period, the subject performed an interfering task of reading aloud. As predicted, the interfering task displayed the greatest detrimental effect early in practice.

Withdrawal of Knowledge of Results

The withdrawal of knowledge of results, viewed from a behaviorist's position, could be analogous to the withdrawal of reinforcement. Were a behaviorist to make this analogy he would expect the extinction of the response being learned to occur. Can we have the same expectations in the motor domain? Would you

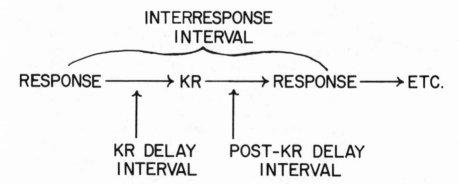

FIG. 4.3. Taken from Adams (1971). Graphic representation of the interresponse interval. The time periods before and after the presentation of knowledge results determine the delay and postknowledge of results delay interval.

continuously administer knowledge of results to an athlete for fear that his or her skill would dissipate? According to Adams' theory, the effect of withdrawing knowledge of results would be dependent on the stage of learning at which the withdrawal occurred. I have previously described the *perceptual trace* as weak early in learning with most corrections dependent on external knowledge of results. With these conditions existing, the learner has no reliable reference with which to detect and correct errors other than the primary source of error information, knowledge of results. Its withdrawal marks not only the cessation of information but the termination of *perceptual trace* development, resulting in a deficit in performance.

Adams' theory predicts that should the withdrawal occur late in practice, performance would not deteriorate and could even improve. The *perceptual trace* in the *Motor Stage* is strong and well-defined and provides ample information for detecting and correcting errors. Hence, the learner may perform the task, generate his or her own error information, and alter subsequent responses accordingly, all in the absence of external knowledge of results. Some evidence has been found to support these predictions. Bilodeau, Bilodeau, and Schumsky (1959) varied the number of initial trials with knowledge of results (0, 2, 6, or 19), with each group receiving knowledge of results on the final trials (5). They observed that learning did not take place without knowledge of results, and that performance decrements occurred when knowledge of results was withdrawn.

Newell (1974) also tested subjects' ability to reproduce a 9.5-inch movement in 150 msec in a knowledge of results-withdrawal paradigm. Seventy-seven trials were administered to six experimental groups. Knowledge of results was withdrawn after 2, 7, 17, 32, 52 trials or not at all. Figure 4.4 shows the effects of knowledge of results withdrawal after progressively more trials with knowledge of results. When knowledge of results is withdrawn early in the course of learning, performance degrades quickly. As more knowledge of results is given, the detrimental effect of knowledge of results withdrawal is attenuated. The *perceptual trace* in the group receiving 52 trials of knowledge of results is strong enough to allow that group to continue to perform at the same level as those with continuous knowledge of results. Since Adams' first theoretical statement, much research has been directed toward this end, knowledge of results withdrawal being a popular technique.

Recall and Recognition

A particularly popular approach to substantiating Adams' theory was to find evidence to distinguish the *memory trace* from the *perceptual trace:* functionally, a distinction between recall and recognition. This distinction in slow movements was difficult to make because both recall and recognition could be operating, and overall accuracy would be determined by the recognition trace because sufficient time was provided. Marshall (1972), using two different tasks

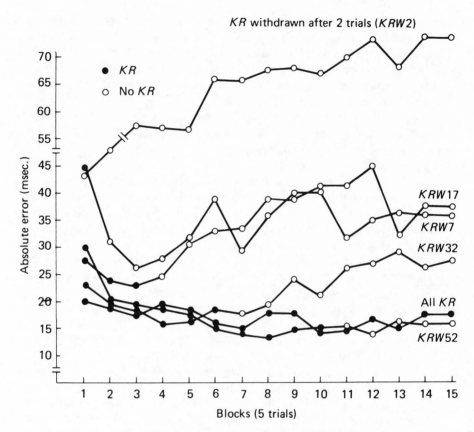

FIG. 4.4.   Taken from Newell (1974). Absolute error for knowledge of results withdrawal as a function of trial blocks.

and measures, was unable to discriminate recall and recognition in a slow movement task. Schmidt and White (1972) and Newell and Chew (1974) utilized rapid-timing movement tasks, reducing the duration of the task, thereby precluding the use of proprioceptive feedback on any one trial. Thus, the recall of the movement was a function of the memory trace, whereas the recognition of the correctness of the attempt came after the response was made. In both these studies, actual error scores were interpreted as indicants of the *memory-trace* strength, and the difference between the actual error and the subjects' own estimated error was considered as indicant of the *perceptual-trace* strength, accompanied by subjective confidence ratings of performance. Schmidt and White (1972) also considered the correlation between these two error scores an index of the strength of the *perceptual trace*. The results of Schmidt and White (1972) revealed that both traces developed with practice and knowledge of results and continued to remain strong after knowledge of results withdrawal late in practice. Newell and Chew (1974) manipulated the amount of feedback in addition to withdrawing knowledge of results and observed a decrement in recognition measures that did not arise in measures of recall, thus substantiating their independence.

Searching for evidence of different memory states in slow movements, Kelso (1978) reasoned that if the accuracy of slow movements was governed by recognition only then the response mode should not affect performance. He compared two groups learning a criterion movement under either active (subject moves to target) or passive (experimenter moves subject to target) conditions. During learning no differences were found between groups, but when knowledge of results was withdrawn the active group's performance deteriorated, whereas the passive group remained relatively stable. The explanation offered suggested that in the case of active movements conscious recognition of peripheral feedback is not necessary if they are substantially preprogrammed, relying on recall mechanisms and knowledge of results for movement regulation. The differences between groups are also representative of a common finding in the verbal literature, namely, the superiority of recognition over recall of information.

EXPERIMENTAL EVIDENCE AGAINST ADAMS' THEORY

In the long run, a theory must be judged by its predictions and how well these predictions survive empirical observation. Further, it would be naive not to expect a theory to undergo some modifications as more data became available. Adams' closed-loop theory has generated a considerable number of experiments attempting to support or negate it empirically. Not all the research aimed at testing this theory has been supportive.

Learning Without Knowledge of Results

Adams contended that knowledge of results is necessary for the learning of a self-paced, graded positioning task. There is evidence to the contrary; that subjects can indeed learn when no external error information is provided. Wrisberg and Schmidt (1975) required blindfolded subjects to move to a stop and reproduce the stop's location on the next attempt. After 12 trials without knowledge of results, error decreased significantly indicating that an error detection mechanism had developed independently of knowledge of results and vision.

Research conducted in my own lab has produced learning without knowledge of results when movement information was presented in an organized fashion. Diewert and Stelmach (1978) found that when knowledge-of-results and no-knowledge-of-results groups were presented with movement distances in a sequential order, no differences between groups developed as learning progressed over trials. In a similar study by Diggles (1979), subjects receiving criterion-movement distances in an organized sequence, but without knowledge of results, performed as well as subjects receiving knowledge of results and a random sequence of movements. In those conditions where all things were equal except for the organization of the targets, Adams' theory would have predicted no differences between sequential and random presentations. The occurrence of these differences suggest that some variable other than feedback consequences influences the storage of movement information (Diewart & Stelmach, 1978; Diggles, 1979). These results tend to minimize the contributions of knowledge of results and feedback as proposed by Adams and to emphasize more cognitive factors.

Feedback

Adams originally proposed that all modalities contributed equally to the development of the *perceptual trace*. In a study that attempted to determine the relative importance of visual and proprioceptive feedback, Adams, Gopher, and Lintern (1977) documented the contributions of each modality. The effects of modality and their combinations were studied in either augmented or minimized conditions. The authors found that in a slow positioning task, both sources of feedback were determiners of performance. However, visual feedback proved to be the more salient source. When the two were in combination, vision dominated and even degraded the use or proprioceptive feedback. The findings suggest that the contribution of the separate modalities in the development of the *perceptual trace* may be viewed differentially.

The findings with respect to augmented proprioceptive feedback are not as convincing as supporters of Adams' theory might wish. Manipulation of this variable has largely consisted of increasing resistance or tension of the responding apparatus. In studies by Jones (1972) and Stelmach (1973), increased tension failed to reduce error relative to conditions where tension was minimal. Similarly, Keele and Ells (1972) altered the tension requirements from criterion to reproduction movements, reasoning that such different conditions of feedback should damage performance. Reproduction accuracy, however, was not affected by this manipulation. Kelso (1977) succeeded in demonstrating the ability of subjects to reproduce voluntary movements under deprived sensory conditions (by the pressure-cuff technique) as well as under normal conditions. Findings such as these regarding the efficacy of feedback undermine any closed-loop theory, and Adams' theory in particular.

Nonspecificity of Feedback

The specificity Adams attributes to feedback induces an inflexibility not characteristic of human memory. Adams postulated that the memory involved in positioning tasks was based on stored sensory information in the form of two memory states. Unless some translation or transformation is performed on this information, it is inferred that reproduction accuracy is dependent on limb- and task-specific characteristics of the stored trace; that is, the sensory consequences of the criterion act guide the reproduction attempt. The theory predicts that, should the reproduction attempt differ qualitatively from the criterion act while still arriving at the same target, accuracy will suffer. Williams and Rodney (1977) failed to support this prediction when they found constant practice with knowledge of results to the same target to be no better than varied practice (experiencing different locations around the target), also with knowledge of results. Similar findings emerged from studies examining the effects of prior knowledge and strategy (Roy & Diewert, 1975). In these studies, groups differed with respect to their criterion experiences while having common targets. The distinguishing factor between groups was not critical feedback, for these results were equivocal, but instead the presence of prior knowledge of movement termination. These findings demonstrating the capacity to perform tasks with no direct feedback of the target indicate that response-specific feedback is not critical in the memory representation responsible for the act.

In contrast to Adams' feedback-specific memory states, an abstract location code, independent of kinesthetic cues, has been hypothesized (MacNeilage, 1970; Russell, 1976; Selmach & Larish, 1980). Wallace (1976) tested this notion in the form of the target hypothesis (MacNeilage, 1970) for limbs by use of a switched-limb paradigm (Hermelin & O'Connor, 1975). He compared the accuracy of location reproduction when the criterion act was performed by the same limb (identical feedback), the opposite limb from the same direction (dissimilar feedback), and the opposite limb from the opposite direction. He found no difference between same-limb and switched-limb reproduction when direction was held constant, supporting to some extent an abstract memory code for location that does not appear to be limb specific.

Stelmach and Larish (1980) also utilized a switched-limb paradigm to study this abstract location code and feedback utilization for two dimensional targets. Again, same-limb performance did not differ from switched-limb performance when targets were located in near space (within 30 cm of the body's midline). When targets were outside this range, same-limb reproduction was superior to that of the switched-limb condition. The conclusion drawn was that within certain limits movements can be made without reference to specific proprioceptive feedback. Beyond these limits, accurate reproduction must rely on specific sensory consequences. The possibility of an abstract movement code in close proximity to the body would seem to weaken Adams' position on the contents of memory states for movement.

CRITIQUE OF ADAMS' CLOSED-LOOP THEORY

Although Adams' theory was thought at first to be new and innovative, a realistic evaluation finds it to be very similar to those theoretical positions preceding it. Recall that Adams posited his theory in opposition to the strong behavioristic emphasis of the times. However, in reality, his theory is based soundly on the principles of reinforcement theory. Consider, for example, the postulate stating that the strength of a memory representation is a function of practice. The major addition was the consideration paid to cognitive influences in regard to the utilization of knowledge of results in problem solving and error correction. Although this addition was of considerable importance in conceptualizing the role of the performer, the theory made only a modest contribution to understanding skill acquisition.

From a practical standpoint, Adams' theory is subject to some criticism when one questions how a motor act might be performed when that specific act has not been previously attempted. The problem of novel movements has two facets. Because the *memory trace* is a function of practice, what mechanism is used to perform the task the very first time? The *memory trace* is technically nonexistent. What then prescribes, even grossly, the task to be performed? The second facet of the novelty problem addresses the fact that an individual never makes exactly the same movement twice. Two attempts at the same task may be similar, but never identical. If one task is well-learned and exactly defined in terms of direction and extent by its memory trace, how is a slightly different task performed accurately when it does not possess a reference of correctness? (See Chapter 8 for further discussion.)

From a logical viewpoint, further argument concerning slow movement and error correction has been offered (Schmidt, 1975). Adams has posited that as a function of practice the subjects develop error-detection capabilities. Therefore, when a movement is made subjects can readily detect their own errors and give a verbal report; that is, a subjective confidence rating. The criticism that has been lodged against such a notion is that, if the subjects are capable of detecting and identifying their own error, why would they not eliminate this error? It makes little intuitive sense that behavior would be carried out in this manner.

The third criticism concerns the situation in which the learner performs in the absence of knowledge of results. Adams' theory proposes that the strength of the *perceptual trace* is proportional to the frequency of correct responses contributing to the trace, much like the mean value of a distribution. If, during the withdrawal of knowledge of results, the subject makes a response incorrectly, the effect is to weaken the *perceptual trace* much the same as an outlier (extreme score) will shift the distribution mean toward its position. Each successive attempt would be progressively more prone to error. With several errors, the individual's ability to learn without knowledge of results would be in doubt.

The fourth limitation of Adams' theory is a memory storage problem (Schmidt, 1975). A conclusion derived from Adams' theory is that *perceptual* and *memory traces* exist for every movement we make, requiring a one-to-one correspondence between each movement and its memory representation. Considering the repertoire of movements available to human beings, a direct function of the mechanical degrees of freedom of which any system as complex as the human body is capable (Turvey, 1977), one would have a difficult time explaining how countless numbers of motor plans are stored in the central nervous system. Many critics of Adams' theory have suggested that movement must be regulated in a much more parsimonious manner. The answer to this problem may require one to view the items stored as rules for generating the programs instead of storing the programs themselves (Boylls, 1980) or, as is suggested by Schmidt (1976), a generalized motor program for response classes may exist.

Perhaps the major reason the area has turned away from Adams' theory is the difficulty of its application in a broader context. As a theory of motor behavior, it would be hard pressed to explain very complex behaviors such as motor equivalence. Motor equivalence refers to the situation in which similar endproducts are achieved even though different muscle groups have responded: for example, the preservation of individual style whether one writes upon paper or chalkboard (Greene, 1972; Merton, 1972), or the ability of a smoker to speak intelligibly with a pipe in his mouth (MacNeilge, 1970). In this context, the endpoint appears unrelated to the movement producing it, clearly a variability not foreseen in Adams' theory. Adams' theory describes very well a limited portion of human motor behavior but is an inadequate explanation for a far greater percentage. Although this condition represents the source of both its strength and its weakness, it accounts for the demise of the theory more than any other reason.

ACKNOWLEDGMENT

Appreciation and a sincere thanks is extended to Virginia Diggles for her background work and editorial assistance in preparing this chapter.

REFERENCES

Adams, J. A. A closed-loop theory of motor learning. *Journal of Motor Behavior,* 1971, *3,* 111–149.

Adams, J. A. Issues for a closed-loop theory of motor learning. In G. E. Stelmach (Ed.), *Motor control: Issues and trends.* New York: Academic Press, 1976.

Adams, J. A., & Creamer, L. R. Proprioception variables as determiners of anticipatory timing behavior. *Human Factors,* 1962, *4,* 217–222.

Adams, J. A., & Goetz, E. T. Feedback and practice as variables in error detection and correction. *Journal of Motor Behavior,* 1973, *5,* 217–224.

Adams, J. A., Goetz, E. T., & Marshall, P. H. Response feedback in motor learning. *Journal of Experimental Psychology,* 1972, *92,* 391–397.

Adams, J. A., Gopher, D., & Lintern, G. Effects of visual and proprioceptive feedback on motor learning. *Journal of Motor Behavior,* 1977, *9,* 11–12.

Anokhin, P. K. Cybernetics and the integrating activity of the brain. In M. Cole & I. Maltzman (Eds.), *A handbook of contemporary Soviet psychology.* New York: Basic Books, 1969.

Bernstein, A. *The coordination and regulation of movement.* New York: Pergamon Press, 1967.

Bilodeau, E. A., & Bilodeau, I. McD. Variation of temporal intervals among critical events in five studies of knowledge of results. *Journal of Experimental Psychology*, 1958, *55*, 603-612.

Bilodeau, E. A., Bilodeau, I. M., & Schumsky, D. A. Some effects of introducing and withdrawing knowledge of results early and late in practice. *Journal of Experimental Psychology*, 1959, *58*, 142-144.

Boucher, J. L. Higher processes in motor learning. *Journal of Motor Behavior*, 1974, *6*, 131-138.

Boulter, L. R. Evaluation of mechanisms in delay of knowledge of results. *Canadian Journal of Psychology*, 1964, *18*, 281-291.

Bowen, K. R., & Smith, W. M. *The effects of delayed visual feedback upon performance*. Unpublished manuscripts, 1976.

Boylls, C. C. *Personal communication*, Jan. 28, 1980.

Burke, D., & Gibbs, C. B. A comparison of free-moving and pressure levers in a positional control system. *Ergonomics*, 1965, *8*, 23.

Chase, R. A. An information flow model of the organization of motor activity: Part I transduction, transmission and central control of sensory information. *Journal of Nervous and Mental Disease*, 1965, *140*, 239-351.

Chase, R. A., Harvey, S., Standfast, S., Rapin, I., & Sutton, S. Studies on sensory feedback. I: Effects of delayed auditory feedback on speech and key-tapping. *Quarterly Journal of Experimental Psychology*, 1961, *13*, 141-152.

Craske, B. A current view of the processes and mechanisms of prism adaptation. In M. Jeannerod (Ed.), *Aspects of neural plasticity, INSERM*, 1975, *43*, 125-138.

Diewert, G. L., & Stelmach, G. E. Perceptual organization in motor learning. In G. E. Stelmach (Ed.), *Information processing in motor control and learning*. New York: Academic Press, 1978.

Diggles, V. A. *Benefits of organization on learning and retention*. Paper presented at AAHPER Convention, New Orleans, 1979.

Ellis, M. J., Schmidt, R. A., & Wade, W. G. Proprioception variables as determiners of lapsed time estimation. *Human Factors*, 1968, *11*, 577-586.

Fairbanks, G. Systematic research in experimental phonetics: A theory of the speech mechanism as a servomechanism. *Journal of Speech and Hearing Disorders*, 1954, *19*, 133-139.

Fairbanks, G. Selective vocal effects of delayed auditory feedback. *Journal of Speech and Hearing Disorders*, 1955, *20*, 333-346.

Glencross, D. J. Control of skilled movement. *Psychological Bulletin*, 1977, *84*, 14-29.

Goodwin, G. M., McCloskey, D. I., & Matthews, P. B. C. The contribution of muscle afferents to kinesthesia shown by vibration induced illusions of movement and by the effects of paralyzing joint afferents. *Brain*, 1972, *95*, 705-748.

Greene, P. H. Problems of organization of motor systems. In R. Rosen & F. M. Snell (Eds.), *Progress in theoretical biology*. New York: Academic Press, 1972.

Held, R. Plasticity in sensory-motor systems. *Scientific American*, 1967, *213*, 84-94.

Hermelin, B., & O'Connor, N. Location and distance estimates by blind and sighted children. *Quarterly Journal of Experimental Psychology*, 1975, *27*, 295-301.

Holland, D., & Noble, M. E. The effect of physical constraints of a control on tracking performance. *Journal of Experimental Psychology*, 1953, *46*, 353-360.

Jones, B. Outflow and inflow in movement duplication. *Perception and Psychophysics*, 1972, *12*, 95-99.

Kalmus, H., Denes, F., & Fry, D. B. Effect of delayed acoustic feedback on some nonvocal activities. *Nature*, 1975, *175*, 1078.

Keele, S. W. Movement control in skilled motor performance. *Psychological Bulletin*, 1968, *70*, 387-403.

Keele, S. W., & Ells, J. C. Memory characteristics of kinesthetic information. *Journal of Motor Behavior*, 1972, *4*, 127-134.

Kelso, J. A. S. Motor control mechanisms underlying human movement reproduction. *Journal of Experimental Psychology: Human Perception and Performance*, 1977, *3*, 529-543.

Kelso, J. A. S. Recognition and recall in slow movements: Separate memory states? *Journal of Motor Behavior*, 1978, *10*, 69–76.

Kelso, J. A. S., & Stelmach, G. E. Central and peripheral mechanisms in motor control. In G. E. Stelmach (Ed.), *Motor control: Issues and trends*. New York: Academic Press, 1976.

Kelso, J. A. S., Stelmach, G. E., & Wanamaker, W. H. Behavioral and neurologial parameters of the nerver compression block. *Journal of Motor Behavior*, 1974, *6*, 179–190.

Kohler, W. *Gestalt psychology*. New York: Liverwright, 1947.

MacNeilage, P. F. Motor control of serial ordering of speech. *Psychological Review*, 1970, *77*, 182–196.

Marshall, P. H. Recognition and recall in short-term motor memory. *Journal of Experimental Psychology*, 1972, *95*, 147–153.

Merton, P. A. How we control the contraction of our muscles. *Scientific American*, 1972, *226*, 30–37.

Newell, K. M. Knowledge of results and motor learning. *Journal of Motor Behavior*, 1974, *6*, 235–244.

Newell, K. M., & Chew, R. A. Recall and recognition in motor learning. *Journal of Motor Behavior*, 1974, *6*, 245–253.

Roy, E. A., & Diewert, G. L. Encoding kinesthetic extent information. Perception and Psychophysics, 1975, *17*, 559–564.

Russell, D. G. Spatial location cues and movement production. In G. E. Stelmach (Ed.), *Motor control: Issues and trends*. New York: Academic Press, 1976.

Schmidt, R. A. A schema theory of discrete motor-skill learning. *Psychological Review*, 1975, *82*, 225–260.

Schmidt, R. A. Control processes in motor skills. In J. Keogh & R. S. Hutton (Eds.), *Exercise and sport sciences reviews* (Vol. 4). Santa Barbara: Journal Publishing Affiliates, 1976.

Schmidt, R. A., & White, J. L. Evidence for an error detection mechanism in motor skills: A test of Adams' closed-loop theory. *Journal of Motor Behavior*, 1972, *4*, 143–153.

Smith, J. L. Kinesthesis: A model of movement feedback. In R. C. Brown & B. J. Cratty (Eds.), *New perspective of man in action*. Englewood Cliffs, N. J.: Prentice-Hall, 1969, 31–48.

Smith, W. M. Feedback: Real time delayed vision of one's own tracking behavior. *Science*, 1972, *176*, 339–340.

Sokolov, F. N. The modeling properties of the nervous system. In M. Cole & I. Matlzman (Eds.), *A handbook of contemporary Soviet psychology*. New York: Basic Books, 1969.

Stelmach, G. E. Feedback—A determiner of forgetting in short-term motor memory. *Acta Psychologica*, 1973, *37*, 333–339.

Stelmach, G. E. Motor control. In K. Connolly (Ed.), *Psychology surveys*. London: George Allen & Unwin, 1978.

Stelmach, G. E., & Larish, D. D. Egocentric referents in human limb orientation. In G. E. Stelmach & J. Requin (Eds.), *Tutorials in motor behavior*. Amsterdam: North Holland Press, 1980.

Trowbridge, M. H., & Cason, H. An experimental study of Thorndike's theory of learning. *Journal of General Psychology*, 1932, *7*, 245–258.

Turvey, M. T. Preliminaries to a theory of action with reference to vision. In R. E. Shaw & J. Bransford (Eds.), *Perceiving, acting and knowing: Toward an ecological psychology*. Hillsdale, N. J.: Lawrence Erlbaum Associates, 1977.

Wallace, S. A. *The coding of location: A test of the target hypothesis*. Unpublished doctoral dissertation, University of Wisconsin, 1976.

Williams, I. D., & Rodney, M. Intrinsic feedback, interpolation, and the closed-loop theory. *Journal of Motor Behavior*, 1977, *10*, 25–36.

Williams, I. D., & Roy, E. A. Closed-loop control of a ballistic response. *Journal of Motor Behavior*, 1972, *4*, 121–126.

Wrisberg, C. A., & Schmidt, R. A. A note on motor learning without postresponse knowledge of results. *Journal of Motor Behavior*, 1975, *7*, 221–226.

5 Memory for Movement with Emphasis on Short-Term Aspects

George E. Stelmach
University of Wisconsin

INTRODUCTION

Closed-loop theory emphasizes motor learning through the detection and correction of movement error via increased memory strength. Thus, another way to study how we acquire motor skills is to look at the memory aspects of movement information; that is, how the memory representation affects retention of movement information. At first glance, it may seem that the topics of learning and retention are not closely related, but if you simply consider that learning research focuses on what is retained, whereas memory research focuses on what is forgotten, you will see they are related. Although we spend most of our lives learning, our learning is usually indexed by how we retained information. It is impossible to separate completely learning and retention; a concern for one is a matter of emphasis rather than of clear and distinct differences. Unlike the procedures used in learning that require successive attempts to repeat a motor act, retention research usually varies the amount of delay or interfering activity before a movement is repeated.

Retention loss over time involves various types of memory, and it is useful for students of movement to conceptualize these differences. It is assumed that newly presented information is transformed by sensory receptors into a physiological representation, which is briefly stored in a sensory storage buffer. After this brief storage, the representation is identified and transformed into a new code and retained temporarily in another memory called short-term memory (STM). At this point, recycling and organizing of the information insures its transfer to a more permanent memory called long-term memory (LTM). The research findings reported in this chapter are restricted to those of short-term retention. The reader is cautioned that there are subtle differences between these types of memory, and one should be careful in generalizing between the two.

Short-term memory refers to the storage of information that has recently been presented, and its capacity is thought to be limited. This type of memory is extremely important because it must maintain in an active state, not only the items of information, but also the rules and algorithms required for most kinds of problem solving. Consequently, the term *working memory* has been applied to describe its functions (Baddeley, 1976). In STM, recall is usually requested within a matter of seconds and seldom exceeds a minute. The methods employed usually employ strict control of learning periods, intertrial intervals, and manipulate the difficulty of interpolated information-processing tasks.

The methodology used in verbal memory and later adopted by motor-behavior investigators was successful in establishing forgetting curves for discrete items over short periods of time. In these experiments, subjects were presented with to-be-remembered items (words, syllables, etc.) either in pairs or in lists. A retention interval followed the presentation, usually filled with information-processing tasks such as counting backward by threes. At the end of the retention interval the subject was required to recall the to-be-remembered item. The rate of forgetting was rapid with much of the forgetting occurring within the first 20 seconds. These findings astonished psychologists and sparked considerable interest and speculation about human memory. This enthusiasm carried over into motor-learning circles, where motor behaviorists questioned whether similar rapid forgetting would also occur with motor responses. Short-term motor memory research (STMM) began about 15 years ago with the overriding theme of making direct comparisons to verbal memory. Since that time, STMM has emerged as an area of experimental psychology that possesses its own theoretical orientations, methodological problems, and empirical controversies.

Typically in a STMM experiment, a subject makes a movement with a knob, lever, or a linear slide to a defined target location or through a prescribed distance. The target or endpoint of the movement is usually determined by the experimenter. After remaining at the target for a brief time (usually 2 sec), the subject returns the arm to the original starting position, or in some cases to varied starting positions. After some predetermined retention interval, the subject is then asked to reproduce the original movement extent or target without the aid of the experimenter-defined stop. The time between termination of the initial movement and the beginning of the reproduction is called the retention interval and usually ranges from 0–90 sec. On the reproduction movement, the mismatch between the initial and the reproduction movements is recorded in deviation units (inches, degrees, etc.). This deviation score is taken to represent the amount of forgetting that has taken place over a given retention interval. Because a STMM experiment usually consists of many trials, the movement apparatus used is designed to provide a variety of different movement amplitudes and target locations.

The introduction of Adams' closed-loop theory (described in Chapter 4), which stresses the development of an internal standard against which ongoing sensory feedback is compared, sparked extensive research on the manner in which movement information is represented in memory. Associated with each movement, there is thought to be a movement trace laid down in memory as a result of the motor act. How the trace is represented and what strengthens or weakens its representation has been the focal point of retention research. Although not relying on Adams' theory directly, investigators in this area used the concept of trace development extensively. Because the movements usually employed were slow, the prevalent notion has been that precise movements are made by matching ongoing sensory feedback (how the movement feels or is seen or heard) to the memory representation of a preceding or criterion movement. One question asked by investigators in this area is how the retention of simple movement may be improved to prevent loss, either from interfering activity or from disuse over time. Understanding the nature of this representation is important, because it then allows us to suggest ways of strengthening the representation.

EXPLANATION OF FORGETTING

The question of whether movement information was forgotten as rapidly as verbal information was answered in 1966, when Adams and Dijkstra published a study that revealed that the accuracy of reproducing arm movements decreased systematically over time. The procedures used were analogous to those in the verbal area and involved the subject making an arm movement to a defined target and, after a varying delay (0–120 sec), attempting to reproduce that movement. The errors associated with movement replication approximately doubled in magnitude over a 120 sec retention interval. This finding constituted some of the first data, displaying clear evidence that movement information is quickly forgotten. Since that time, the forgetting curve for movement information has been replicated many times, often revealing even more rapid forgetting. For example, I demonstrated that absolute error for reproduction doubled in as little as 20 sec (Stelmach 1969). After it was shown that motoric information was subject to forgetting after brief delays, interest developed in the basic laws underlying the memory representation of such movements. The following types of questions were asked: What are the causes of forgetting, what movement cues are encoded, and how is this information stored and retrieved?

Trace Decay Theory

There have been two main explanations of forgetting that have been used to explain forgetting in STMM. Decay theory assumes that when a criterion act is made, a memory trace is formed that decays spontaneously over retention intervals, making discrimination between traces more difficult. As a result, there will be greater error at recall. In some STMM research, it has been found that with unfilled retention intervals, recall gets progressively worse, leading to the conclusion that activity prior to learning or interpolated between learning and recall is assumed to be independent of forgetting. Due to the type of errors that are generated in movement research, decay interpretations emerge from two types of findings: (1) shrinking with time, producing increased undershooting of the recall attempt (Adams & Dijkstra, 1966); and (2) "fading" with time, producing increased variability at recall (Laabs, 1973). Although the evidence is not convincing, a number of studies have found some evidence to support a trace decay interpretation.

Interference Theory

Interference theory views forgetting as the result of competing responses learned either before or after a criterion item that somehow disrupt memory representation. Retroactive interference refers to the deficit in recall attributable to events occurring between initial presentation and recall, whereas proactive interference refers to the deficit produced by events occurring prior to presentation. The interference theory is an active theory based on the dynamic process of experiencing interpolated events, in contrast to the passive decay theory (Stelmach, 1974). The influence of interference theory on motor memory research is best seen if one inspects the type of paradigm that has been most prominent.

Interference Studies

Proactive Paradigms. In verbal skills, it is well-established that items learned before the presentation of a criterion item can disrupt recall. In STMM, it has been difficult to demonstrate proactive interference, and most studies that have examined the effects of prior trials have found no proactive interference. Exceptions exist in several studies that found proactive interference within a given trial. These studies required subjects to make either 0, 2, or 4 prior responses before making a criterion movement, and then to recall them in the reverse order of presentation. Proactive interference was generated in both the 2- and 4-response conditions, and error increased as a function of the number of prior responses (Ascoli & Schmidt, 1969; Stelmach, 1974). These studies demonstrated that proactive interference can be found within a trial under specific experimental conditions. Just what the nature of this interference is and how it operates has not been determined.

Retroactive Paradigms. The vast majority of studies in STMM have used some form of interpolated activity as an experimental variable. The aim of this research was to document the type of interpolated activity that increases forgetting. The findings have been quite variable: Some studies have shown that interpolated motor activity causes increased absolute error at recall, others have demonstrated changes in constant error, still others have found increases in the variability, and some investigators have been unable to demonstrate interference with interpolated motor activity. Although an overall interpretation is difficult, it appears that increasing the amount of interpolated activity similar to the criterion movement generates increased forgetting. This forgetting generally manifests itself in the form of increased variability (see Stelmach, 1974, for review).

Response-Biasing Paradigms.   Some interpolated movements that deviate from the criterion response have been shown to produce sizeable directional shifts in recall errors. If an interpolated movement is of a greater extent or intensity (force) than the criterion and the subject is required to recall it, recall error is influenced in a positive direction. In a similar manner, if an interpolated movement is of lesser extent or intensity, recall error is shifted in a negative manner (Pepper & Herman, 1970). Another source of biasing was identified by Stelmach (1974), when he found that the longer one stays at an interpolated target and the later an interpolated movement is introduced in the retention interval the greater the directional shift at recall. It has also been shown that response biasing can be reduced by increasing the number of repetitions and by augmenting the feedback of a criterion movement (Stelmach & Kelso, 1975).

Two views, which rely to some extent on the concept of assimilation (see later) have been expressed to account for this phenomenon. Pepper and Herman (1970) postulated a trace interaction theory in which the memory traces of the criterion and interpolated movements interact to yield a memory trace that is a combination of both. The criterion recall response is therefore made with reference to the altered trace representation, and the directional shift at recall is seen as an assimilation effect. Laabs (1973) viewed the reproduction of the criterion movement as being made in reference to an "average" movement trace representing many similar movements and to the criterion trace. Changes in the "average" movement trace that result from interpolated movements are seen as responsible for shifts in recall errors. With forgetting, more emphasis is given to the average movement trace, resulting in a greater directional shift toward it.

Response-biasing effects have also been explained in terms of the relative decay state (memory-trace strength) between movements. This trace interaction view states that the weaker a given trace is relative to a stronger one the more response biasing will occur. On the other hand, the stronger a trace is in comparison to a weak one, the less response biasing will occur (Stelmach, 1974). The data from studies that have manipulated time at an interpolated target, the temporal occurrence of an interpolated movement, and the feedback associated with it have generally been in support of this explanation of response biasing, as is evident subsequently. The relative strength interpretation is an excellent way to account for the multitude of research findings.

Whereas response biasing has been observed many times, its localization is not known. Existing theory provides some broad insight into response biasing but does not pinpoint the mechanisms involved. There are few, if any, differential predictions between the theories postulated to explain response biasing.

MEMORY-REPRESENTATION DEVELOPMENT

Now that it has been established that movement information is quickly forgotten and is subject to interference, the obvious question of importance is can something be done about it? From a practical standpoint, we would like to reduce forgetting as much as possible. In the following section I review studies that suggest that there are ways to prevent memory loss.

Reinforcement

The Adams and Dijkstra (1966) study, reviewed previously, demonstrated rapid forgetting over short retention intervals. These data were interpreted as support for the trace decay notion, which states that stored items lose precision over time due to a fading movement trace. A second aspect of this study was to examine whether memory representation would be strengthened through repeated exposures (reinforcements) to the criterion movement, thereby decreasing the amount of forgetting. Reinforcements were defined as movement repetitions so that subjects made either 1, 6, or 15 movements before the retention interval began. It was found that as the subjects experienced more repetition they became more accurate and forgetting decreased. This data suggests that one way to prevent forgetting is to repeat movements over and over again, thereby strengthening their memory representations. Similarly, Stelmach and Kelso (1975) strengthened the movement trace by means of repetition in a response-biasing paradigm. The subjects made either 0, 5, or 14 repetitions of a criterion movement prior to the presentation of an interpolated location. The results clearly revealed that interference was reduced by increasing the number of repetitions.

Rehearsal

Once a movement has been made and the subject is able to attend to the act, there is a rich opportunity to rehearse a movement during the retention interval. Many of you may think of movement rehearsal as some overt activity, where the subject attempts to actively reproduce the to-be-remembered movement. However, there may be more subtle ways to rehearse that require no overt activity. One method of examining whether there is some covert activity involved in movement retention is to prevent it by completely occupying the subject's attention. The technique used to accomplish this attentional loading involves the imposed processing of some information during the retention interval. The following example is only one of several ways the subject may be engaged in an information-processing task. At the end of a movement, the subject is given a three digit number such as 327 and is instructed to immediately begin counting backwards by three's as rapidly and accurately as possible for the duration of the retention interval (Diewert & Roy, 1978). This task is assumed to fully occupy the subject's processing capacity, leaving no attention available for the movement rehearsal. Using such procedures, Stelmach, Kelso, and Wallace (1975) compared the movement accuracy at the end of a 20-second retention interval between a group that counted versus one that did not. They found that subjects required to count during the interval performed with less accuracy, indicating that some covert rehearsal is necessary to prevent retention loss.

Another form of rehearsal involves providing the subject the opportunity to experience certain aspects of a movement for a longer period of time. For example, by allowing the subject to remain at the endpoint of a movement provides the increased time to rehearse the sensory feedback associated with the final position. In this case, the subject attends to the proprioceptive cues available from the maintained limb. In an experiment investigating this type of rehearsal, Wallace and Stelmach (1975) varied the amount of time subjects spent at the endpoint of a criterion movement. The three conditions required removing the hand from the movement endpoint either immediately, after 2 seconds, or after 5 seconds before the retention interval began. Inspection of the recall scores at the completion of a 15-second retention interval revealed that the longer the subject spent at the endpoint the less forgetting occurred. The data indicated that, if the subject was allowed longer rehearsal of the sensory aspects of a movement, retention losses were smaller, supporting the facilitation of covert activity in memory-trace development.

It has been shown that with increased practice and augmented feedback there is less forgetting. However, a question of major interest is whether once the memory representation is strengthened can we also expect it to remain resistant to interfering activity? Stelmach and Kelso (1975) performed two experiments that suggest that heightening the memory representation prevents forgetting. In one experiment we used repetition, whereas in other additional feedback was provided through vision, audition, and heightened proprioception. Regardless of whether the hypothesized trace was strengthened via repetition or increased feedback associated with the movement, performance was more accurate and there was more resistance to interfering activity.

Labeling

Verbal labels would seem to provide a rich source of information to aid the subject in the recall of motor responses. Through the years there have been anecdotal reports that subjects used verbal labels for movement. A few studies,

Burwitz (1974) and Posner and Konick (1966), reported that subjects practiced labeling to assist movement retention. However, whereas the use of verbal labels have usually been acknowledged, they have been discounted as being too inexact to assist in the precision required for accurate movement. In 1974, I postulated that an effective strategy to recall the to-be-remembered movements would be to produce a verbal label for each newly presented movement. In 1977, Shea tested that notion by having subjects associate verbal labels to various movements. With each curvilinear movement, subjects were verbally given either a relevant label, an irrelevant label, or no label. The relevant labels were chosen so that they were representative of the hours on a clock face such as 9:00, 12:00, and 3:00. Thus, the relevant labels also had a high imaginal component. In this study, Shea found that verbal labels improved performance and reduced forgetting. The striking part of the data was that with a verbal label no forgetting occurred up to a 60-second retention interval. In another study demonstrating the importance of verbal and imaginal labels, Shea (1977) reported that movement reproductions could be shifted by giving a label that was slightly descriptive. In this case labels were given that were either larger ($+$) or smaller ($-$) than the actual movement. The verbal labels shifted the errors in the direction of the label bias. These studies provide evidence that the use of a relevant verbal label can aid the retention of movement information and is a valuable mnemonic strategy. Thus, the subject can be viewed as an active organizer capable of using both the cues that are present in the environment and those of past experience.

Perceptual Organization

It is well-known and accepted that the human is a limited information processor (Broadbent, 1958) with respect to both the absolute amount of information that can be processed and the processing capacity over time. If the memory representation of movement is comprised merely of the sensory consequences produced by the movement, the limited processing capacity would be easily overwhelmed when the complexity or number of items to be remembered substantially increased. Thus, it has been assumed that some form of organization of perceived events is necessary to allow processing of movements of even minimal complexity and load. The organization presented to or determined by the subject permits processing of large amounts of information within the bounds of the limited capacity. This suggests a dynamic role for the subject in a learning situation, where feedback is supplemented by higher-order strategies and organization.

The importance of practice and feedback has been stressed with little reference to the effect of structured movement on memory representation. Is experiment-defined organization an important factor in learning and retention of movement information? An experiment by Nacson (1973) suggested that the learning of movement information is not merely a function of repetition or feedback, but that it is facilitated by the order of movement presentation or organization. In a series of experiments (Diewert & Stelmach, 1978), experimenter-defined organization was examined in learning five discrete arm movements to determine how a sequential order compared to a random order in aiding memory representation. In agreement with the findings of Nacson, a sequential presentation of movements resulted in markedly better performance than did a random presentation sequence (Fig. 5.1). These studies clearly demonstrated the importance of the experimenter structuring the environment for the learner. The organized structure allowed the subject to better retain the sensory consequences from the movement presumably by higher-order cognitive activity.

Whereas experimenter-defined organization facilitated memory representation, it is important to know whether the benefit of structured movements is maintained outside the condition of sequential presentation. If recall of movement is tied to its position in a sequence, then the experimenter-defined organization examined lacks generality and implies that an intact and rigid memory constellation has been established. However, if performance is not affected by the removal of the structure at recall, the organization presented in learning is a potential variable in facilitating individual memory representation. In a subsequent experiment examining these questions (Diewert & Stelmach, 1978), subjects learned under an organized sequence and were later switched to a random sequence during a retention phase. It was found that the benefits of experimenter-defined organization were not limited to the structured situations in which they were learned. Movement components learned under an organized regime can be performed as well as in a novel situation (Fig. 5.2)

With some understanding of experimenter-defined organization, it is of interest to examine whether organization imposed by the subject also aids retention. Subject-defined organization is analogous to free recall where the subject is permitted to recall the movements in any order desired, thereby allowing subjects to impose their own structure to the movement sequence. As in the previous experiments, the subjects were given five movements in either sequential or random orders but were also allowed to recall the movements in any order they wished. Not surprisingly, most subjects chose to recall in a sequential order. However, the surprising finding occurred when subjects were allowed to freely recall; those who learned under organized sequences performed with much more accuracy. In fact, it made little difference whether the subjects received knowledge of results after each reproduction. Such an unexpected finding demonstrated the potential of organizational factors in motor behavior. Thus, just as with the findings of experimenter-defined organization, subject-defined organization has also proven to be a strong variable in motor learning. However, it appears that organization best facilitates the memory representation in a situation where the subject initiates the organization. The most important conclusion of these experiments is that memory representation of movement can be enhanced by perceptual organization, which is a set-back for those closed-loop theorists who have

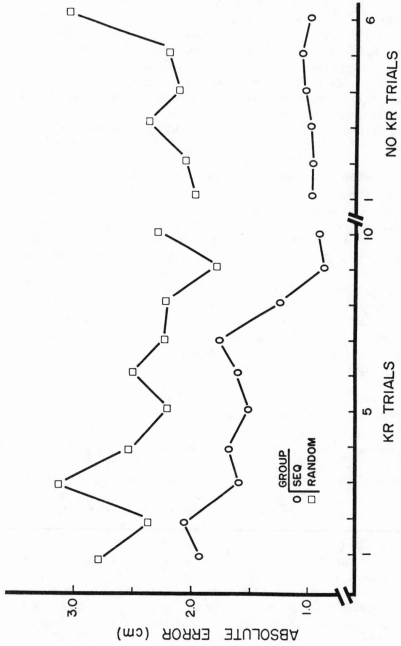

FIG. 5.1. Taken from Diewert and Stelmach (1978). Mean absolute error for random and sequential movement sequences plotted as a function of knowledge of results and no knowledge of results trials.

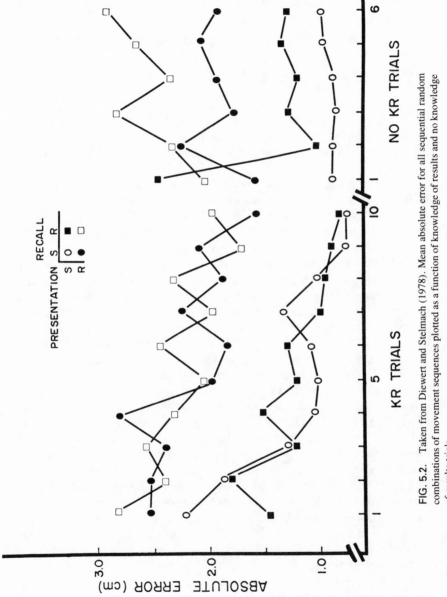

FIG. 5.2. Taken from Diewert and Stelmach (1978). Mean absolute error for all sequential random combinations of movement sequences plotted as a function of knowledge of results and no knowledge of results trials.

advocated that movement-memory representation is dependent entirely on feedback and practice. Whereas these experiments do not identify the mechanism involved, they do stress the importance of cognitive activity in motor behavior.

MECHANISMS INVOLVED IN MOVEMENT RETENTION

In short-term retention conditions where an individual is asked to make a movement and is later asked to produce it, very precise motor coordination is involved. This motor coordination may involve such factors as the manner in which the movement was made, the neurological stimuli activated, the movement cues available, and how the movement information is represented in memory. As the short-term motor-memory area developed, scientists became more concerned about the basic mechanisms that underlie positioning responses, and attempts were made to isolate and examine the role of various types of movement information used by the central nervous system to form the memory representation of movement. The preoccupation with how this representation is formed forced motor-behavior scientists to systematically examine the input domains that contribute to the formation of the memory representation.

There are a variety of information sources that can contribute to the development of a memory representation (e.g., vision and audition). On the other hand, there are many situations in which the learner must depend on cues arising as the result of his or her own movements, per se. Such cues are thought to be based on proprioception, the encompassing term for the modality subserving the sense of position and movement. In addition, it has been hypothesized that the central nervous system also has mechanisms available by which it can inform itself as to the intended output. Thus, movement information can be considered as "peripheral" in the sense that it arises from proprioceptive receptor organs stimulated as a result of movement; or "central" in the sense that internal information is generated by the occurrence of overt movement.

Most of the studies concerned with the coding, repetition, and retention characteristics of movement information have focused on the proprioceptive modality. Proprioceptive information was altered by reducing the subjects' ability to use such cues as distance, direction, location, rate, and muscular effort. Additionally, some investigators examined the role of motor outflow to determine if it is used to aid reproduction accuracy. The instigation of this type of inquiry forced many motor-behavior researchers to examine the neurophysiological literature, thereby starting a shift in orientation from memory research per se to that of motor control (Kelso & Stelmach, 1976).

Proprioception and Movement Retention

Most of the studies concerned with the coding and retention characteristics of movement information have focused on the proprioceptive modality, in part because of the rich tradition of closed-loop theory. In the past, it was assumed that feedback from the periphery is responsible for establishing an internal memory representation that guides and controls movement. The importance of proprioceptive information in movement control is generally assessed by either reducing or increasing its presence during the performance of a motor task. Its importance is inferred if either a reduction of its presence hinders performance or if a heightening of its presence facilitates performance. A number of techniques have been devised to determine whether proprioceptive information is important for movement retention.

A common variable that has been manipulated to determine the saliency of proprioceptive information has been the amount of tension required to move a lever or joystick. The assumption is that the amount of proprioceptive input is increased as a function of increased lever resistance. Although this method has been extensively used in tracking tasks with some success (Burke & Gibbs, 1965; Holland & Noble, 1953), its potency in short-term retention experiments has yielded minimal support (Adams, Marshall, & Goetz, 1972; Jones, 1974; Stelmach, 1973). Adams et al. (1972) found evidence that retention loss is reduced by increased tension, whereas Jones (1974) and Stelmach (1968) found increased tension to be of no assistance.

Why has there been success with this variable in tracking studies and failure with it in short-term retention studies? Jones (1974) has suggested that verbal or visual knowledge of results usually accompanied the increased tension in tracking studies, thus making it difficult to determine which variable was most important. However, knowledge of results was not provided in any of the Adams et al., Jones, or Stelmach experiments. Another explanation suggests that subjects in minimal-tension conditions may already be performing optimally under task constraints. Thus, any benefit of increased tension may be masked because of floor effects. A final reason, offered by Bahrick (1957), is that increased tension can only become a potent variable when the subject learns to use it.

The most direct method of assessing whether proprioception affects motor performance is to eliminate it and examine the deficits, if any, that occur. The procedure usually followed in animal studies is to surgically eliminate joint and tactile information, either before or after learning movement patterns have been established, and observe the resultant motor performance (Taub, Perella, & Barro, 1973). However, surgical deafferentation in humans is not practical because the damage produced is not reversible. Some motor-behavior workers have therefore utilized techniques that cause only temporary insensitivity of some proprioceptive receptors.

Kelso (1975) used a procedure where joint and cutaneous receptors in the hand were rendered insentient via the inflation of a child's sphygmomanometer cuff at the wrist. His subjects performed in a short-term retention paradigm where they reproduced movements that were made to prescribed targets. Performance was found to be markedly reduced by the temporary loss of some proprioceptive information. However, in conditions where the subjects selected their own movements to a location, the reduction of sensory information had little effect. Thus, it can be concluded that proprioception is important in movements where the experimenter defines the target; that is, movements that are made without a terminal goal are encoded primarily via proprioception.

Storage Codes and Movement Retention

In short-term memory research, students of motor behavior have generally assumed that certain aspects of a criterion movement are encoded and stored in memory and later decoded for reproduction purposes. Thus, a major focus of contemporary research on the retention of motor skills has been on the identification of the types of information that are coded and stored in memory. In movement situations where there are no visual or auditory cues, intrinsic information is derived from the movement itself. Such sensory information is based on proprioception, which can provide a variety of useful movement cues such as acceleration, amplitude, direction, force, location, and velocity. By far the most researched topic of these has been the coding of distance and location cues. Researchers have attempted to isolate these cues and determine their retention characteristics. A major effort has gone into determining whether a movement is remembered via information based on the location occupied by the limb after a movement or on the extent or distance through which the limb moved. Three basic questions have been asked regarding the retention characteristics of distance and location information: Are these two cues initially stored and registered equally?; can these two cues be maintained in memory for short retention intervals?; and, does the maintenance in memory of distance and location require attention or central processing?.

Although Leuba (1909) and Woodworth (1899) discussed the separation and isolation of movement cues many years ago, Laabs (1973) was the first modern-day investigator to use a paradigm that separated distance and location cues. His experimental procedure forced subjects to rely on either distance or location cues by making the opposing cues unreliable. For example, location cues were rendered unreliable by having subjects make movements that replicate a previous movement extent from variable starting points, thereby producing a reproduction attempt that utilized different starting and ending locations while preserving movement extent. Distance information was discriminated against in a similar manner. After a movement to a location, the reproduction movement was initiated from a different starting point that caused the distance information to be unreliable. For the most part, this experimental technique has been adopted by most investigators who have examined the distance versus location issue.

Laabs (1973) found that location information was well-retained, unless a task preventing rehearsal was present, whereas distance information decayed rapidly and was unaffected by interpolated information-processing activity. Based on these findings, Laabs speculated that distance information was not centrally represented, and that distance and location cues were stored differentially. Most studies (Diewert, 1975; Marteniuk, 1973; Stelmach & Kelso, 1973) that have examined the storage of distance and location information have found that location information is codable only under special conditions, and that location information is always more precise than distance information (Marteniuk & Roy, 1972; Posner, 1967; Stelmach & Kelso, 1975). Moreover, when the cues are compared after interpolated processing activity, location information is almost always affected, whereas distance information has produced rather mixed results. In summary, it has been shown that location information is better stored and maintained initially than distance information, and that this process has been shown to be attention demanding.

More recently, Kelso (1977) investigated the neurological substrate underlying memory for location and extent with preselected movements. Subjects were required to recall either the end location or the extent of a movement under two feedback conditions. In one condition, joint and cutaneous feedback from the responding hand was reduced using a nerve compression block, and, in the other condition, feedback from the hand was unaltered. The results showed that reproduction accuracy was significantly impaired under the feedback-reduced condition only for distance information (but see Chapter 7 and 11 for other interpretations of these data). Apparently, subjects were able to relocate the finger at a position in space without joint feedback. In a subsequent study, Roy and Williams (1978) found similar results; location reproduction accuracy was unaffected by feedback reduction, whereas reproduction accuracy for distance information was significantly reduced when joint feedback was unavailable. Many have taken these findings as further evidence that some movement cues are differentially stored and utilized in the memory of movement information (but see Chapters 7 and 11 for other interpretation of these data).

Because there are no known distance receptors, Stelmach and McCracken (1978) questioned the usefulness of postulating separate and independent storage codes for distance and location cues. They speculated that location information may influence distance representation. For example, distance information may be extrapolated from the start and finish locations of the criterion movement, and both cues could be centrally processed but perhaps at different levels. In a series of four experiments, the availability of movement information was manipulated in a distance-reproduction paradigm. Location information was altered by varying the time spent at the movement endpoints, and distance information was manipulated by either omitting, disrupting, or augmenting the dynamic phase of the movement. The results of these experiments, when taken together, reveal the interdependence of the two movement cues and argue that distance memory representation is dependent on the relative amount of distance and location information present in the criterion movement. These findings have been taken as evidence against the dual storage hypothesis for movement cues. Nevertheless, they do not alter the findings that location information is much more strongly represented in memory than movement extent information.

Motor Outflow and Movement Retention

Whereas it is generally accepted that certain effector and receptor mechanisms may subserve the storage and retention of movement information, there is little consensus as to the nature and utility of the information that each mechanism provides. The debate is an old one and continues among psychologists and physiologists alike; some have argued that voluntary movements are based on central mechanisms (Evarts, 1971; Jones, 1974; Kelso & Stelmach, 1976), whereas others have stressed the role of feedback (Adams, 1976; Goodwin, McCloskey, & Matthews, 1972).

For years there has been speculation that motor commands may perform functions other than the initiation of muscular contraction. For example, motor outflow may affect conscious or subconscious processes, or they may modify incoming sensory signals. Further, it is conceivable that motor outflow may influence higher sensory areas concerned with movement perception. Whereas the discussion of efferent information has employed varying terminology— corollary discharge (Sperry, 1950), efference copy (Festinger & Cannon, 1965), feedforward (MacKay, 1966), efference monitoring (Jones, 1972, 1974), and motor outflow (Paillard & Brouchon, 1968), the central ideas are the same. As motor commands are being relayed to spinal motoneuron pools, they are presumably recirculated in or monitored by the central nervous system so that the central nervous system is aware of the course of the action about to occur.

The most common way of studying the contrast between properties of efferent and afferent codes is to compare movements that are actively or passively presented. One of the first investigators to document the importance of motor outflow in movement was Lashley (1917). He observed a patient who had suffered a gunshot wound that had severed nearly all proprioceptive pathways of the lower limbs. It was found that in spite of not being able to perceive passive movement the patient could duplicate his own active movements reasonably well. In a short-term retention paradigm, Marteniuk (1973) demonstrated that active movement not only resulted in better immediate reproduction, but that it also retained better than passively induced movement. These results have been interpreted as meaning that memory codes resulting from efferent information are more precise and have superior retention characteristics than those codes arising primarily from afferent information. Similar findings have also been reported by Kelso (1975), who found that active movement reproduction was superior to passive reproduction over varying retention intervals. In related work, Paillard and Brouchon (1968) reported that the accuracy of active arm movements was far superior to those of passive in a variety of movement conditions and over variable periods of delay.

Other evidence that suggests the importance of motor output for movement coding has been provided by Jones (1972, 1974). In a series of experiments using a reproduction task, he found that subjects reproduced voluntary movements equally well from variable and constant starting positions. He reasoned that, as long as efferent commands for movement extent are the same for the criterion and recall movements, no deficits in motor recall occur. Thus, it is the efferent aspect of the movement that is crucial, and proprioception was relegated to a secondary and insignificant role.

The most common theoretical construct used by students of motor behavior to explain the superiority of active goal-oriented movement is that of collorary discharge. According to the corollary-discharge concept, active movement contains two sets of signals: one, a downward discharge to the effector organs; and two, a simultaneous, central discharge from motor to sensory systems preparing them for the anticipated consequences of the motor act. It is assumed that the latter discharge is responsible for the heightened movement coding that leads to a stronger memory representation. Work is continuing on the corollary-discharge hypothesis, and time will tell whether it is solely responsible for the superior recall in movements that possess active components.

The Preselection Effect

When a blindfolded individual makes a voluntary movement of his or her own choice and is later asked to reproduce that movement, considerable enhancement of the performance occurs in comparison to conditions where the subject moves or is moved passively to an experimenter-defined target (Stelmach, Kelso, & McCullagh, 1976; Stelmach, Kelso, & Wallace, 1975). The superior reproduction accuracy of subject-defined movement has been demonstrated with slow- to moderate-paced movements (Kelso, 1975, 1977; Marteniuk, 1973; Stelmach et al., 1976), rapid movements (Jones, 1972, 1974; Stelmach et al., 1975), and across a variety of movement amplitudes (see Kelso & Wallace, 1978, for review). This phenomena has been labeled the "preselection effect" and has generated much research to account for this robust finding. For the most part, the debate has focused on the theoretical mechanisms that underlie these types of movement.

There have been several views posited to account for the superior reproduction accuracy of preselected over constrained movements. The first of these emphasizes the cognitive aspects of preselection, stressing for example, the possible differences in the attention demands of preselected and constrained movements. The cognitive view further points to the greater availability of task-related information that may allow preselected subjects to formulate encoding strategies. Unique to this view is the rejection of the role of efferent information in producing superior performance (Kelso & Wallace, 1978).

In contrast to the cognitive view, some theories have stressed the importance of internal efferent information available in preselected but not constrained movements. Stelmach et al. (1975) initially interpreted the preselection effect as support for the corollary-discharge hypothesis where, as a result of preselection, a corollary motor signal activates appropriate or relevant sensory areas, thereby presetting them for the sensory consequences of the motor act. Thus, under preselected conditions, sensory processing centers in the central nervous system are prepared to receive peripheral information, whereas under nonpreselected conditions this does not occur.

In reviewing the theoretical accounts of preselection, Kelso and Wallace (1978) invoke the term *image* as one of several possible explanations of why self-defined movements are so robust and resistant to forgetting. The availability of an image may constitute one of the major differences between preselected and constrained movements. According to Kelso and Wallace, the role of the image in preselected movement may be to generate anticipatory signals that prepare the individual to accept certain kinds of information. The main advantage of this proposal is that the afferent signal and the input are in compatible codes. In other words, the internal, anticipatory image, and the organization and discharge of motor commands (efference) are intrinsically bound together (Kelso & Wallace, 1978).

The preselection effect described in the foregoing paragraph has received an enormous amount of attention and is still vigorously debated. What has intrigued students of motor behavior is the potency of this phenomena in an area that has a reputation for ambiguous findings. Nevertheless, further research is needed to determine the exact theoretical context of preselection. Regardless of this outcome, the work on preselection suggests that useful information is available to the performance prior to movement. It seems feasible to suggest that the performer's attention should be focused on what is intended to be done, rather than merely directing attention to the sensory aspects of a motor act.

Memory Storage Through a Spatial Coordinate System

The fact that preselected movements do not appear to be affected by the reduction of proprioception information and that location cues are so robust has stimulated some investigators to speculate about how movement information is represented in memory. As a result, some investigators have adopted MacNeilage's (1970) target hypothesis as a useful concept to explain movement storage. The target hypothesis was originally developed by MacNeilage to overcome some perplexing problems in speech production. The basic problem for MacNeilage was how an individual could position the oral articulators to a required location specific to a given phoneme from virtually any starting position. Because a feedback-regulated model would have difficulty in explaining such behavior, MacNeilage proposed a three-dimensional coordinate system as the primary agent for generating the necessary motor pattern. This system was presumed to be comprised of the invariant relationships between the articulators that have been built up over time through experience. That quality that remains invariant regarding a given phoneme and that must be stored in memory is the required articulatory end-points within the coordinate system.

Russell (1974) suggested that the target hypothesis could explain the ability of subjects in short-term retention studies to reproduce a limb location from different starting positions. For example, after making a criterion movement to a particular location, this position would be stored in a space-coordinate system in the form of an abstract code. As such, the spatial coordinate system is proposed as a representation of physical space, within which invariant descriptors (anchor points) correspond to objective spatial positions. The spatial positions of targets are defined with respect to the absolute coordinates and, when it becomes necessary to orient to a specific target, the anchor points are thought to facilitate motor action. For the target hypothesis to be a viable explanation of motor control, it must be shown that spatial location can be accessed in memory, independent of the movements responsible for their initial storage, and that accurate movements can be reproduced from starting positions and directions not associated with initial storage. In the work of Laabs (1973), Kelso (1977), Stelmach, Kelso, and Wallace (1975), and Bizzi, Polit, and Morasso (1976), among others, it has indeed been shown that varied starting positions have no affect on limb localization.

Further support for the target hypothesis comes from work of Wallace (1976), who reported two experiments where the subjects had to reproduce a location with the opposite limb to that used for the initial movement. Under these conditions, it was argued that stored proprioceptive feedback of the criterion location could not be directly used for the reproduction because the switched-limb technique forced the subject to rely upon a more abstract location code derived from the criterion location. The results indicated that when direction of the movement was held constant, opposite-limb reproduction was equal to same-limb reproduction, and this result has been interpreted as providing support for the target hypothesis.

With the acknowledged importance of spatial orientation and the apparent importance of the space-coordinate system to orientation, Stelmach and Larish (1980) used the switched-limb paradigm to examine spatial localization within the context of egocentric space. In the first two experiments, one dimensional movements were made vertically upward and horizontally away from the body, respectively, with reproduction attempts being made with the same or switched limb. The results of both experiments revealed that same-limb accuracy was superior only at target positions located beyond earlier-defined body referents. The results seemed to suggest that orientation of the limb could be mediated by a spatial location code if movements remained within the confines of an egocentric reference system defined by body referents. To test this assertion, an additional experiment examined same- and switched-limb performance in two-dimensional space. Based on the previous findings, three targets were selected to represent positions within the bounds of the reference system, and three targets were selected to represent positions outside the bounds of the reference system. Providing the Stelmach and Larish (1980) interpretation is correct, the expected pattern of results is as follows: same- and switched-limb accuracy will be equivalent when limb orientation remains inside the egocentric reference system, whereas same-limb accuracy will be superior when limb orientation is beyond the influence of the reference system. In addition, switched-limb accuracy inside the reference system will be superior to that outside.

At locations defined a priori as inside egocentric space (location near the body midline), accuracy was not different between the limb conditions. At locations defined a priori as outside egocentric space, the same-limb condition was superior to the switched-limb condition. On the basis of these data, one is compelled to believe that efficient motor control by the spatial code is possible only when localization is made within the egocentric reference system. These data support MacNeilage's target hypothesis but suggest restrictions to its generality. When body referent points are available, the accuracy of spatial positioning proceeds independently of the movement originally responsible for creating the spatial location code. Moreover, beyond the limits of this body-based reference system, accurate spatial positioning becomes dependent on direct proprioceptive information.

In general, the reviewed studies imply that accurate limb orientation need not be executed on the basis of remembered sensory consequences and suggest that a spatial coordinate system may mediate the storage of movement information. From the perspective of economy, such an assertion is appealing, as it permits a certain degree of flexibility in the central nervous system's ability to represent movement information.

CONCLUDING COMMENTS

One of the major contemporary issues in motor-behavior research concerns the development of an internal memory representation, postulated as necessary for guiding and controlling movement. This chapter addressed this issue by examining the vast amount of research on the short-term retention of simple motor responses. In contrast to the previous chapter the discussion was not limited to any one theory but presented several viewpoints attempting to stress important findings. From a broad perspective it was pointed out that much of the work in this area focused on developing a memory representation of movement information that was similar in theoretical context to that of Adams' view for developing a memory reference. Most of this work was concerned with examining the causes of forgetting and stressed strategies to improve memory representation, including the importance of cognitive activity.

The final part of the retention section dealt with the mechanisms involved in the retention of movement information. At issue here was the type of movement information used by the central nervous system in reproduction tasks. The primary questions concerned the type of movement information that was encoded, the receptors and effectors involved, and the manner in which movement information is stored. The results discussed did not provide complete answers, but they did suggest the importance of certain types of cues, receptors, and effectors. Unfortunately, the current state of the art does not provide a comprehensive understanding of the mechanisms that underlie movement representation. Thus, a major challenge facing students of motor behavior lies in elucidating the manner in which central and peripheral processes interact to guide movement.

The present discussions have been undertaken with the conviction that students can be introduced to the areas of motor learning and memory through a systematic simplification of essential theoretical constructs and supporting data. Consequently, many nuances, details, and qualifications have been left out. Despite the attempt at simplification, an effort has been made to provide students with an image of the vitality, controversy, and excitement in these research areas. Let the student of motor behavior be warned that as in any area of active scientific research the major issues in motor learning and memory research are rapidly changing; what is known today may be modified tomorrow.

ACKNOWLEDGMENT

Appreciation and a sincere thanks is extended to Virginia Diggles for her editorial assistance in preparing this chapter.

REFERENCES

Adams, J. A. Issues for a closed-loop theory of motor learning. In G. E. Stelmach (Ed.), *Motor control: Issues and trends*. New York: Academic Press, 1976.

Adams, J. A., & Dijkstra, S. Short-term memory for motor responses. *Journal of Experimental Psychology*, 1966, *71*, 314–318.

Adams, J. A., Marshall, P. H., & Goetz, E. T., Response feedback in motor learning. *Journal of Experimental Psychology*, 1972, *92*, 391–397.

Ascoli, K. M., & Schmidt, R. A. Proactive interference in short-term motor retention. *Journal of Motor Behavior*, 1969, *1*, 29–36.

Baddeley, A. D. *The psychology of memory*. New York: Basic Books, 1976.

Bahrick, H. P. An analysis of stimulus variables influencing the proprioceptive control of movements. *Psychological Review*, 1957, *64*, 324–328.

Bizzi, E., Polit, A., & Morasso, P. Mechanisms underlying achievement of final head position. *Journal of Neurophysiology*, 1976, *39*, 435–444.

Broadbent, D. E. *Perception and communication*. London: Pergamon Press, 1958.

Burke, D., & Gibbs, C. B. A comparison of free-moving and pressure levers in a positional control system. *Ergonomics*, 1965, *8*, 23.

Burwitz, L. Short-term motor memory as a function of feedback and interpolated activity. *Journal of Experimental Psychology*, 1974, *102*, 338–340.

Diewert, G. L. Retention and coding in motor short-term memory: A comparison of storage codes for distance and location information. *Journal of Motor Behavior*, 1975, *7*, 183–190.

Diewert, G. L., & Roy, E. A. Coding strategy for memory of movement extent information. *Journal of Experimental Psychology*, 1978, *4*, 666–675.

Diewert, G. L., & Stelmach, G. E. Perceptual organization in motor learning. In G. E. Stelmach (Ed.), *Information processing in motor control and learning*. New York: Academic Press, 1978.

Evarts, E. V. Feedback and corollary discharge: A merging of the concepts. *Neurosciences Research Program Bulletin*, 1971, *9*, 86–112.

Festinger, L., & Cannon, L. K. Information about spatial location based on knowledge about efference. *Psychological Review*, 1965, *72*, 373–384.

Goodwin, G. M., McCloskey, D. I., & Matthews, P. B. C. The contribution of muscle afferents to kinesthesia shown by vibration induced illusions of movement and by the effects of paralyzing joint afferents. *Brain*, 1972, *95*, 705–748.

Holland, D., & Noble, M. E. The effect of physical constraints of a control on tracking performance. *Journal of Experimental Psychology*, 1953, *46*, 353–360.

Jones, B. Outflow and inflow in movement duplication. *Perception and Psychophysics*, 1972, *12*, 95–99.

Jones, B. Role of central monitoring of efference in short-term memory for movements. *Journal of Experimental Psychology*, 1974, *102*, 37–43.

Keele, S. W., & Ells, J. C. Memory characteristics of kinesthetic information. *Journal of Motor Behavior*, 1972, *4*, 127–134.

Kelso, J. A. S. *Planning efferent and receptor components in movement coding*. Unpublished doctoral dissertation, University of Wisconsin, 1975.

Kelso, J. A. S. Motor control mechanisms underlying human movement reproduction. *Journal of Experimental Psychology: Human Perception and Performance*, 1977, *3*, 529–543.

Kelso, J. A. S., & Stelmach, G. E. Central and peripheral mechanisms in motor control. In G. E. Stelmach (Ed.), *Motor control: Issues and trends*. New York: Academic Press, 1976.

Kelso, J. A. S., & Wallace, S. A. Conscious mechanisms in movement. In G. E. Stelmach (Ed.), *Information processing in motor control and learning*. New York: Academic Press, 1978.

Laabs, G. J. Retention characteristics of different reproduction cues in motor short-term memory. *Journal of Experimental Psychology*, 1973, *100*, 168–177.

Lashley, K. S. The accuracy of movement in the absence of excitation from the moving organ. *The American Journal of Psychology*, 1917, *43*, 169–199.

Leuba, J. H. Influence of the duration and rate of arm movements upon judgments of their length. *American Journal of Psychology*, 1909, *20*, 374–385.

MacKay, D. M. Cerebral organization and the conscious control of action. In J. C. Eccles (Ed.), *Brain and conscious experience*. Berlin: Springer-Verlag, 1966.

MacNeilage, P. F. Motor control of serial ordering of speech. *Psychological Review*, 1970, *77*, 182–196.

Marteniuk, R. G. Retention characteristics of short-term cues. *Journal of Motor Behavior*, 1973, *5*, 312–317.

Marteniuk, R. G., & Roy, E. A. The codability of kinesthetic location and distance information. *Acta Psychologica*, 1972, *36*, 471–479.

Nacson, J. Organization of practice and acquisition of simple motor task. In *Proceedings of the First Canadian Congress for the Multi-disciplinary Study of Sport and Physical Activity*, Montreal, Canada, 1973.

Paillard, J., & Brouchon, M. Active and passive movements in the calibration of position sense. In

S. J. Freedman (Ed.), *The neuropsychology of spatially oriented behavior*. Homewood, Ill.: Dorsey, 1968.

Pepper, R. L., & Herman, L. M. Decay and interference effects in the short-term retention of a discrete motor act. *Journal of Experimental Psychology, Monograph Supplement*, 1970, *83*, 1-18.

Posner, M. I. Characteristics of visual and kinesthetic memory codes. *Journal of Experimental Psychology*, 1967, *75*, 103-107.

Posner, M. I., & Konick, A. T. On the role of interference in short-term retention. *Journal of Experimental Psychology*, 1966, *72*, 221-231.

Roy, E. A., & Williams, I. D. Memory for location and extent: The influence of reduction of joint feedback information. In G. C. Roberts & K. M. Newell (Eds.), *Psychology of motor behavior and sport*. Champaign, Ill.: Human Kinetics Publishers, 1978.

Russell, D. G. Location cues and the generation of movement. A paper presented at the North American Society for the Psychology of Sport and Physical Activity, Anaheim, Calif. 1974.

Shea, J. B. Effects of labelling on motor short-term memory. *Journal of Experimental Psychology: Human Learning and Memory*, 1977, *3*, 92-99.

Sperry, R. W. Neural basis of the spontaneous optokinetic response produced by visual invasion. *Journal of Comparative and Physiological Psychology*, 1950, *43*, 482-489.

Stelmach, G. E. Short-term motor retention as a function of response similarity. *Journal of Motor Behavior*, 1969, *1*, 33-44.

Stelmach, G. E. Feedback—A determiner of forgetting in short-term motor memory. *Acta Psychologica*, 1973, *37*, 333-339.

Stelmach, G. E. Retention of motor skills. In J. Wilmore (Ed.), *Exercise and sport sciences review*, San Francisco: Academic Press, 1974.

Stelmach, G. E., & Kelso, J. A. S. Memory trace strength and response biasing in short-term motor memory. *Memory and Cognition*, 1975, *3*, 58-67.

Stelmach, G. E., Kelso, J. A. S., & McCullagh, P. D. Preselection and response biasing in short-term motor memory. *Memory and Cognition*, 1976, *4*, 62-66.

Stelmach, G. E., Kelso, J. A. S., & Wallace, S. A. Preselection in short-term motor memory. *Journal of Experimental Psychology: Human Learning and Memory*, 1975, *1*, 745-755.

Stelmach, G. E., & Larish, D. D. Egocentric referents in human limb orientation. In G. E. Stelmach & J. Requin (Eds.), *Tutorials in motor behavior*. Amsterdam: North Holland Press, 1980.

Stelmach, G. E., & McCracken, H. D. Storage codes for movement information. In J. Requin (Ed.), *Attention and performance VII*. Hillsdale, N.J.: Lawrence Erlbaum Associates, 1978.

Taub, E., Perrella, P. N., & Barro, G. Behavioral development following forelimb deafferentation on day of birth in monkeys with and without blinding. *Science*, 1973, *181*, 959-960.

Wallace, S. A. The coding of location: A test of the target hypothesis. Unpublished doctoral dissertation, University of Wisconsin, 1976.

Wallace, S. A., & Stelmach, G. E. Proprioceptive encoding in preselected and constrained movements. In *Movement 7, Canadian Psycho-Motor Learning and Sports Psychology Symposium*, 1975.

Woodworth, R. S. Accuracy of voluntary movement. *Psychological Review, Monograph Supplement*, 1899, *3*, 1-114.

III

FROM COMPONENT ANALYSIS TO MOTOR PROGRAMS

Editor's Remarks (Chapters 6 and 7)

Thus far, we have dealt primarily with the control and learning of quite slow, discrete movements. In the next set of chapters by Steven Keele and Richard Schmidt, the emphasis is shifted to highly practiced skills that often involve very rapid action. For reasons that are probably already obvious, a closed-loop account of such actions seems inadequate; instead, the idea is that a whole pattern can be generated without any requirement that peripheral information be constantly used to update and adjust the movement. Centrally generated movement patterns or motor programs are thought to be represented in certain, as yet unclear, neural structures. Chapter 7 by Steven Keele (who had much to do with the development of the idea in motor-behavior circles) and Chapters 8 and 9 by Richard Schmidt (who has worked a great deal on clarifying the notion) address numerous issues regarding motor programs: how programs are learned, their relationship to feedback, the hierarchical nature of motor programs, what parameters are contained in the motor programs, how programs may be translated into muscle action, and so on.

Before elaborating on the program concept, however, Keele (Chapter 6) presents a more traditional approach to motor skills—common in industrial time and motion analysis—that breaks the skill up into its task components and asks how each component changes with practice. Certain variables, for example, compatibility and the probability of expected events, have well-known effects on the time it takes to make decisions. Keele suggests a number of interesting applications of these concepts to sports skills. Knowing ahead of time what stimulus is about to appear vastly reduces decision time, and in theory, the skilled basketball player or boxer could use such "cues" to anticipate what is most likely to happen next. In short, Keele advances, in his words, the "quite speculative" hypothesis that highly skilled behavior is as much cognitive as it is perceptual or motor.

Keele's suggestion is a challenging one because it "lifts" skill out of the perceptual-motor domain and drops it firmly in the bag of "cognition." But maybe we should stop and ponder a while before taking this step. Certainly, some of the skills that Keele discusses such as chess seem categorizable as cognitive acts. But others, such as Mohammed Ali's ability to avoid punches, seem less so. Just because Mohammed Ali's decision times and movement times are not much different than those of the ordinary man or woman on the street does not necessarily imply that his skilled behavior falls in the cognitive domain and that the "redundancy inherent in the situation is stored in [Mohammed Ali's] memory." Rather than appealing to cognitive operations to give meaning to incoming stimuli, it might be that the information being *picked up* becomes more and more subtle and precise as skill develops. This alternative, the theory of information pick up (Gibson, J. J. *The senses considered as perceptual systems,* Houghton Mifflin: Boston, 1966; *The ecological approach to visual perception,* Houghton Mifflin: Boston, 1979), argues that the skilled performer resonates to the information and becomes attuned to it over time. For this contrasting view, information is *always* available, and hence there is no need to access stored knowledge structures for purposes of prediction and anticipation. Well... there goes the gauntlet. Will highly learned skills fall under the rubric of cognition as Keele suggests, or will they remain for the student of perception and action? Does highly skilled behavior necessarily implicate the presence of an abstract structure stored in memory (Schmidt, Chapters 8 & 9)? I think we will all stand to benefit, perhaps more from a rigorous attempt to provide an answer to questions like these than from the answers themselves.

6 Component Analysis and Conceptions of Skill

Steven W. Keele
University of Oregon

The more one practices a skill, the more the skill improves. In fact, for some purposes it is best to think that no real limit exists for the degree of improvement. This is illustrated in Fig. 6.1 from Crossman (1959), showing the speed with which operators of a cigar-making machine make cigars. Different operators practiced on the machine for up to 7 years and made up to 10 million cigars. What is interesting is that performance bottomed out only after 2 years of practice. The apparent reason for lack of improvement after 2 years is not the human but the machine itself. Operators with that amount of experience approached very close to the cycle time of the machine, which is indicated by the horizontal dotted line. It would appear that improvement on this simple skill would have continued for a much longer time were it not for machine limitations.

There is an additional point to make about the practice curve in Fig. 6.1. The horizontal and vertical axes are plotted on a logarithmic scale, and this leads to a bit of an illusion. At first glance one might think that the skill improved linearly with practice—that's really not true because both axes are on a log–log scale. A feature of a logarithmic scale is that is compresses large values so, in fact, the amount of improvement declines with increasing practice. This general formulation, a linear decrease in the log of performance with the log of practice, has been labeled DeJong's Law by Crossman.

Now improvement occurs not just within an individual but also across individuals over the course of generations. Ryder, Carr, and Herget (1976) examined the improvement of running speed over the years 1930 to 1970 for distances ranging from 100 yards to 15 miles. Over successive years runners have become faster and faster, and the relationship between speed and year shows no evidence

143

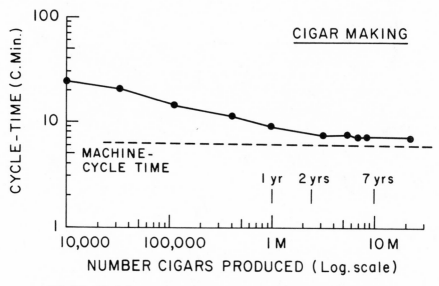

FIG. 6.1.   The influence of over 7 years practice (and 10,000,000 cigars) on the speed of making cigars. Each point represents a different operator. The logarithm of cycle time reduces linearly with the logarithm of amount of practice until a point near the minimum cycle time of the machine is reached (from Crossman, 1959).

of leveling off. One might conclude that there really is no clear limit to human speed.

Much of the improvement with practice might be due to factors not of interest here—better conditioning, better equipment, selection from a greater population of possible athletes, and so on—but likely even in running, with modern coaching, the very, very intensive practice engaged in by the modern runner leads to improved technique, not just improved condition. Many years ago Bernstein (1967) showed, for example, that the motion of the body parts of a world-class runner were much more complex than those of ordinary runners, implying that technique, and not just conditioning, improves with practice.

The task in Chapters 6 and 7 is to gain theoretical perspectives on what it means to say that practice yields improved technique. To the extent that we can generate useful perspectives, we may be able to intervene and more quickly improve skilled performance or produce a higher level of skill. These chapters cover three different perspectives on why skills improve. The first might be called the component-analysis perspective: A person decides what action is required, executes it, evaluates the results, makes another decision, and then a further action, and so on. From this perspective, knowing the variables that influence decision time and movement time suggests ways to increase the efficiency of skills. This is an old and time-honored approach in industrial time and motion analysis, where the goal is to reduce time of assembly-line skills. Much of this perspective has already been covered in a chapter by Stelmach and receives only a review here.

A more speculative perspective then is developed. Fast-action skills characterized by a rapidly changing environment or arrangement of people—skills such as race-car driving, basketball, soccer, boxing, and so on—should be viewed not just as depending on perceptual and motor abilities, things like reaction time and movement time, but also as depending very heavily on a variety of cognitive abilities. The best performers may be ones that are strong in particular cognitive capacities rather than just perceptual or motor capacities.

The second chapter is concerned with a third perspective, the concept of a motor program, a notion that a series of actions become melded into a unitary movement pattern that can be executed without constant decision and correction.

COMPONENT ANALYSIS

Component analysis posits two primary components that enter into skill, a decision component and an action component. People are assumed to assess a situation, make a decision, select a movement or some other action, and then execute that action. Duration of the decision component can be assessed by reaction times, and duration of movement action components can be assessed by movement time. Once we know what variables influence reaction and movement time, we may be able to intervene in some way to reduce them.

Reaction Time

Reaction time abstractly defined is a measure of the time from the signal onset until movement to the signal begins. For example, reaction time is the time from when a player yields a cue that he is shooting a basketball until an opponent begins a leap to block the shot.

Number of Alternatives.   Perhaps the major variable to influence reaction time is the number of possible situations that can arise and the number of possible responses that can be made in those situations. The greater the uncertainty about what's going to happen, the longer reaction time to decide what response to make.

Figure 6.2 shows some very old data from Merkel, published in 1885 (see Woodworth, 1938). In a sense these data have never been improved on, though they have been replicated several times since. Merkel simply asked people to press buttons to the appearance of Arabic and Roman numerals. People were told in advance exactly which digits they could expect. In a two-choice situation, for example, Merkel might tell a subject to expect either the Roman numeral II or the Arabic numeral 5. The subject would not know which of those two would occur,

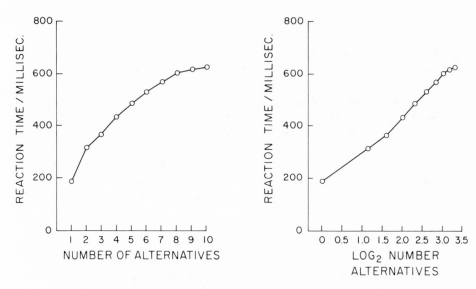

FIG. 6.2.   Reaction time as a function of number of alternative choices: The more choice, the slower reaction time. The right panel shows the same data as the left except number of choices is plotted on a logarithmic scale (based on data of Merkel, reported in Woodworth, 1938).

but when one did he pressed the button that corresponded to that numeral. For four choices, four numerals would be specified, any one of which could occur on a trial. The left of Fig. 6.2 depicts how reaction time depends on the number of alternative digits ranging from one to 10. Reaction time arises from a minimum of about 200 milliseconds up to around 600 milliseconds for 10 choices. The data plotted this way produce a curvilinear relationship. In other words, the effect on reaction time of adding one more alternative is less when there are already a large number of alternatives than where there are only a few alternatives. Another way of stating this result is that reaction time is a logarithmic function of the number of alternatives. The right-hand graph of Fig. 6.2 simply involves replotting the data, converting the horizontal axis to the logarithm of the number of alternatives, or what is sometimes called bits of information. With that transformation, reaction time is seen to be a linear function of the logarithm of the number of alternatives. Practice on a task like Merkel's both lowers the curve (reduces the intercept) and reduces the steepness of the function (reduces the slope).

Does this simple result of Merkel's have practical implications for skill learning? One implication is that coaches should carefully define situations that require specific responses. Carefully defining them will reduce RT by effectively reducing the number of possible situations and responses to be considered, and then practicing each situation-response combination should vastly reduce RT.

In basketball an offensive player very often holds the ball in front or only slightly to the side. In ordinary, garden-variety basketball few defensive players take the opportunity to slap the ball away. The offensive player slips by the defensive opponent and goes pell-mell for the basket. Few defensive teammates take the opportunity to take a single sideway step and draw an offensive foul. Naturally, most coaches make mention of such common situations and appropriate responses, but they give little systematic practice. Would it be useful to produce numerous slides or brief film clips that illustrate a small, defined set of offensive moves of the sort mentioned and flash them briefly, requiring the defensive player to say as rapidly as possible what should be done? A contrived setting of this sort could be effective in reducing the uncertainty and also would give extensive practice in recognizing the situations and quickly selecting a response.

Probability of Alternatives.   A variable closely related to the number of alternatives but one that requires special mention is that of probability of alternatives. In most situations, of the possible things that can happen, some are more probable than others. The astute sportsman should notice which possibilities are the most common, and that person will then react much faster to them.

Table 6.1 presents data from an experiment by Fitts, Peterson, and Wolpe (1963). The task was simply to name whatever digit was shown. Subjects were given four sessions of practice on this simple task and their reaction times were measured. For one group, all the digits from 1–9 were equally likely (i.e., probability of .11 for each digit). For a second group, the number 1 occurred with a higher probability, .24, and the remaining 8 digits each had a probability of about .09. The thing to notice is that the more probable event is responded to more rapidly than the equally likely events. Conversely, the less-probable events, those that occur 9% of the time, are responded to a bit more slowly than in the equally probable case. In yet another group, the probability of the number 1 was 75%, and the probabilities of the remaining digits were each 3%. In a final

TABLE 6.1
Reaction Time as a Function of Probability
(Fitts, Peterson, & Wolpe, 1963)

	Condition	*Reaction Time*
Group 1	Equiprobable ($P = .11$)	390 milliseconds
Group 2	Hi probability = .24	375 milliseconds
	Lo probability = .095	405 milliseconds
Group 3	Hi probability = .75	320 milliseconds
	Lo probability = .031	425 milliseconds
Group 4	Hi probability = .94	285 milliseconds
	Lo probability = .008	440 milliseconds

case involving another group of subjects, one alternative occurred 94% of the time, and the other ones occurred about 1% of the time. Again, with practice, the more probable the event the faster the reaction time. But at the same time, when a less-probable event occurs there is some cost; the reaction time is lengthened.

Let's concentrate for a moment on the last condition involving the .94 and .01 probabilities, which come from the same group, and contrast their reaction times with the equally probable group (.11). When an expected event occurs, the respondent gains what might be called reaction-time benefit. But when the unexpected or the unpredicted events occur, then the respondent suffers what might be called reaction-time cost. More formally, benefit can be defined as the reaction time in the neutral condition when each of the alternatives are equally likely, in this case .11, minus the reaction time to a high-probability event—that event that occurs 94% of the time. Subtracting the reaction times in those two situations yields a sizeable benefit of 105 milliseconds. Clearly, there is a great advantage in expecting the high probability event, especially in a setting where fast decisions mean success. On the other hand, there is a cost. Subtracting the neutral reaction time from reaction time to the low-probability event yields a cost, in this case about 50 milliseconds. With this cost, why is predictability advantageous overall? Of course, the high-probability event occurs most of the time. So if one anticipates, then a benefit is obtained. In this case a benefit would occur 94% of the time. Only a small percentage of the time would the performer get the cost. So although there is a cost to unexpected things, by their very nature, unexpected things occur less frequently, and overall a great advantage accrues to using the probabilities.

There is one other aspect of the probability notion that should be made explicit: In many settings over a long period, one event is no more probable than another. For example, in a football game the pass receiver may just as likely turn left as turn right over the course of a game. But cues may alter the probabilities at a particular time; a certain cue may anticipate the movement, making one movement much more probable than another at that time.

What are some implications of the probability notion for improvement of sport? Sport is to a very, very large extent a probability game, and it is wise to keep that in mind. The task of the offensive player is to make things unpredictable, as much as possible, and to induce the defensive player to predict the wrong thing. This should be a primary emphasis of any coach. Teach your players how to make the offense unpredictable. Practically everyone acknowledges this is why a good fastball pitcher unpredictably throws other pitches. Otherwise, the fastball would lose much of its own effectiveness. But the same principle applies to a much wider domain than pitching.

On the other hand, the defensive player should always search for the cues that tell what will most likely happen next and learn to avoid cues, "fakes," that the offensive player is using to fool. Some basketball coaches say to watch the bellybutton on an opposing player, for it is less likely to fool you than the head or hand. Of course if you're dealing with an offensive player who telegraphs movements with the head or eyes, then the astute player should use those cues to anticipate what most likely is to happen next. Anticipation vastly reduces reaction time.

Compatibility.   Consider one final variable that influences reaction time—the variable of compatibility. Reaction time is often slow not because there is too much choice but because the response is not a natural one for that situation. Consider the data of Figure 6.3 from Broadbent and Gregory (1962). Vibrators were placed under the fingers. In the compatible situations people pressed the finger that was vibrated. In the incompatible situation the task was simply to respond not with the vibrated finger but with the mirror-image finger. For example, if the left index finger was vibrated, the subject should press the right index finger. As seen in the data, incompatibility greatly slows reaction time. Moreover, the effect of compatibility was considerably greater for four choice than for two choice. Other studies have shown that even in very simple situations, poor compatibility still lowers reaction time after dozens of practice sessions.

Despite the simplicity of the compatibility principle, it is very commonly ignored, at least in the design of machines and other complex systems. Consider, for example, the 10-speed bicycle. In approaching a hill, what direction should the levers be moved to gear down and ease pedaling? On almost all 10-speeds the

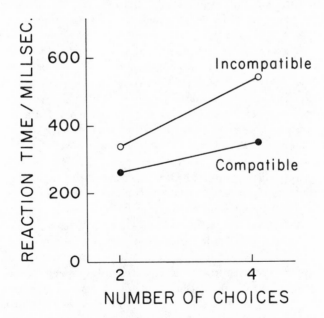

FIG. 6.3.   Reaction time as a function of number of choices and compatibility. The detrimental effects of poor compatibility are magnified the more the number of choices (based on data of Broadbent & Gregory, 1962).

answer depends on the lever: The right lever is moved back and the left one forward. Most cyclists undoubtedly are aware of times when this inconsistency resulted in a shifting error just at the wrong time. On some machines, such as automobiles or airplanes, poor compatibility is a life-or-death matter. In fact, a good many airplane accidents and near accidents in World War II were attributed to poor compatibility (Fitts & Jones, 1961).

An applied psychologist cannot overemphasize the compatibility problem because it is so omnipresent. A near maxim of the applied psychologist is: When a decision speed problem exists, change the system to make it more compatible; don't change the person.

Movement Time

Once a decision is made concerning some necessary action, movement of some body part must occur to carry out the action. The efficiency of skilled performance typically depends on either speed or precision of the movement, or more often a combination of the two. The baseball player tries to compromise by choosing a speed of bat swing that is likely to move the ball an acceptable distance, but also a movement precise enough so the ball is hit in the first place.

What kinds of variables influence movement time? Most obviously, movement time increases with distance of movement. But this can be quite a misleading principle. Two examples illustrate situations in which movement time depends little or not at all on distance, at least within bounds. The maximum rate at which the finger or arm can be moved back and forth is rather independent of distance and lies somewhere around 6 cycles per second. Also, one can write on the blackboard nearly as fast as writing small on paper, despite the fact that an enormous difference exists in distance moved.

Obviously, factors other than distance must be considered. For many decades time and motion engineers in industry have been concerned with movement speed, and among other things they have realized that movement time depends on precision of movement, not just distance. From that knowledge they constructed extensive tables giving movement time for different combinations of distance and precision. But in 1954 Paul Fitts discovered a very simple and hence elegant manner of combining distance and precision into a single formulation, and his formulation is now called Fitts' Law. Figure 6.4, based on a later study by Fitts and Peterson (1964), illustrates that formulation. Fitts and Peterson varied the distance that one moved a stylus with the arm to hit a target. The distance of movement varied from 3 to 12 inches in length and the width of the target varied from ⅛ to 1 inch. What affected movement time was not the distance per se, nor the width per se, but only the ratio of the distance to the width. If two different distance-width combinations had exactly the same ratio, then they had about the same movement time. For example, moving 3 inches to a

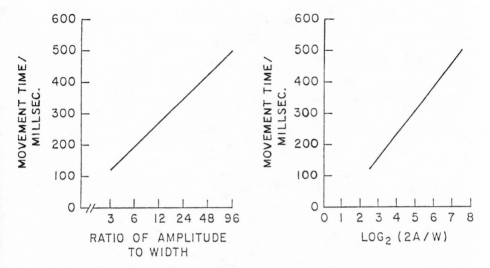

FIG. 6.4. The left panel portrays movement time as a function of the ratio of movement amplitude to target width. Note that successive ratios double. The right panel portarys the same data but explicitly notes the *logarithm* of the amplitude to width ratio.

target ¼ inch wide, which is a 12 to 1 ratio of distance to width, produces the same movement time as a movement of 12 inches to a 1-inch wide target. Distance and width are exactly compensatory. The left-hand panel of Fig. 6.4. shows how movement time relates to the distance–width ratio. Movement time increases from about 125 milliseconds for a short movement of 3 inches to a 1-inch target, to about 500 milliseconds for a long movement of 12 inches to a narrow target of ⅛ inch. Notice that ratios on the horizontal axis successively double: 3, 6, 12, 24, 48, and 96. The horizontal axis is essentially a logarithmic scale. The right-hand panel of Fig. 6.4. shows the same results but with the horizontal scale relabeled as $\log_2(\frac{2A}{W})$, where A is amplitude of movement and W is target width. The value has come to be called the index of difficulty. Fitts' Law then relates movement time (MT) to the index of difficulty by the equation $MT = a + b \log_2(\frac{2A}{W})$. If one knows the constants a and b, movement time of the arm for any combination of amplitude and width can be estimated.

The real importance of Fitts' Law lies in the idea that distance and precision are complementary to each other. It explains why excursion of the finger takes the same amount of time regardless of amplitude: The larger the amplitude, the less the precision, and hence those movements are carried out in the same amount of time. Write your name as fast as you can on a piece of paper in small letters, perhaps only ⅛-inch high. Write your name as fast as you can on the blackboard. The latter involves an enormously larger length of movement, and

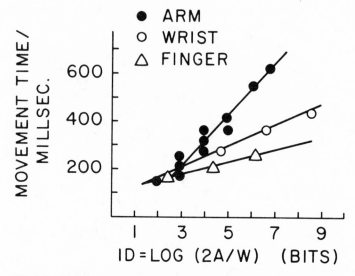

FIG. 6.5. Movement time as a function of the index of difficulty of the movement for movements made under a microscope by finger, or by wrist, or by normal movements of the arm (from Langolf, Chaffin, & Foulke, 1976).

yet those two handwritings take similar amounts of time. The reason is that though the length is vastly increased for writing on the board, the precision is vastly decreased. The ratio of precision-to-length remains more or less constant, and hence movement time is essentially the same.

Numerous studies show Fitts' Law to generalize to movements other than simple arm movements. For example, the basic motivation of a study by Langolf, Chaffin, and Foulke (1976) came from a new industrial problem. In modern electronics much assembly of parts is done under a low-power microscope so that only movement of the finger or wrist, not arm, is required. Thus, a need exists for establishing time standards for microscopic work. Langolf and colleagues investigated movement time to targets of different width for arm movements of different distance, for short-wrist movements about ½ inch in length, and for finger movements about 1/10 inch in length. The two shorter movements were performed under a seven-power microscope. Figure 6.5 shows Fitts' Law to provide a good description of arm, wrist, and finger. However, these differ from each other in one detail: The finger is faster and more accurate than the wrist, and the wrist is faster and more accurate than the arm. Fitts' Law now underlies time standards for microscopic work.

What is the underlying nature of the movement system that yields Fitts' Law? In the last few years it has become clear that no single idea yields an exact quantitative prediction in line with this law, but there are a couple of factors that seem to be involved. One factor is the intrinsic accuracy of the motor system when visual feedback is unavailable. When the eyes are closed during a movement (or the lights are turned off), an average movement will miss the target by about 7% of the total distance moved. To consistently hit a target, therefore, vision must be used to correct the movement, and the longer the distances of the movement *or* the narrower the target, the more correction is necessary. Because correction takes time, movement time (*MT*) obviously will depend both on amplitude and target width. So Fitts' Law depends partly on accuracy of the movement system and the time to process visual feedback.

A second factor underlying Fitts' Law has been investigated by Schmidt and his colleagues (reported in Chapter 8). The faster a movement is to be made, the greater the force that must be imparted to start a movement, and the greater the opposing force to stop movement as the target is neared. But greater force results in less precision. Thus, if one needs precision, moving slowly will result in a more precise movement even without visual feedback. In some unknown quantitative mix, visual feedback and accuracy due to force combine to produce Fitts' Law.

Is there any sense in which the law can be used to help improve skilled performance? The quantitative aspects of Fitts' Law probably will find most use in nonsports settings, as in assembly-line tasks where the most efficient combination of movements is desired. But there are perhaps qualitative implications for sport. Fitts' Law makes it very clear that speed and accuracy trade off. And Schmidt's analysis of underlying processes makes it clear that the tradeoff is partly due to inaccuracy in increasing force in order to increase speed. A principle then would be this: Make a slow movement whenever accuracy is the prime concern. A slow bat swing will result in a higher batting average. A slow stroke of the cue in pool will be more accurate than a slam. Perhaps a long arm movement in shooting a basketball in which a modest force has sufficient time to generate the needed velocity will be more accurate than an impulsive movement. Moreover, the movement should not be slowed before the release of the ball, for the stopping impulse imparts another source of error.

When speed as well as accuracy is of major concern, Fitts' Law again provides some perspective. It shows that movement in fact takes a sizeable chunk of total time in a skill. Speed can be greatly increased by reducing the number of component motions or by making each motion either shorter or less precise. Consider shaving with a blade razor. Given that speed is of interest, would you choose a single-edge or a double-edge razor?

WHAT DOES IT MEAN TO BE SKILLED?

Consider fast-action sports—things like boxing, race-car driving, soccer, basketball, and football. Then think of the tremendously gifted athlete, the very best, and ask what it is that makes that person so good? Is it incredibly fast reaction times, lightning movements, precise depth perception, or very good accuracy in the movement system? A fair summary is that investigations have not found components of that sort to be a large factor, if a factor at all, in the success of most sport skills (Marteniuk, 1974). We cannot say with certainty that the super athlete is particularly fast on reaction time, particularly fast and accurate on his movements, and so on, though there is some question whether the issue has been properly investigated. The same can be said about motor patterns—a topic covered in the next chapter. You've probably seen athletes that have the very best of technique, the best of form, yet they are not outstanding. Something is missing, and that something has to do with how effectively the knowledge about the game can be mustered at critical times. This leads to yet another perspective on high-level skill, one that emphasizes the great deal of practice necessary to become an expert.

The role of practice has not been carefully explored and conceptualized on sport, but work on cognitive skills provides potentially important guidelines for this path. One well-studied skill is chess, and we may ask what makes the master player or the grand master in chess? Is it some incredible general ability or is it just a great deal of practice? A study by Chase and Simon (1973) that followed up on an earlier one by DeGroot casts light on the problem. An arrangement of 24 chess pieces from a real middle-game situation was flashed before subjects for 5 seconds. Then the subjects were given a board and the same 24 peices and told to reproduce the chess positions. It is important to note that there are so many, many possible middle-game arrangements that even a master with all his practice is very unlikely to have seen the particular middle-game arrangements chosen. This experiment was done with a master in chess at Carnegie–Mellon University, a class-A player, who qualified as very good but not as good as a master, and a beginner. On the first 5-second exposure the master player got about 16 of the pieces in the correct position; the class-A player got only about 8 peices in the correct position; the novice got only about 4 pieces in the correct position. Moreover, the master took fewer trials to be able to reproduce accurately the entire 24-piece board.

What makes the master so much better on this memory task? A common notion is that the master has some super capability that other people do not, in this case perhaps a super memory. A simple change in procedure rules that hypothesis out. The chess pieces, rather than being placed as they would be in a real game, are placed at random positions on the board. After a 5-second exposure the master now does somewhat poorer than either the novice or the class-A player. Perhaps he does poorer because random positions conflict with previous knowledge, or perhaps this master actually has a *poorer* memory, not better! The point is that the superior memory performance demonstrated with real chess positions seems to be specific to the fact that the master has practiced thousands upon thousands of hours with chess. In that time the chess master has acquired thousands of chess patterns that are stored in long-term memory so that when he sees a real game, rather than seeing twenty odd pieces arranged at random, the chess master actually sees only a few meaningful patterns. The novice in contrast sees 24 randomly scattered pieces. This sort of research led Chase and Simon (1973) to suggest that the main element in most skills is the acquisition of patterns that are stored in long-term memory and stored there as a result of very extensive practice. How long does it take to become a master? According to Chase, perhaps 10,000–15,000 hours.

Consider another example that leads to a similar viewpoint (Hunter, 1968). Dr. Aietken is a professor of mathematics and a mathematical wizard. For example: "He is asked to express as a decimal the fraction 4 over 47. He is silent for 4 seconds then begins to speak the answer at a nearly uniform rate of one digit every three-quarters of a second: 'point 0 8 5 1 0 6 3 8 2 9 7 8 7 2 3 4 0 4 2 5 5 3 1 9 1 4. That's about as far as I can carry it.' The total time between presentation of the problem and this moment is 24 seconds. He discusses the problem for one minute and then continues the answer at the same rate as before. 'Yes, 1 9 1 4 8 9, I can get that.' He pauses for 5 seconds. '3 6 1 7 0 2 1 2 7 6 5 9 5 7 4 4 5 8.' (p. 341)"

One might well wonder what amazing abilities Professor Aietken had inherited? But although we don't know whether inherited abilities may partly underlie his wizardry, an analysis of his capabilities soon makes it clear that something very similar to that with the chess master is going on. With years and years of practice doing problems in his head, Professor Aietken has stored a large mass of relevant information in long-term memory. That information falls into three categories: One, he has stored a large array of number facts. For example, most of us have learned multiplication talbes up to 12 times 12. It's not clear how extensive his multiplication tables are, but descriptions of his ability suggest they may be as large as 100 times 100. So, given an arbitrary number like 1961, he recognizes it as the product of 37×53. And he knows for all the numbers up to 1500 whether they are prime, and if not, their factors. A second memory store besides basic number facts consists of a vast array of calculation strategies, ways to work with numbers in different settings. And finally, a peculiarity that comes about from great practice is that Professor Aietken exhibits unitization of large numbers. To him, any two-or three-digit number is as simple and presumably as easy to remember as a one-digit number is for us. Whereas for us a string of two-digit numbers, like 23, 35, 49, 16 is more difficult to remember than a string of single-digit numbers, we would infer that such is not the case for him, because each number from 0 to 1000 is more or less a single unit. To appreciate the idea of a unit consider 1776. Most Americans would have little trouble remembering that among a longer string because it is a single unit, an important historical date. You could be given a set of four or five four-digit numbers of *that* sort and be able to remember them because you've unitized them. Unitization appears to result when many facts become associated with a particular number, and so for Professor Aietken unitization is probably a by-product of his other knowledge about numbers.

The analysis of Professor Aietken suggests again that a major component of extreme skill is the extensive repertoire of facts, procedures, and recognizable patterns that result from extensive practice. Undoubtedly, the same is true of sport skills.

But a nagging doubt persists that only practice explains the super star. Other people may have had as extensive practice as a star and have the physical features necessary for success in a particular sport and yet they are not the superstars. What might be involved? In the last part of this chapter, we speculate that fast-action skills might fruitfully be thought of not as perceptual-motor skills, but as cognitive skills. The idea is quite speculative; some of our own ongoing research is directed at the idea, but it is largely untested. But consider both an informal experiment with Muhammed Ali, one of the outstanding athletes of our time, and a more formal experiment with pilots and bus drivers.

Some years ago, when Muhammed Ali was in his prime, *Sports Illustrated* (May 5, 1969) measured his reaction and movement times. A light flashed and Ali lashed out to smash a board 16 inches away. Reaction time was reported as 190 milliseconds, but it is unclear from the description whether that value also included the 40-millisecond movement time. If the 40 milliseconds is subtracted, 150 milliseconds remains as a reaction time. The point made by *Sports Illustrated* was, firstly, that Muhammed Ali was incredibly quick, and, secondly, that the quickness accounted, in part, for his success. However, it is not clear that the times are incredibly quick. Observations of reaction and movement time suggest that other people are equally fast. Instead, the numbers have a hidden meaning. Presumably, any other world-class boxer also has a movement time of about 40 milliseconds. Once the movement begins, it would be absolutely impossible for Ali to react in time to avoid the punch if he waits until the start of the punch to begin his reaction, because the reaction process takes at best 150 milliseconds, much longer than movement time. Yet Ali was adept at avoiding punches. His success must lie more in the anticipation of punches before they start.

A probable key to most people adept at fast-action skills is that they typically react not to the start of movement, but instead they use cues in the situation to tell what probably will happen next; they anticipate. This constitutes a cognitive skill. Redundancy inherent in the situation is stored in memory. The skilled person has quick access to that knowledge structure that allows prediction and anticipation.

Some formal experiments conducted by Daniel Kahneman and colleagues (Gopher & Kahneman, 1971; Kahneman, Ben–Ishai, & Lotan, 1973) explore another cognitive skill, which might be called attentional flexibility. They studied bus-driver accidents among Israeli bus drivers and pilot success among Israeli pilots. Their prediction task was dichotic listening. A high or low tone indicated from which ear to report digits. Then a succession of pairs of words occurred, one member of each pair in the left ear, and the other member in the right ear. Some of the words were digits, and whenever a digit occurred in the ear indicated by the tone, it was to be repeated back. This went on for 16 word pairs, and then with no break another tone reassessed which ear was relevant. Part 2 of the task then began, and it also involved repeating digits from the indicated ear.

Dichotic listening performance on part 1, which followed the first tone, correlated little if at all with either bus-driving accidents or pilot success. But performance on part 2, following the second tone, correlated modestly with the number of bus-driving accidents. People who did relatively poorly on part 2 tended toward more accidents. Moreover, people who did well on part 2 tended to succeed in pilot school, and, among accomplished pilots, those assigned to faster aircraft, which require more skill, did better than those assigned to slower aircraft.

Why would a task like dichotic listening, which requires little in the way of motor activity, correlate with two different motor skills? Kahneman and colleagues suggest that when the second tone occurs there is very little time to switch attention to another ear. At that point in time some people fall a little bit behind, and then they make more errors on part 2. Those people in turn tend to have more accidents or lower pilot ratings. Why? Presumably, bus-driving accidents are caused when one fails to switch attention rapidly enough from the task at hand to deal with an unexpected event that potentially can cause an accident. Likewise, at times high-speed flying requires rapid switching of attention from one task component to another.

The studies of Kahneman and colleagues suggest, therefore, that a basic cognitive ability, the ability to rapidly switch attention, might help predict success on fast-action motor skills.

What other cognitive abilities besides attentional flexibility and the ability to rapidly draw on knowledge of a task's redundancy might be considered? Another potential ability we might refer to as time sharing. Most fast-action skills require the performer to do several things at once, such as watching several opponents, executing a pattern, and remembering the coach's instructions. Several investigators have speculated that some people might be better than others at time sharing on two or more tasks, and that such an ability would be predictive of skill. Damos (1978) in fact produced some evidence for this view. One of her tasks involved tracking a moving spot on a screen, and another task required rapid key presses with the free hand in response to visual digits. She found in one pilot sample that reaction time to digits when time shared with tracking was correlated with piloting proficiency, but her report doesn't mention the correlation between the time-shared score and piloting performance for a second sample of pilots, who may not have been so successful. Other research in fact has generated controversy on whether a time-sharing ability in fact exists. Sverko (1977) ran subjects on reaction time, tracking, discrimination, and mental arithmetic tasks both alone and in all combinations of two tasks. A person's ability to time share one combination of two tasks had no relation to the ability to time share another combination. Similarly, Hawkins, Rodriquez, and Reicher (1979) found virtually no correlation in the ability to rapidly respond to one set of two signals with ability to rapidly respond to another set of two signals when the difficulty level, modality of signal (visual or auditory), and nature of the response (verbal or manual) were changed from one situation to another. (A detailed report of Hawkins work, related work on flexibility of attention, and individual differences in repetitive speed appears in Keele and Hawkins, 1982).

So although Damos' work suggests some promise for time-sharing capability as a cognitive factor that might underlie motor skill, other work raises serious questions as to whether people do in fact differ from one another on a general ability to time share.

Another promising cognitive ability that might underlie high-level skill is spatial awareness or sense of direction. Some outstanding athletes seem to have an uncanny sense where various other players and parts of their immediate environment are, even though they themselves and the opponents have moved since last viewed. It is as though they take note of trajectories, can remember them very well for a few seconds, and can very rapidly draw on that spatial information. But no investigator has yet objectively shown that the successful athlete has a better than normal sense of direction. Nonetheless, people do differ from one another on at least one type of sense of direction. Kozlowski and Bryant (1977) showed that college students who reported they had a good sense of direction indeed tended to be more accurate in locating campus buildings on a map, pointing to unseen campus locations, and at indicating where they had been after being led through an underground maze. Whether this sort of ability is one factor underlying athletic prowess remains to be demonstrated.

Summary.   We know from outstanding skill other than sport that success depends largely on extended practice involving thousands of hours. In that time people accumulate a "vocabulary" of thousands of patterns (or situations) that they can recognize, and they build an extensive repetoire of strategies and responses to deal with those patterns. Beyond that, little is known about the abilities that make some people so astoundingly skilled. Undoubtedly, practice is equally important for success in sports. But beyond practice, are there particular perceptual or motor abilities that are important? Past research has had little success in identifying at least general perceptual-motor abilities that cut across more than one sport. Alternatively, but largely untested, is the possibility that certain cognitive abilities are important to sports success—things like attentional flexibility, sense of direction, speed of drawing on cues that predict subsequent events, and the like. Hopefully, these kinds of issues will draw more investigation in future years.

We might finally note that, although reaction time as discussed in the first part of the chapter probably is not indicative of skill, reaction time measures may well play an important role in the endeavor to identify important cognitive abilities. It can be used to measure the speed of attentional shifting, the speed to draw on redundant cues that predict what will happen next, the speed of accessing spatial information, and so on. Reaction time should be viewed not as a basic ability in itself but rather as a technique to be used in measuring these other abilities.

REFERENCES

Bernstein, N. *The coordination and regulation of movement.* London: Pergamon Press, 1967.

Broadbent, D. E., & Gregory, M. Donder's B- and C-reactions and S–R compatibility. *Journal of Experimental Psychology,* 1962, *63,* 575–578.

Chase, W. G., & Simon, H. A. The mind's eye in chess. In W. G. Chase (Ed.), *Visual information processing.* New York and London: Academic Press, 1973.

Crossman, E. R. F. W. A theory of the acquisition of speed-skill. *Ergonomics,* 1959, *2,* 153–166.

Damos, D. Residual attention as a predictor of pilot performance. *Human Factors,* 1978, *20,* 435–440.

Fitts, Paul M. The information capacity of the human motor system in controlling the amplitude of movement. *Journal of Experimental Psychology,* 1954, *47,* 381–391.

Fitts, P. M., & Jones, R. E. Analysis of factors contributing to 460 "pilot error" experiences in operating aircraft controls. In H. W. Sinaiko (Ed.), *Selected papers on human factors in the design and use of control systems.* New York: Dover, 1961.

Fitts, P. M., & Peterson, J. R. Information capacity of discrete motor responses. *Journal of Experimental Psychology,* 1964, *67,* 103–112.

Fitts, P. M., Peterson, J. R., & Wolpe, G. Cognitive aspects of information processing: II, adjustments to stimulus redundancy. *Journal of Experimental Psychology,* 1963, *65,* 423–432.

Gopher, D., & Kahneman, D. Individual differences in attention and the prediction of flight criteria. *Perceptual and Motor Skills,* 1971, *33,* 1335–1342.

Hawkins, H. L., Rodriguez, E., & Reicher, G. M. *Is time sharing a general ability?* (Tech. Rep. No. 3), Center for Cognitive and Perceptual Research. University of Oregon, Eugene, 1979.

Hunter, I. M. L. Mental calculation. In P. C. Wason & P. N. Johnson–Laird (Eds.), *Thinking and reasoning.* Baltimore: Penguin, 1968.

Kahneman, D., Ben–Ishai, R., & Lotan, M. Relation of a test of attention to road accidents. *Journal of Applied Psychology,* 1973, *58,* 113–115.

Keele, S. W. & Hawkins, H. L. Explorations of individual differences relevant to high level skill. *Journal of Motor Behavior,* 1982 (in press).

Kozlowski, L. T., & Bryant, K. J. Sense of direction, spatial orientation, and cognitive maps. *Journal of Experimental Psychology: Human Perception and Performance.* 1977, *3,* 590–598.

Langolf, G. D., Chaffin, D. B., & Foulke, J. A. An investigation of Fitt's Law using a wide range of movement amplitudes. *Journal of Motor Behavior,* 1976, *8,* 113–128.

Marteniuk, R. G. Individual differences in motor performance and learning. In J. H. Wilmore (Ed.), *Exercise and sport sciences review* (Vol. 2). New York: Academic Press, 1974.

Ryder, H. W., Carr, H. J., & Herget, P. Future performance in foot racing. *Scientific American,* 1976, *234,* 109–119.

Sverko, B. Individual differences in time-sharing performance. *Acta Instituti Psychologici,* 1977, *79,* 17–30.

Woodworth, R. S. *Experimental Psychology.* New York: Henry Holt, 1938.

7

Learning and Control of Coordinated Motor Patterns: The Programming Perspective

Steven W. Keele
University of Oregon

The component-analysis approach to motor skill leaves the impression that improvement of skill is a mere matter of decreasing decision time and selecting more efficient movements. Yet, even the most cursory look at skill suggests there is more than that. People learn to coordinate several movements into a smooth pattern—a field-goal kick, a dive, and so on. There are two implications. One is that, rather than requiring each movement component to be evaluated and another decision made, a whole series of movements often occurs in response to just a single decision. In other words, as practice proceeds it is not just that decision time is reduced, but some decisions drop out altogether as they become redundant when a pattern of movement can be made. As a result attention is freed for more global decisions about the task. The skilled basketball dribbler, for example, can stop worrying about the dribble itself and look for passing opportunities or detect circumstances that require the dribble to be altered. Second, as movements become coordinated, two or more movements may overlap in time as when one learns to coordinate hands, arms, and legs in a tennis serve.

A formal demonstration of the development of a motor pattern with practice was provided in a very simple study by Pew (1966). Subjects attempted to keep a constantly moving dot centered on a line. Pressing a left-hand key accelerated the dot leftward; pressing a right-hand key accelerated it rightward. To keep the dot centered they had to alternately press the keys. The results for two men both early and late in practice are shown in Fig. 7.1. The pulses on the keys send the dot back and forth across the center line, and the graph portrays that movement over time. Early in practice behavior is rather erratic. Note the irregularity in pulse height and in interpulse interval. People appear to make a movement, evaluate

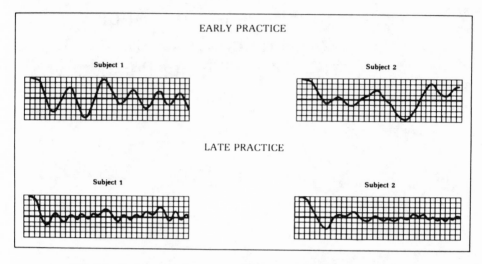

EARLY PRACTICE

Subject 1   Subject 2

LATE PRACTICE

Subject 1   Subject 2

FIG. 7.1.   Position of a dot on an oscilloscope screen as a function of time.
Pressing two keys results in dot movement back and forth across a center line.
Results are shown for two people both early and late in practice (based on Pew,
1966).

the results of the movement, select another, and so on. This mode of operation is
sometimes called closed-loop behavior, (see Chapter 4).

Later in practice, the movement pulses become much more regular, and the
records suggest that subjects execute a pattern of responses with only periodic
correction. Subject 1 appears to emit a regular series of pulses without modification until he drifts off target, and then a single correction is made. Subject 2 also
emits a regular pattern, but as he drifts off, rather than making a single correction, he modulates the pattern by holding one key down slightly longer than the
other, thus producing a slow drift to the other side. After practice, control of the
skill at one level appears open loop. Feedback is still used, but it influences not
each movement alone but the whole movement pattern.

An issue to be addressed is this. Once a patterned movement is established,
how is it controlled? One view that might arise from a strictly closed-loop
interpretation is that, although each movement no longer is under strict visual
control, control has shifted to other sensory modalities. In particular, each sub-
movement of the pattern generates kinesthetic feedback from the internal sense
organs of the body—the joint receptors, the muscle and tendon-stretch receptors,
and the tactile senses. According to one such view, the kinesthetic feedback from
each part of the movement stimulates the next part. According to another such
view, a movement occurs until the kinesthetic feedback matches an internal
reference, specifying what the kinesthetic feedback should be like, and then
another part of the movement is initiated. But an alternative view is that the entire

pattern is represented in some neural structure independent of feedback. Such a neural structure is called a motor program. This view does not mean that visual and kinesthetic feedback are not important—they definitely are. But the feedback, rather than driving the movement pattern, serves to evaluate the outcome of the pattern, to allow modification when needed, and to set parameters such as speed, amplitude, and responding limb for the program. Later we expand on this feedback notion and look at some applications to skill learning, but, firstly, we must examine whether feedback is actually needed to drive the pattern.

EXPERIMENTAL EVIDENCE FOR MOTOR PROGRAMS

How does one go about determining whether neural structures that would be called motor programs exist independent of feedback? Three approaches are described. Two of these approaches are described later, and those are ones that can be applied to people. The other approach involves animals in which not only can visual feedback be removed by blindfolding but kinesthetic feedback can be removed by surgery.

Animal Studies

A peculiarity of the vertebrate nervous system is that nerves subserving the arms and legs come into and out of the spinal cord between the vertebrae in different bundles. The so-called efferent nerves come out the front (ventral) side of the spinal cord and carry messages to the muscles, causing them to move. When muscles move, they activate sensory receptors in the joints, skin, muscles, and tendons, and the impulses generated are carried back to the central nervous system by afferent nerves. The afferent and efferent nerves are intermixed, except right next to the spinal cord where they separate, and the afferents (the sensory nerves) enter into the posterior (dorsal side) of the spinal cord. This anatomical fact allows a surgeon to cut the dorsal roots, eliminating kinesthetic sensation, whereas leaving the ventral roots, with their efferent nerves that drive the muscles, intact. What is the result on motor performance?

Some years ago Taub and Berman (1968) performed this sort of surgery on monkeys and observed the effects on locomotory and grasping behavior. When a single forelimb was first deafferented (i.e., the sensory roots were cut), the animal did not use that forelimb for locomotion and was reluctant to grasp with it, though grasping would occur if use of the intact forelimb was not allowed. The de-afferented forelimb, however, was not paralyzed, for when the good forelimb was restrained by a straitjacket for a few days, the monkey began to use the deafferented one in wlaking and climbing, and such use persisted even when the straitjacket on the intact limb was removed. When not one but both forelimbs were deafferented, the straitjacket experience was not needed and the monkey ambulated even when blindfolded. Later studies by Taub, Perrella, and Barro (1973) deafferented forelimbs only a few hours after birth, and with only modest delays in development, the monkeys eventually ran, walked, climbed, and jumped rather naturally.

What do we conclude from the studies of Taub and his colleagues? A complex, coordinated series of movements can occur without the visual or kinesthetic feedback that typically accompanies that movement. This suggests that the movement is controlled by a motor program.

However interesting, there is one aspect that prevents us from extrapolating these results too far to human skill. And that result is that the program for locomotion is probably inborn and largely contained in the spinal cord. Thus, it does not represent many of the programs for human skill that involve a large degree of learning. It is worth noting, however, that the deafferented monkeys have fair limb control for grasping, and that may not be susceptible to the same criticism; that act could be controlled more centrally than the spinal level. Moreover, the deafferented monkeys can learn to move their arms in a rather arbitrary pattern, such as tapping the head, to obtain a food reward.

A variety of other animal studies also demonstrate coordinated skill without normal sensory feedback, and not all of these involve locomotion. For example, later we talk more about the fine motor skill exhibited by birds when they sing. That skill is sometimes partly learned but nonetheless appears under program control. Consider also a study by Fentress (1973) concerned with grooming patterns in mice. One grooming sequence in adult mice is as follows: The mouse moves both forepaws simultaneously over its head and to the mouth. As the paws near the mouth, the tongue extends. In another grooming pattern a single forelimb crosses over the head, and as it passes the eye the eye blinks. When baby mice only 1-day old have their forelimbs removed, at a later age (30 days) when grooming typically occurs, exactly the same grooming sequence manifests itself. As the shoulders rotate the tongue licks or the eye blinks at just the right time, even though there is no limb to make contact and even though the limb, not being present, can provide no feedback. Apparently, the grooming sequences are under strict program control and because eyes, tongue, and limbs all participate, the program probably is not spinally mediated. Again, however, the program appears genetically determined and it is not a learned skill.

So at least some animal skills are under program—not feedback—control. Feedback, as will be seen, is an important element of the total system, but not in generating movement. Let's turn to some human studies that make a related point.

Human Studies

In humans removing kinesthetic feedback is not so feasible because, of course, we don't want to surgically and irreversibly deprive people of kinesthesis. Nonsurgical methods of temporarily removing feedback have their own special problems. For these reasons more indirect approaches have been developed for humans, and these approaches yield important additional clues to the nature of motor programs beyond the issue of feedback and its effect on motor control.

A set of studies by Stuart Klapp and colleagues follow a completely different logic than deafferentation. If a movement pattern is programmed rather than being driven by feedback from already occurring subparts of the movement pattern, then it is conceivable that the program is "called up" or readied in some manner before it is executed. This is much like the notion of loading a program in a computer. The more complex the program, the longer it may take to load. If this supposition is true, then reaction time from a signal to move until the actual beginning of movement should be longer for acts requiring more complex programs. Whereas such a result would be consistent with program theory, it would be inconsistent with any feedback theory that postulates that a later component of movement is not readied until it is stimulated by feedback from an earlier component.

Klapp, Anderson, and Berrian (1973) tested this notion using word pronunciation. They flashed one-syllable and two-syllable words on a screen and simply asked people to name them. If two-syllable words take longer to program before beginning to speak, then the reaction time between the word and the start of the utterance should be increased for two-syllable words. Note that reaction time, not duration of speaking the word, is the time of concern. Table 7.1 shows the results, and as expected the time to begin pronunciation of a two-syllable word is just slightly (15 milliseconds) but reliably greater than the time to begin pronunciation of a one-syllable word.

However, there are alternative explanations. Perhaps two-syllable words take longer not to program but to perceive. To eliminate that possibility, Klapp and colleagues asked people to categorize each word as an animal or not. Here the word must still be perceived, but the category response bears no relationship to the number of syllables. Column two of the table shows the syllable effect to disappear, so because perception of the words is still present, the syllable effect must not be in perception. Also, if subjects are asked not to name words but pictures, the syllable effect reappears. Of course, when naming pictures, syllables are a property of the response, not the picture.

TABLE 7.1
Reaction Time in Milliseconds to Respond to One- and
Two-Syllable Words (Klapp, Anderson, & Berrian, 1973)

No. Syllables	Word Naming	Categorization	Picture Naming
1	518	696	619
2	533	697	633
Difference	15	1	14

This and a variety of other studies by Klapp and his associates suggest that learned human movement patterns are stored as a motor program independent of feedback. The more complicated the program, the longer it takes to prepare it for execution.

Now consider a study by David Rosenbaum (1977) that uses yet another approach to the program problem. Suppose you perform an act with one arm and then with the other. Perhaps the same program is used for both arms, identical in every respect except that a different arm is specified. Suppose now the act is repeated with one arm so vigorously that fatigue occurs. What is the source of fatigue? Is it only in the arm? Or is it also in the program? If we can show that fatigue transfers from one arm to the other when the same act is performed, but not to such a degree when a different act is performed, this would constitute evidence for a motor program.

One of Rosenbaum's several studies went this way: With one arm subjects either cranked a handle round and round as rapidly as possible for 30 seconds, which is fairly strenuous, or twisted a handle back and forth for 30 seconds. Then with very little rest they either cranked or twisted with the *other* arm for 30 seconds. Interest resides in the cranking or twisting rate of the second movement as a function of the nature of the first movement, and Tab. 7.2 shows those results. The table shows the number of cranks or twists in 30 seconds of the second task when it is preceded by either cranking or twisting on the first task.

What should be noted is the very slight decrement in cranking or twisting when the act was preceded on the other hand by a movement of the *same* type. Why? What has been fatigued? Rosenbaum argues that extra fatigue due to transferring the same movement to the other arm implies that the two arms share a common motor program and that such a program can be fatigued. If fatigue were only general and had no program specificity, then there should be no difference in performance of the second task as a function of the first hand task.

To summarize, animal studies and human studies all suggest that at least some skills are under motor-program control. What does this mean? Firstly, although feedback has its purposes, feedback does not stimulate succeeding parts of the

TABLE 7.2
Number of Movements in 30 sec by
Second Arm as a Function of the First Arm
Movement and Second Arm Movement
(Rosenbaum, 1977)

		Second Arm	
		Crank	*Twist*
First Arm	Crank	106.7	167.4
	Twist	111.2	165.0

movement, because movements occur in a coordinated way without feedback. Such coordination is seen in deafferented monkeys, in mice with no forelimbs, and in birds with no voice feedback. Secondly, a sequence of movement may be prepared or called up before movement begins. This was seen in the Klapp et al. naming studies. And thirdly, the same skill representation may subserve more than one limb.

Later, this conception of motor programs is examined in more detail by partly building on some deeper implications of the Rosenbaum study. And exactly how a program is translated into movement is examined. But at this point it seems best to examine how feedback enters into the total movement system and consider some possible implications.

Feedback in the Development and Performance of a Skill

The study of bird-song development has been quite instrumental in conceptualizing one manner in which feedback might enter into the acquisition and maintenance of a skill. Bird song would appear to be an appropriate model of skill because, like human speech, it involves very fine coordination of a succession of movements. In addition, the songs of greatest interest in this context are from birds that exhibit some learning of the song: Song dialect differs from one region to another, and the particular dialect is clearly learned rather than inherited. Because the song is partly learned, it may provide a better model of human skill than walking in monkeys or grooming in mice. Species studied in this context include the White-crowned Sparrow and the Oregon Junco.

The basic phenomena are outlined by Nottebohm (1970). If a young bird is taken from the nest within a few days of hatching and is reared never having heard an adult song, then when it learns to sing the following spring, the resultant song is very crude. If, however, the young bird is repeatedly exposed over several weeks to an adult song, then many months later in the spring it will develop a normal song. This implies the bird must store in memory a template or representation of what the song sounds like and such a template is a necessary precursor to actual song development.

Now suppose a bird acquires the adult template, but *before* learning to sing it is deafened so that it cannot hear itself (Konishi, 1965). In this circumstance the bird also fails to learn a proper song. In fact, what song it learns is even worse than for the bird that can hear but has no template. Conceptually, this means the bird must be receptive to its own feedback, which it compares to the stored template.

Finally, suppose a bird is deafened *after* it has learned the song well. In this circumstance the song persists for at least a year and probably more. Moreover, a bird that knows the song well can have nerves cut that render the muscles on one side or the other of the bird's voice box inoperative (Nottebohm, 1970). As a result some song segments are lost entirely, but the remaining segments occur just at the appropriate times interspersed with blanks for the missing parts. These manipulations demonstrate that once a motor program is established the song can persist without its normal feedback.

Figure 7.2 shows a general model of skill learning and performance that the studies of monkeys, mice, and birds and the studies of word naming and arm cranking or twisting lead us toward. Some part or parts of the brain send a pattern of impulses through the nerves to excite the muscles to move in some pattern. Those parts of the brain are collectively labeled the movement generator or motor-program center. Movement of the muscles produces feedback. That feedback can include sounds as in speech, in bird song, or in the sounds of machinery operated by muscular movement. That feedback can include visual effects, and it can include kinesthetic feedback from movement senses embedded in the body—the joint, skin, and stretch receptors. The feedback goes to a comparison center where it is compared to a template of what the feedback should be like at that moment in time. If feedback mismatches the template, the program must be altered. When the skill is learned well enough so that feedback almost always

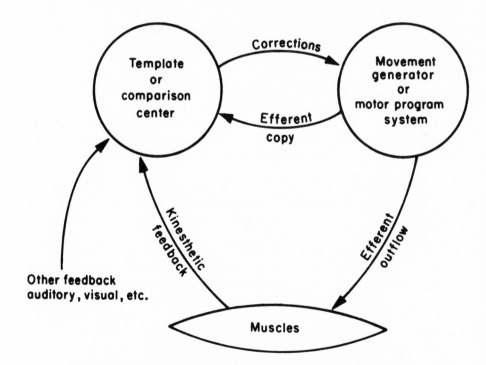

FIG. 7.2. A model of skill learning and performance. A motor program sends signals to the muscles. The movement of the muscles produce feedback that returns to a comparison center where the feedback is compared to a template of expected feedback. If a mismatch occurs, corrections are issued.

matches the template, feedback sometimes can be eliminated and the program can proceed on its own. However, for most human skills feedback must persist indefinitely to continually adjust the program to changing situations. The point is that feedback is used not to drive the motor pattern but to correct it when the program falls in error. Feedback is the monitor of success or failure.

This view of feedback is cursory. Without a doubt feedback has other functions, but this analysis captures one major function, the role of feedback as a monitor and source of correction for motor programs.

Application of the Program—Feedback Model

The Suzuki technique of teaching children to play stringed instruments such as violins bears a remarkable correspondence to the model of how feedback leads to development of a motor program. In the full-fledged technique, according to Pronko (1969), the parents of a child select a single, great piece of music that involves the stringed instrument of interest and play it over and over to an infant, sometimes even before the child has learned to speak. Only when the child shows signs of recognizing the music is another piece selected. This frequent exposure to great music continues until the child is perhaps 4 or 5 years old. Analogous to bird-song development, by that time the child presumably has several high quality templates of what good music should sound like. At that time the child is introduced to the violin. The child learns to play not by reading notes, but by ear. Judging from the theory of program development, the secret of success is that the child uses his or her extensive template repertoire to recognize when the violin produces good or bad sounds and then uses that comparison to correct subsequent movement. Pronko claims the technique teaches excellent and world-class performance with the stringed instruments.

Likely, most use of Suzuki's technique is less extreme. Nevertheless, the main ingredients, the extensive exposure to the ideal feedback that later will become relevant and the learning by comparison of actual to stored feedback, are probably important ideas for application. A related application has been to teaching the deaf child to speak. A problem faced by a deaf child acquiring speech, according to our model, is that the deaf child has neither template nor feedback to match to the template, so there is no basis for knowing whether the correct movement sequence was issued. The model of program acquisition suggests that perhaps some artificial source of feedback and an artificial template could be used. Although those props might be awkward outside the learning laboratory, once a proper speech program is acquired the feedback could be dropped, as in deafferentation of the monkey or deafening in the bird, and the speech program might persist.

This basic notion was tested by Nickerson, Kalikow, and Stevens (1976). They extracted a variety of features from throat vibrations and the acoustic wave form and transformed them to video display. Figure 7.3 portrays one procedure

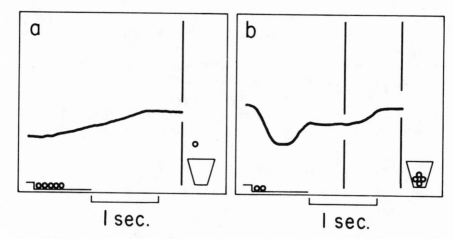

FIG. 7.3. A display used in teaching the deaf to speak. The height of a "ball" moving across an oscilloscopic display is controlled by voice pitch, and if the desired pitch is produced the ball passes through a window and drops in a basket. The right panel portrays a more complicated voice-pitch pattern with two windows (based on Nickerson, Kalikow, & Stevens, 1976).

called ball game. When a child starts to speak, a ball moves across an oscilloscope screen. The height of the ball is controlled by some speech feature, such as pitch of the voice. If pitch is properly controlled, the ball passes through a slot, drops in a basket, and a smiling face appears. More complex pitch patterns can be trained by inserting two slots at different heights as shown in the right-hand panel.

Another technique a little closer to the logic of the model in Fig. 7.2 is illustrated in Fig. 7.4. The teacher utters a consonant–vowel combination, such as "be." Features of the teacher's vowel are extracted and displayed in the left-hand member of the pair of figures. The vertical dimension represents voice frequencies, and the energy at each frequency is portrayed by width. The frequency by energy diagram for the vowel "e" looks a bit like an hourglass. Other voice features are portrayed at the same time. The student attempts to produce an utterance, which is portrayed on the right, that matches the teacher's utterance.

By analogy to the model of program acquisition, a source of feedback is provided that varies with speech of the deaf child. The child compares the feedback to a model or template. If a mismatch occurs the motor sequence is altered. When a motor program is formed, then that feedback can be removed, as obviously the child cannot carry it around in the real world. Nickerson and colleagues report this method to provide some success in teaching the deaf child to speak.

Are there applications of the program-feedback model to skills of sport? At this time successful applications are not apparent. Perhaps this is because good

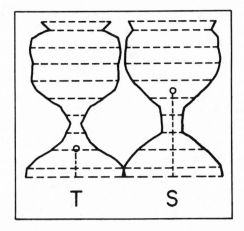

FIG. 7.4. Another display to aid teaching the deaf to speak. The ē sound from the word "be" is portrayed. A teacher's vocalization is shown on the left and the student produces a match, as portrayed on the right. The width of the figure represents energy at different voice frequencies, the dotted lines indicate a voiced consonant, and the height of the "balloon" indicates voice pitch (from Nickerson, Kalikow, & Stevens, 1976).

applications sometimes are very difficult to demonstrate. But to illustrate a direction that application might take, consider a study by Alex Carre (1972). Although it didn't produce positive results, it does nicely suggest the logic of an approach.

Carre taught novices to throw the discus. The logic of the model in Fig. 7.2 says that to acquire the skill one must have some kind of template that specifies what constitutes good form. Secondly, the learner must have some type of feedback that can readily be compared to the model. The problem with normal feedback in throwing the discus is that people cannot see their own body in action very well, so they must infer form from feel. That inference may be inaccurate. Also, the body moves so rapidly and the act of generating the movement requires so much attention that sufficient time may not be available to monitor all the movements. Typically, there is also a problem of establishing the template. A coach may demonstrate technique, but that demonstration may not be readily available for later use. Two techniques seek to remedy these problems: A model performer can be shown repeatedly on loop film. This provides the template. Likewise, the learner's performance can be displayed on videotape replay. Surprisingly, most research has been unable to demonstrate the utility of either technique. Why?

Carre's notion was that the model of skill acquisition developed here requires *both* adequate template and matched feedback for effective learning. A model of performance with inadequate feedback should be of little use. Likewise, excellent feedback with no model should be of little use. Instead, one should have both model performance *and* feedback, and they should be in the same form.

To evaluate the notion, Carre pretested subjects for distance of discus throw on Day 1. The following three sessions were devoted to practice. And on the fifth session the learners were retested and their improvement determined. During the practice sessions some subjects were given instructor's comment, others were periodically shown video feedback of their own performance, others obtained both instructor comment and video replay, and yet a fourth group received neither of these feedback sources. Another variable was presence or absence of model: Some subjects received no model except for an initial demonstration on the pretest day, for another group the instructor gave periodic demonstrations during practice, and for a third group a video tape model was shown periodically. Theory predicts that those people exposed to *both* model and video feedback should improve the most.

Table 7.3 shows the improvement in meters throwing the discus from first day to last day for each combination of model and feedback. Unfortunately, there are no reliable differences among the improvements in distance. One method is as good as another. One can speculate on reasons for the failure. Perhaps discus throwing by the novice is more a matter of strength, and at that stage of expertise, technique adds little. In support, none of the groups show appreciable improvement. Or perhaps modeling and feedback didn't capture the critical aspects of the discus throw. Or perhaps the model portrayed in Fig. 7.2 is not useful for this skill. The usefulness of the theory of program acquisition for sports application is, therefore, still open to question.

FURTHER ISSUES CONCERNING MOTOR PROGRAMS

The preceding discussion provides a general scheme of how program and feedback interact in a more complete system, and how that scheme might be applied. At this point it is useful to delve further into the idea of a motor program. Two issues turn out to be partly related. One is this: Should a program be considered

TABLE 7.3
Improvement in Meters in Discus Throw
from Pretest to Posttest (Carre, 1972)

| | *Feedback* | | | |
	Control	*Instructor*	*Video*	*Both*
Control	.21	2.01	2.67	1.56
Model Live	1.84	2.04	1.75	.85
Video	.64	.82	2.32	1.50

as a string of muscle commands, or should it be considered as a much more abstract representation of hierarchical form that runs from general idea of the skill to the general sequence of action, to specification of limb, speed, size, and the like, and finally to particular muscles. The second and related issue concerns how programs get translated into actual movement.

The Hierarchic Conception of Programs

The notion of a program as a hierarchic structure was earlier introduced by Rosenbaum's study of cranking or twisting motions first with one arm and then the other. Rosenbaum found that fatigue induced by moving one arm transfers to a greater degree to the other arm if the same motion is required. This in turn implies that portions of a program are more abstract than particular muscles or arms. It is as though the program specifies some sequence of action in the environment and then arm is specified next. A similar point, and perhaps a more dramatic one, is made by the examples of writing in Fig. 7.5 taken from Raibert (1977). The top writing example was produced by the right hand, the hand normally used. The second is from large writing (here photographically reduced in size) produced by the right arm. The third is left-hand writing. In the fourth, a

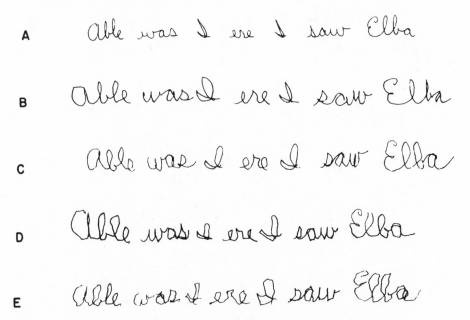

FIG. 7.5.   Five samples of writing produced by the same person using the right hand (top), right arm, left hand, mouth gripping the pen, and pen taped to right foot (bottom). The samples are remarkably similar despite different muscles being used (from Raibert, 1977).

pen was taped to the right foot, and the final sample was produced by a pen held in the mouth. Although the use of unusual muscle groups in writing produces "shakier" movement, clearly the basic writing pattern is similar throughout. This observation suggests the same writing program is drawn on by diverse muscle systems.

Consider another phenomenon studied by Summers (1975). Subjects responded to nine lights by pressing keys. The lights occurred in a particular order over and over, and part of the task was to learn the order so that it could be produced without the lights as a cue. In addition to learning the order of lights, subjects learned to respond with a particular time sequence designated slow–fast–fast. A pause of 500 msec occurred before one response and was followed by three rapid pulses with only 100-msec pause between them. This was followed by another pause and then three rapid pulses. To these pause times must be added the time for which the keys are held down, and when that is done, the long and short interpulse intervals are in about a 2-to-1 ratio. That time structure constitutes a natural rhythm. The top curve of Fig. 7.6 portrays the timing of a sequence at this stage of practice and without the lights as a cue to timing and sequencing.

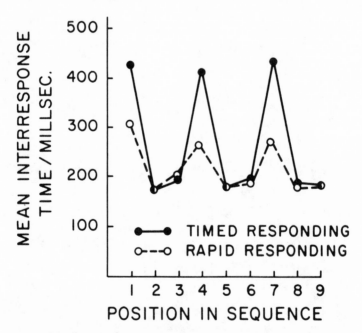

FIG. 7.6. Interresponse times for different positions within a sequence for timed responding or rapid responding without regard to the timing. The previously learned time structure nonetheless effects rapid responding (based on Summers, 1975).

Following the initial training, subjects in Summer's study were told to ignore the timing structure they had just learned and instead respond as fast as they could. The results of that manipulation are shown in the bottom curve of Fig. 7.6. The interesting aspect of the data is that although people did increase response speed they were unable to rid themselves of the time structure.

The point of Summer's work is similar to that of the handwriting example and to Rosenbaum's work. The program is general, consisting of both sequence order and *relative* timing. But the same program appears implemented at slow and fast speeds because the relative timing is maintained.

These and other studies suggest that programs should be thought of not as a sequence of muscle movements but as a hierarchic memory structure in which the skill is first specified at a gross level, and then at successive levels of the hierarchy more and more specificity is added. As one descends the hierarchy, speed, intensity, size, limb, and finally particular muscles are specified.

Consider basketball shooting as a concrete example of how this hierarchic conception might have useful implications. Some years back in basketball the skilled player learned a variety of very different shots. There was the set shot from the perimeter in which the feet stayed on the floor. Sometimes set shots were two-handed. There was the free throw that sometimes was like the set shot, but sometimes people used both hands and threw the ball underhanded. There was the lay in, the hook shot, and finally the jump shot. Most of these are basically quite different shots; you might say each involves a different program. Modern shooting appears a bit different. A large number of the shots all seem to be variations on a common theme, the basic jump shot. Inside and outside shots, free throws, and short hooks all have similarities. It is as though at an abstract level the programs are the same, or at least have many common elements, but they differ mostly in specifics lower in the hierarchy. In other words older players appeared to have learned several different programs. Newer players appear to learn more variations on a basic program. Perhaps the latter is both much more efficient and much more flexible. Certainly modern shooting percentages are much higher. Perhaps one goal of coaching should be to devise similar procedures underlying a variety of movements.

Role of Reflexes in Motor Patterns

We've emphasized that when one learns a program, the product starts with an abstract representation, to which specifications are added. The same program manifests itself in different limbs, at different speeds, in different sizes, and the like. Eventually, particular muscle combinations are chosen. One must ask whether the performer must learn all the details of the hierarchy down to the smallest muscle twitches. Some investigations suggest no: At least to some extent the final coordination of different muscles is already built into the organism. What the learner does is learn particular goals at an abstract level. At lower levels some part of those goals are automatically translated into action. To put the notion another way, in theory the human body has many more possible ways that it could move than it actually does, because body movements are partly constrained by patterns already built into the organism. We've already suggested this is true of locomotion patterns in animals. Consider another illustration of this idea involving tonic neck reflexes, one set of many reflexes of the human body. This illustration, although by no means conclusive, is highly suggestive of the notion that much final selection of movement is based on already-existent motor patterns.

Figure 7.7 shows a classic neck reflex exhibited by babies with certain diseases and by animals with certain brain surgery. When the head is twisted in one direction, both the arm and leg extend on the side toward which the head is pointing and flex on the opposite side. The same reflex occurs when the head is tilted to the side rather than rotated. When the head is tilted forward, all four limbs tend to flex, and when the head is tilted back, all four limbs extend.

These reflexes are not necessary actions in adults. You can certainly turn your head without getting accompanying extension and flexion of the limbs. However, it is conceivable that if people did use those reflex patterns in appropriate circumstances it would incur advantages, and in an important study by Hellebrandt, Horitz, Partridge, and Walters (1956) such advantges were found. They

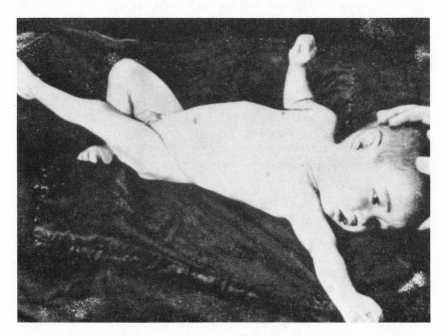

FIG. 7.7.   The tonic neck reflex. Turning the head to one side results in limb extension on that side and flexion on the other side (from Fukuda, 1961).

asked people to repeatedly move a lever with either the left or the right wrist until near exhaustion. Power in the wrist was exerted by flexion in some instances and by extension in others. Moreover, people either looked toward the moving wrist or away.

From the tonic neck reflex one would predict a gain in extension power by looking at the wrist. One should gain flexion power by turning the head away. Figure 7.8 shows the decrement in responding with successive bouts of the exercise. The flexion response is shown on the left and the extension response is shown on the right; the head is turned either to the same side as the wrist (termed ipsilateral) or to the opposite side (termed contralateral). We see a striking confirmation of the predictions: Ipsilateral head turning facilitates extension, contralateral head turning facilitates flexion. Moreover, even when people are not instructed to turn their heads, they spontaneously do so under fatigue. Finally, when using both wrists simultaneously, flexion of both wrists is facilitated by bending the head forward, and extension of both is facilitated by tilting the head back. When movements are in accord with the tonic neck reflex, therefore, additional strength is conferred.

Of course, applications of the tonic neck reflex to sports that require strength are straightforward. Given that the reflex pattern facilitates strength, one might expect they would commonly find their way into sports. In a remarkable photoes-

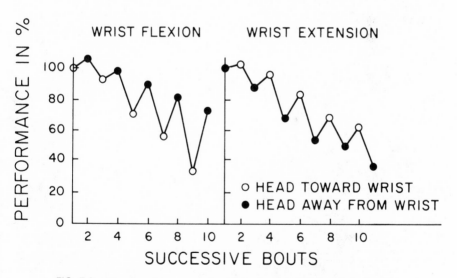

FIG. 7.8. The strength on successive bouts of weight lifting with the hand is portrayed. With successive bouts, strength declines when plotted as a percentage of first-bout performance. When weights are lifted by flexing the wrist, strength is greater when the head is turned away; when weights are lifted by extension, strength is greater when the head is turned toward the hand (based on Helle-brandt et al., 1956).

say by a Japanese investigator, Tadashi Fukuda (1961), many skilled performers were in fact captured on film showing the classic neck reflex.

Figure 7.9 shows a baseball player jumping for a ball. The head is turned in the direction of the ball and the limbs on that side show extension. The limbs on the other side show flexion just as in the classic reflex. This observation is better appreciated by noting that there is no apparent reason other than the reflex why the contralateral limbs should be flexed. Similar reflex patterns for high jumping,

FIG. 7.9.   A baseball player leaping for a ball exhibits the same pattern as the tonic neck reflex. Note especially the extreme flexion on the side opposite the direction of head turning (from Fukuda, 1961).

soccer, fencing, diving, and the like were photographed by Fukuda. A further illustration from judo is shown in Fig. 7.10. One opponent is about to throw another. The throw will be accomplished by lifting with the left leg and pulling in with the left arm, both of which are flexions, and by extending the right leg and throwing the right arm into extension. The pattern seems to be stimulated by throwing the head to the proper side just at the correct moment.

FIG. 7.10. The judo competitor on the left is establishing a move to throw the one on the right. The right arm and leg are being extended and the left leg and arm flexed. The pattern is preceded by turning the head down, as in the tonic neck reflex (from Fukuda, 1961).

In addition to the appearance of the reflex pattern in sports, dancers and artists often portray the reflex, and Fig. 7.11 shows one example from Japanese art.

Figure 7.12 illustrates that in some situations one reflex overrides another. When the baseball player jumps up, the tonic neck reflex rules, but when sideways movement is imposed as well, a vestibular reflex appears to overrule the neck reflex and alter the pattern.

Let us summarize the general point: A motor program is a hierarchical representation of action that proceeds from general goals to specific selection of muscles. Much of the learning is concentrated at higher levels in the hierarchy that specify the general sequence of action. Lower levels are free for alternative specification such as speed or arm. Final details may partly be taken care of by innate reflex patterns.

FIG. 7.11.   The same pattern as in the tonic neck reflex portrayed in a piece of Japanese art (from Fukuda, 1961).

FIG. 7.12. When a leap by a baseball player involves sideways movement, a vestibular reflex, which involves extension of all four limbs, appears to override the tonic neck reflex even though the head is turned (Fukuda, 1961).

Translation of Program to Actual Action

How does a program finally make contact with the muscles? Probably no single answer suffices. Nevertheless, we can show that one process probably is not commonly used and that another commonly may be.

There are two possible routes from brain to muscle action. An efferent nerve, called an alphamotoneuron, travels from the spinal cord ending on muscle fibers. One route of muscle activation would be for the brain to send a message through the spinal cord *direct* to the muscle fibers, causing contraction. But, in addition, a specialized muscle fiber called a muscle spindle is slipped in among the other fibers. Activation of the spindles does not cause sufficient force to move the limb. Activation does, however, contract that fiber itself and, because the ends are fixed, it stretches the middle region of the spindle called the equatorial region. In the equatorial region lies stretch receptors that fire when stretched and send impulses back to the spinal cord where, among other things, they feed back on the nerves that go directly to the other muscle fibers. Thus, another mode whereby the brain could get muscles to operate is as follows: The brain sends messages not to the main muscle fibers but only to the spindles via the so-called gammaneurons. The spindles contract exciting the stretch receptor. These in turn send signals back to the spinal cord to activate the alphaneurons going to the main muscle fibers, and the limb moves. The limb moves until it relaxes the stretch receptor at which point it stops (see Chapter 2 for details).

This system is just like power steering on a car. Twisting the steering wheel sets a small device that amplifies power with a hydraulic pump to turn the road wheels. When the road wheels reach the position specified by turning the steering wheel, the hydraulic pump stops. With power steering there is no direct connection from steering wheel to road wheels.

This follow-up servomechanism, as it is called, seems much more complex than the direct route of stimulating muscle fibers. Yet it has a potential advantage in that it is a location-seeking device. The brain does not need to know where the limb is to accurately direct it to a new location. It only needs to set the spindle for the new location, and the primary muscle will follow no matter where it is currently set. However, the follow-up servo theory appears incorrect in general. Nevertheless, the notion is not wasted, because it leads to an elaboration of the direct notion whereby muscle fibers are directly stimulated through the alphaneurons.

What is wrong with the follow-up servo conception? Recall the deafferentation studies of monkeys. Deafferentation cuts the feedback from muscle spindle to spinal cord, interrupting the cycle from stretch receptor to spinal cord to main muscle fibers, so deafferentation should eliminate coordinated movement. But it does not. Moreover, according to the follow-up servo idea, the muscle spindles should become active before the other muscle fibers, because the former controls the latter. But such seems not to be the case; the spindles and muscles are excited more or less simultaneously (Vallbo, 1971).

A key to the way the movement system may commonly work was recently provided by Bizzi, Polit, and Morasso (1976) in a study of monkey head movements and a study by Kelso (1977) of human finger movements. Bizzi and colleagues placed monkeys in a chair and trained them to move their eyes and head to a spot of light that was turned on. During movement lights were turned off, so the monkey had no visual feedback whether the head was turned the correct amount. In addition the vestibular apparatus in the inner ear was removed so there was no vestibular feedback. The only source of sensory information once movement was started was neck kinesthesis. The monkey is seated in a chair and attached to the head is a clutch. When the head begins to move, the clutch can be engaged to a set of weights that effectively make the head heavier, or the clutch can engage a spring that tends to retard movement of the head.

Figure 7.13a shows a record of normal head movement with distance of head movement plotted against time. The head starts slowly, picks up speed, and then slows down, finally stopping at the target area. Figure 7.13b shows the head to be retarded when the spring is engaged, and when the spring is released, the head moves to its normal position. When the head is made heavier by engaging the weights, the head overshoots its normal stopping position and then comes back, (Fig. 7.13c). Recall the monkey has no vestibular information and no visual cues once movement begins. Does this mean that the corrective movements portrayed in Fig. 7.13b and c depend on neck kinesthesis? To determine the answer Bizzi and colleagues next deafferented the neck by severing the sensory nerve fibers. The results are shown in Fig. 7.13d, e, and f for unimpeded, spring retarded, and weighted movements. As can be seen, very similar courses of movement occur without kinesthesis as occur with it. The same correction occurs when the spring is released. The same correction occurs to overshooting when a weight is added to the head. Because no known source of feedback is available to apprise the

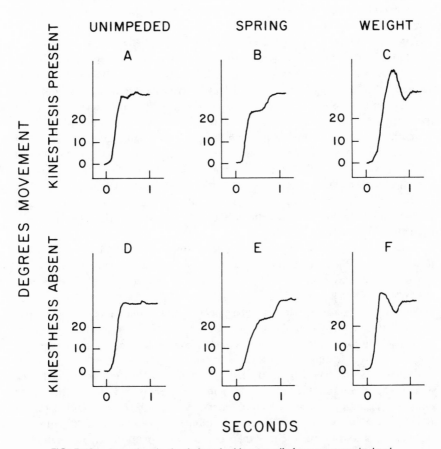

FIG. 7.13. A monkey in the dark and with no vestibular sense turns its head toward a light that extinguishes as soon as movement begins. In panels a, b, and c the monkey has normal neck kinesthesis, and in panels d, e, and f kinesthesis is removed. The curves show amount of movement as a function of time for unimpeded movement, movement where a spring momentarily impedes the full extent of movement and then is removed and movement with a weight attached to the head (based on Bizzi, Polit, & Morasso, 1976).

animal of the need for correction, how is it done? The answer seems to reside in what we may call a rubber-band model.

The neck and limbs have muscles arranged in pairs. Imagine them as rubber bands. As one muscle, the so-called agonist, is activated, it moves the limb (or head). A muscle on the other side, called the antagonist, stretches. The antagonist is the muscle that would produce movement in the opposite direction were it the more strongly activated. The limb stops when forces due to contraction of the agonist and stretch in the antagonist exactly balance. The rubber-band model shows us that the location of the limb or head reaches a position solely determined by the balance of forces due to inputs to the two muscles and external forces.

You should now be able to account for the results of Bizzi et al. All feedback is removed. The monkey programs tensions of the agonist and antagonist by sending nervous activity through the alphaneurons to the muscles. As the agonist contracts the head begins to move, but as it does, so the antagonist stretches, building up a force that tends to retard movement. When the retarding force of the antagonist matches the contractive force of the agonist, the head stops. If a spring is added, it acts in concert with the antagonist and keeps the head from fully turning. Once that spring is removed, the balance of forces is changed, and the head will shift to the originally programmed spot. When the weights are added, it changes the inertia of the head, making it harder to start and stop. But final resting place will depend only on initially programmed tensions. Though feedback may modify the corrections, the movement is largely self-correcting, occurring without feedback.

Recently, Kelso (1977) found striking confirmation of the rubber-band model in a very nice study of human finger movements. The procedure was this: A blood pressure cuff applied to the upper arm was inflated until blood supply to the lower arm was shut off. In about 20 minutes all finger sensation was lost, but at that stage there was also motor impairment. At that point a pressure cuff is put on the wrist and the one on the arm is removed. This keeps a fresh blood supply from reaching the fingers, and they remain without sensation. But the fingers are largely operated by muscles in the forearm, and they are refreshed and can move the fingers. Subjects cannot feel their forefingers when they are placed in a particular position, but they can move them. A subject is told to move the finger either a certain distance or to a certain location. After the initial movement, the finger is then moved to a new starting position, which cannot be felt, and again the subject is told to move either the same distance or to the same location as previously. The subject is quite successful; in fact, the location response shows no more deficit than the distance response when the cuff is applied and the finger can no longer be felt as compared to a case with normal feeling. This means that subjects can program location in the absence of finger feedback. Because the subject can't feel the starting position in order to calculate the distance to be moved, it must be that location is programmed by sending an amount of neural activity to the agonist and antagonist muscles that would generate the same tensions as in a preceding movement. As dictated by the rubber-band model, the finger will move to the same terminal location regardless of starting location. Location seeking is instrumented by opposing tensions in agonist and antagonist muscles, not by achieving felt position.

This model of agonist–antagonist programming captures an essential idea of the follow-up servo model but does it without the necessity of sensory feedback. It explains how limbs can seek out locations independent of the preceding location. Let us tie up one loose end. If the original follow-up servo mechanism that involves muscle spindles sensitive to stretch is incorrect, then what is the function of the spindle system. Apparently, the spindle system operates simultaneously with the direct alpha route, providing a source of correction when unexpected posturbations in the environment alter movement. In essence, the spindle system is a monitor of movement rather than a direct stimulant of movement (c.f., Keele & Summers, 1976 for a more complete explanation).

The simple yet elegant notion of agonist-antagonist programming may have far-reaching consequences for our understanding of skill. This chapter has argued that at the highest levels a motor program is an abstract representation of a sequence of action that is more or less independent of the muscles to carry it out. If the representation at that abstract level specifies a sequence of locations, then a rather natural translation occurs between the abstract representation of location and setting muscles to seek out those locations.

REFERENCES

Bizzi, E., Polit, A., & Morasso, P. Mechanisms underlying achievement of final head position. *Journal Neurophysiology* 1976, *39*, 435–444.

Carre, F. A. *Effects of imitative learning and augmented feedback on the initial stages of learning a novel complex motor skill.* Unpublished doctoral dissertation, University of Oregon, 1972.

Fentress, J. C. Development of grooming in mice with amputated forelimbs. *Science,* 1973, *179* 704–705.

Fukuda, Tadashi. Studies on human dynamic postures from the viewpoint of postural reflexes. *Acta Oto-Laryngologica,* 1961, *161,* 1–52.

Hellebrandt, F. A., Houtz, Sara Jane, Partridge, Miriam J., & Walters, C. Etta. Tonic neck reflexes in exercises of stress in man. *American Journal of Physical Medicine,* 1956, *35,* 144–159.

Keele, S. W., & Summers, J. J. The structure of motor programs. In G. E. Stelmach (Ed.) *Motor Control: Issues and Trends.* New York: Academic Press, 1976.

Kelso, J. A. Scott. Motor control mechanisms underlying human movement reproduction. *Journal of Experimental Psychology: Human Perception and Performance,* 1977, *3,* 529–543.

Klapp, Stuart T., Anderson, Wallace G., & Berrian, Raymond W. Implicit speech in reading, reconsidered. *Journal of Experimental Psychology,* 1973, *100,* 368–374.

Konishi, M. The role of auditory feedback in the control of vocalization in the white-crowned sparrow. *Z. Tierpsychologie,* 1965, *22,* 770–783.

Nickerson, R. S., Kalikow, D. N., & Stevens, K. N. Computer-aided speech training for the deaf. *Journal of Speech and Hearing Disorders,* 1976, *41,* 120–132.

Nottebohm, F. Ontogeny of bird song, *Science*, 1970, *167*, 950-956.

Pew, R. W. Acquisition of hierarchical control over the temporal organization of a skill. *Journal of Experimental Psychology*, 1966, *71*, 764-771.

Pronko, N. H. On learning to play the violin at age four without tears. *Psychology Today*, 1969, *2*, 52.

Raibert, M. H. *Motor control and learning by the state space model*. Unpublished doctoral dissertation, Massachusetts Institute of Technology, 1977.

Rosenbaum, David A. Selective adaptation of "Command Neurons" in the human motor system. *Neuropsychologia*, 1977, *15*, 81-91.

Summers, Jeffery J. The role of timing in motor program representation. *Journal of Motor Behavior*, 1975, *7*, 229-241.

Taub, E., & Berman, A. J. Movement and learning in the absence of sensory feedback. In S. J. Freedman (Ed.), *The neuropsychology of spatially oriented behavior*. Homewood, Ill.: Dorsey, 1968.

Taub, E. Perrello, P., & Barro, G. Behavioral development after forelimb deafferentation on day of birth in monkeys with and without blinding. *Science*, 1973, *181*, 959-960.

Vallbo, A. B. Muscle spindle response at the onset of isometric voluntary contractions in man: Time difference between fusimotor and skeletomotor effects. *Journal of Physiology*, 1971, *218*, 405-431.

IV GENERALIZED MOTOR PROGRAMS AND SCHEMAS FOR MOVEMENT

Editor's Remarks (Chapters 8 and 9)

In Chapters 8 and 9, Richard Schmidt treats us to an in-depth discussion of the nature of motor programs and their interaction with peripheral feedback. Schmidt draws several distinctions that seem of heuristic value. One is between slow and fast movements, research into which allows one to differentiate between the types of errors that people make during movement. More important perhaps is that a clearer definition of the motor-program concept emerges. In Schmidt's view, because of feedback processing limitations, errors of program *selection* cannot be corrected within short periods of time. On the other hand, errors in *execution* can be handled by low-level peripheral reflex adjustments without any need to alter the program itself.

This analysis, as Schmidt admits, is only part of the story. How, one asks, are we to account for the remarkable context sensitivity of the action system? There must be lawful statements that we can make about how environmental information is used during the course of activity. One of the most elegant experiments in the movement literature discussed by Schmidt in Chapter 8 shows that a spinal cat walking on a treadmill produces *different* reactions to the *same* stimulus (a tap to the paw), depending on where in the step cycle the stimulus is applied. Schmidt analogizes this behavior to an IF statement in the computer language

FORTRAN; that is, IF a tap to the paw occurs here, then DO this; IF there, DO that. But maybe this analogy is too arbitrary and does not quite capture the significance of the cat's action. By this I mean that the IF statement does not provide any insight into why only functionally specific kinds of reaction occur in response to the same stimulus—the fact that, when the cat's paw is tapped during the recovery phase of the step cycle, the paw is lifted much higher than usual as if to avoid an object in the cat's path. This behavior is significant in that it performs an *adaptive function* for the animal. Perhaps what needs to be considered here is the role that evolution may play in economizing the task of the motor system through constraints that limit its operation to behaviorally useful acts. This view, if correct, forces us to consider the still poorly understood *function* of the motor system—a step that may require us to integrate data from evolution and ethology as well as psychology and physiology. Such a step, one ventures to guess, may well take us away from the currently dominant language of inputs and responses and the rigid relations that hold between them and force us to develop a new terminology for action.

An important contribution of Schmidt and his colleagues—introduced in these chapters—stems from their concern for the role of variability in movement control, and the way in which physical variables such as mass, distance, and time combine to affect movement outcomes. This line of research has proved productive and a clear set of predictions have been generated. The basic idea is that the variability in IMPULSE (the area under the force-time curve of a movement) is causally related to the variability in accuracy of response. As Keele mentioned earlier, this proposal may allow us to explain the underpinnings of Fitts Law, at least for rapid movements. Suffice to point out here that the initial predictions are undergoing some revisions, as the analysis and the questions become refined. Interestingly, spatial and temporal accuracy actually *decrease* as the force requirements of rapid actions approach the subject's maximum. The reader would do well to consult recent papers by Schmidt and Sherwood (An inverted-U relation between spatial error and force requirements in rapid limb movements. *Journal of Experimental Psychology: Human Perception and Performance,* in press) for the spatial accuracy data, and Newell, Carlton, and Carlton (The relation of impulse to response timing error. *Journal of Motor Behavior,* in press) for the timing evidence.

8

More on Motor Programs

Richard A. Schmidt
University of California, Los Angeles

In studying the published research literature on motor behavior, I find it easy to come to the conclusion that motor responses are of basically two types. The notion of categorizing things into dichotomies certainly has precedent in all fields of science; in fact, Robert Benchley, the English humorist, believed that the people of the world can be neatly divided into two classes: (1) those people who believe that the world can be divided into two kinds of people; and (2) those people who do not. I want to begin this chapter with a discussion of why I think the literature indicates that motor responses can be dichotomized, and then I turn to a more complete discussion of one of those kinds of movements.

TWO KINDS OF MOVEMENTS

In particular, the division is along the lines of how long movements take in time. The first category contains movements that are very short in time (on the order of 200 msec or less), whereas the second category contains movements that last considerably longer than that (e.g., a few seconds). Speaking very subjectively, when we perform a movement that is very rapid, such as a kicking or striking response, we seem to plan the movement in advance and then "let it fly." We do not seem to have conscious control over the movement's execution for a short period of time, and often we find ourselves making an originally planned movement when something has happened in the environment that indicates that the movement is now clearly inappropriate (e.g., the batter who swings at a very bad pitch). On the other hand, movements that are long in time seem to have ample opportunity for conscious control; we can determine if the movement is going to be incorrect, and we can make changes in the response as the movement is progressing (e.g., steering a car down the road, or drinking a mug of beer). So at this superficial level of analysis at least, it appears that some movements (with short movement times) appear to be carried out without the possibility of conscious involvement, whereas other movements (those with longer movement times) clearly appear to be modifiable via feedback during the movement. I am particularly interested in those movements that do not seem to be controlled through these conscious feedback-based processes, and what intrigues me is how these movements are planned and organized in advance.

CLOSED-LOOP CONTROL

Firstly, let me describe a very simple model of movement control that has two states in it: (1) an executive, which one can think of as a decision maker; and (2) an effector, which one can think of as a mechanism that carries out orders (Fig. 8.1). The executive sends instructions (commands) to the effector and the effector acts on them (i. e., makes movements). When movements are made, information about error in the movement is returned to the executive, and this information is called *feedback*. This is the simplest *closed-loop* model we can imagine. An executive makes decisions about what needs to be done, instructions are sent to some other "level" in the system that calls for action, the effector acts, and

FIG. 8.1.   A simple closed-loop control system.

then feedback information is sent to the executive indicating how accurately it was done (or whether it was done at all).

Consider a simple response where I start with my hand in one place, and I move quickly to a target a few centimeters away. One model to explain how I control my limbs during a movement like this would be the simple closed-loop model in Fig. 8.1. In effect, it says something like this. I start moving, with some initial instruction to the effectors (the muscles) to get the response going in essentially the right direction, and then I evaluate my feedback. Am I there yet? Am I on course? If the answer is ''no,'' the executive computes a correction and issues another instruction. That instruction moves me along a little farther, and then I evaluate the feedback again. I keep going through this process of evaluating where I am and whether I am there yet, and eventually I ''home in on'' the target. It is similar to the idea of setting the thermostat on your home heater to a new value that is far higher than the present temperature; the system constantly evaluates its own state until the temperature eventually arrives at the value to which you have set the thermostat.

Next, I would like to evaluate that model and ask whether it is reasonable to think that movements are controlled like this when they are fast in time. I think we would all agree that when they are slow in time it is reasonable to think that movements might be controlled this way; I start moving slowly and I can (consciously) guide my hand onto the target so that I make no errors at all. But what if the movement is rapid, like throwing, kicking, and hitting responses that are so typical of sport activities? The potential problem for this kind of movement is related to how fast the system can produce and analyze its own feedback and issue corrections. And if I cannot perform those processes very rapidly, then I must raise serious questions about whether the model in Fig. 8.1 works for fast movement.

Feedback Processing

I want to describe three experiments with widely different kinds of paradigms, techniques for collecting data, tasks, and experimenters; all of them point to the same conclusion: Humans have a very difficult time processing feedback information and making corrections. The difficulty is manifested by the fact that the processes are very slow.

The first experiment is by Henry and Harrison (1961). Subjects began standing, with the knuckle of the right hand on a reaction key. A warning light would come on, then there was a variable delay period that the subject could not anticipate, then there was a stimulus to which the subject moved his hand as quickly as possible in a forward–upward direction to trip a string that was in front of the body. The goal was to minimize the amount of time from when the stimulus light came on until the string was tripped; the *reaction time* was the time from the stimulus light until the movement started, and *movement time* was the interval from the start of the movement until the string was tripped. The subjects were encouraged to perform the entire movement as quickly as possible.

In this particular example, reaction time was about 200 msec, and movement time was just about 200 msec as well. (Movement time can be anything we choose it to be, depending on what we ask the subject to do; coincidentally, it happened to be about the same as reaction time in this case.) Then, in addition to the main task, there was another task. Should another light come on, the subject's task was to stop the response, reverse his limb, or otherwise keep from tripping the string. About 40% of the time no "stop" light came on; but on the other 60% of the trials, the "stop" indicated that the response should be inhibited. The stop light came on at various times after the stimulus light: 100, 190, 270, or 350 msec. The subjects held an accelerometer in the right hand, and when they began to stop their response, the accelerometer stopped a clock; the authors measured the time it required from the start of the response until the reversal. It turns out that about 200 msec was required after the presentation of the stop light for the subject to "put on the brakes" and *begin* to stop the limb. To what extent can the subject in fact inhibit the response? Only when the stop light came on 100 msec after the "go" stimulus was the subject able to begin to decelerate before the string was tripped. When the stop light came on at 190, 270, or 350 msec after the stimulus light, the movement was never inhibited. This means, therefore, that the 190-msec stop stimulus was illuminated before the movement began, and yet the movement was carried out to completion essentially without modification anyway. Even though, in the 100-msec condition, the subject could *begin* to stop the limb before tripping the string, the limb was traveling very fast by then; as it requires a lot of force and time to stop a limb that heavy going that fast, the string was tripped anyway.

The point is this. It appears that, when the warning light comes on, the subject prepares to make the response. Either slightly before or slightly after the stimulus light comes on, the subject preplans a movement that is then initiated, with the movement being carried out as planned; it seems to be very resistant to being changed both slightly before it is initiated and during its actual performance. Certainly this evidence says that whenever there is a signal during a 200-msec movement that calls for a change, the subject cannot do anything about it until the movement is complete. It appears that people have a great deal of difficulty dealing with information in the evironment that says "do something else"; in this case, "doing something else" means stopping the movement.

The next experiment really says the same thing but in a different way. Slater–Hammel (1960) had subjects watch a clock whose hand swept at one revolution per sec. The clock hand started at zero, and the subject's job was to hold an index finger on a key until such a time that lifting the finger would stop the clock hand exactly at "8"; obviously, if you wait until you see the clock hand arrive at "8" and then "instruct yourself" to pull your finger off the key, the clock hand is going to be quite a bit past 8 before the finger response occurs.

Occasionally, the clock hand would stop at different places before it reached 8, and the subject could not predict whether or when it would stop. If it stopped before 8, the subject's job was to do "nothing" (i. e., to hold the finger on the key as before). But if it did not stop before reaching 8, the subject's job was to initiate a response and stop the clock. This is a slightly different situation from that in the previous experiment (Henry & Harrison, 1961), because in the previous case the subject had to execute another movement (a stopping action) in response to a sudden light. In this case the subject has to do nothing in response to the second stimulus to perform the overall task perfectly. How much time does it require for subjects to inhibit a response that is already planned but not yet initiated? Alternatively, when does the subject give him- or herself an internal signal that says "go"? This signal, when it finally occurs, produces a response that is irrevocable, and this experiment should tell us when it occurs.

Slater–Hammel's major result is in Fig. 8.2, where the probability of inhibiting the response is plotted against the time before 8 that the clock hand stopped. This is the probability of "successfully doing nothing," which sounds silly, but perhaps we can see that "doing nothing" is an act in itself. When the clock hand stops 500 msec before reaching 8, the probability of success is almost 1; subjects always inhibit the response when the hand stops at 3, 500 msec before 8. When the hand stops very close to 8, they can never inhibit the response, and the probability is equal to zero.

The 50% point—the point at which the person achieves success 50% of the time—is about at 168 msec.[1] When the clock hand stops 168 msec before reaching 8, the subject cannot inhibit the response more than 50% of the time.

To me these data say that the the person issues an order to move; once this order has been issued, the subject moves, almost without regard to what happens in the next few hundred milliseconds. We do this experiment in the lab sections for our undergraduate motor-learning course; one sensation students report is that they see that the clock hand has stopped, and then later the hand comes up. Students report that they seem to have no control over their hand for this brief period. The value of 168 msec is a very long time when one considers time intervals that occur in rapid sports events (for example, it requires about 600 msec for the baseball to travel from the pitcher to the batter in baseball).

The first experiment (from Henry & Harrison, 1961) seems to say that when one receives a signal to do something and then one initiates it, then it is very difficult to stop doing that particular act. Slater–Hammel's (1960) data, on the other hand, say that when one initiates a signal to oneself to do something, it is very difficult to inhibit that response when told to do something else (in this case,

---

[1]Slater–Hammel showed a 26-msec constant error, indicating that the subjects were, on the average, 26 msec late in responding. When we add 26 msec to the 50% point in Fig. 8.2, we arrive at the value of 168 msec as the estimate of the interval at which subjects could inhibit their responses successfully 50% of the time.

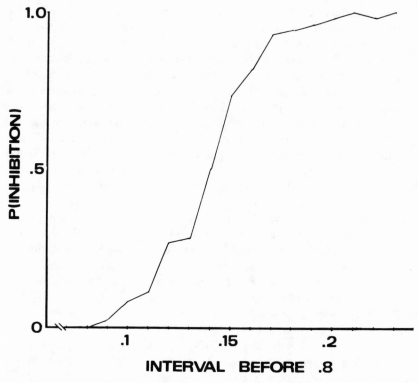

FIG. 8.2.   The probability of successfully inhibiting a response as a function of the interval before "8" that the clock hand stopped (from Slater–Hammel, 1960).

nothing). The idea from both studies is that a person has a prestructured set of commands that are necessary in order to move; when those commands are issued, that result occurs regardless of anything that happens in the next few hundred milliseconds.

Keele and Posner (1968) asked the same sort of question again in a very different kind of way. The problem was to what extent visual feedback information about a rapid movement can "get into" the response and alter it. They had subjects move from a starting key to a target in predetermined movement times; subjects were trained (via practice trials with knowledge of results) to move in either 150, 250, 350, or 450 msec. Then, after the subjects were trained to make the movement with the correct movement time, Keele and Posner occasionally (unpredictable to the subjects) turned the lights off when the subjects left the starting position; the remainder of the movement had to be made in the dark. The question was how accurate people were in the light versus dark. If the lights are off, of course, the subjects cannot monitor the visual information about their movement.

Table 8.1 gives the probability of *missing* the target as a function of the instructed movement time and whether the lights were on or off. When the movement time was 150 msec, the probability of missing the target was about the same for the "lights-on" and "lights-off" conditions. This tells us that vision was not used in those movements. When subjects were instructed to move in 250 msec, there began to be an advantage for the "light on" condition, but it was not a very big difference. When the movement became longer in time yet, there was about a two-to-one advantage (lights on versus off) in accuracy, and when the movement was slower yet—450 msec—there was a three-to-one advantage for the lights-on condition. What all of this suggests is that only when the movement times are long (more than 200 msec) could vision be used in controlling the movement. As the movement times decrease, vision is used less and less to a point somewhere between 190 and 260 msec where vision cannot be used at all.

It should be mentioned that there has been a serious challenge to this conclusion recently from our laboratory. Hawkins, Zelaznik, and Kisselburgh (1979) argued that Keele and Posner's method whereby subjects could not predict whether the lights would be on possibly led to a strategy whereby subjects tended to ignore vision. When Hawkins et al. repeated the Keele–Posner experiment, but using long series of trials where the lights would always be on or always be off so that the use of vision would not be discouraged, they found less movement error for the lights-on condition with movement times as short as 100 msec. Such evidence could suggest that the use of visual information is far faster than Keele and Posner's data indicate. Obviously, more work is going to have to be done on this issue.

Let me summarize what all these three studies say. They say to me that people have a very difficult time processing and using information about the ongoing course of movements, especially when the movements are fast. When the movements are, for example, 200 msec or less, there is serious doubt as to whether people can make use of environmental information indicating that something different should be done. Returning to the simple closed-loop model in Fig. 8.1, it seems to require 200 msec to go around the loop once.

TABLE 8.1
Proportion of Target Misses and Mean Movement Times (msec)
As a Function of the Instructed Movement Time
and Lighting Conditions (from Keele & Posner, 1968)

	Instructed Movement Time							
	150		*250*		*350*		*450*	
Lights	*ON*	*OFF*	*ON*	*OFF*	*ON*	*OFF*	*ON*	*OFF*
Probability of Missing	.68	.69	.47	.58	.28	.52	.15	.47
Actual Movement Time	190	185	267	254	357	338	441	424

A critical question is this: If I make the same movement that Keele and Posner did, but in 100 msec, how do I control that limb during that 100-msec movement? If we think that we control the limb by some sort of ongoing conscious feedback analysis, then there does not seem to be sufficient time to process the feedback information in these rapid moves. Numerous studies (Wadman, Denier van der Gon, Geuze, & Mol, 1979) have been done on the patterns of activity in agonist and antagonist muscles in these rapid movements. A typical pattern that is seen invovles the contraction of the agonist, its relaxation and the contraction of the antagonist, and then the simultaneous contraction of the agonist and antagonist so that the limb is "clamped" into its position at the target. A fundamental question that we must ask is, by what process do I perform these particular changes in muscle activation? Or, what turns off the agonist and turns on the antagonist at the proper time in the movement? One way of thinking is that the person processes the information from the movement until the limb is halfway there, and then the feedback information triggers the antagonists and the movement comes to a stop. That kind of an explanation does not satisfy me because, if it indeed takes 200 msec to process feedback information, then the movement will have been completed for 100 msec before the instructions to turn off the agonist can be issued. Another explanation that many people have given is one in which subjects structure their movement in advance, and this structure is termed the *motor program.*

THE MOTOR PROGRAM

The motor program is usually thought of as an abstract memory structure that is prepared in advance of the movement to be produced. When the program is "triggered off" by some environmental (or internal) event, the program results in the movement being produced, without there being very much possibility of modification or interruption of the response from events that occur in the environment.

What kinds of things need to be specified in order that the movement be performed? First of all, *which muscles* are to contract must be determined. Imagine now a complex act—like throwing a baseball—that involves a series of muscles from various parts of the body; the set of muscles associated with the throw must be defined. The second thing that has to be determined is the *order of contraction.* Order information must be important because I usually cannot have the muscles that stop the response contracting before the muscles that start it; also, the many muscles involved in such an act must contract in the proper sequence. The third component to be determined is termed *phasing,* which refers to the temporal relationships among the set of contractions within the sequence. In a certain act, the onset of Muscle B follows the onset of Muscle A by only 5 msec, for example, where the onset Muscle C follows the onset of Muscle B by

50 msec. Clearly, there can be no accuracy in phasing without the proper order of contractions; but given that the order is correct, phasing determines the fine details of *when* the various muscles contract in relation to each other. The fourth element that must be determined is *relative force*. Some of the muscles involved in the movement contract very little, whereas others might be involved nearly maximally. The program appears to be able to govern the relationships among the forces in the various contracting muscle.

The best analogy to the motor program that I have been able to find is the simple phonograph record, where the record is the program and the movements of the speakers can be considered as similar to the movements in the muscles controlled by the program. Firstly, if something goes wrong with the muscles (the speakers), the program goes on for a while as if nothing had happened. Wadman et al. (1979), in a study cited previously, had subjects make rapid arm movements of a handle to a new position. Suddenly, without the subject being able to predict when, the lever was clamped into place at the starting position so that the limb would not move at all when the subject exerted force on it. The authors found that the pattern of EMG was completely unaffected (relative to the EMG pattern when the limb was moved in the normal fashion) for the first 110 msec, and that there were only minor modifications thereafter. Thus, the pattern of agonist-on, agonist-off, etc., mentioned earlier, was maintained even though the limb did not move at all. Alternatively, we could say that there is no feedback loop from the sound of the speakers back to the record that can create modification in the record's output, at least for 100 msec. Also, when the movements were shorter in time, feedback appeared to be able to alter the movement somewhat earlier.

Other ways in which the program can be thought of as being like a record are that the record has information about which events are to occur (drumbeat rather than the voice), the order (drumbeat before the voice), the phasing among the events (in music, rhythm, which defines the intervals between sounds), and the relative force (where the first drumbeat of a series is always louder than the second). Of course, we do not have phonograph records in the head, but the usefulness of analogies (sometimes called models) is that they help us to understand how the human system might "work" by relating some of its common properties to systems about which we already know (e.g., phonograph records). See also Schmidt (1982) for a more complete discussion.

Next, we consider some other evidence for the motor-program idea, some of it from other species. (See previous chapter for more details.) There is evidence that the "face-washing" behavior of rodents is the result of programmed instructions "wired-in" at birth (Fentress, 1973). Wilson (1961) has shown in locusts that, when afferent nerves are severed (so that the insect can't "feel" its own wings), a single electrical stimulation is sufficient to cause the wings to beat, much as if the insect was in flight. Deafferented monkeys (whose afferent nerves are cut surgically) can run, climb, and groom themselves nearly normally (Taub

& Berman, 1968); there are decrements in fine finger movements, though. There is evidence that the running and walking patterns in cats and cockroaches are programmed (Pearson, 1976). It appears that patterns like these, necessary for survival, are built in genetically as programs in the central nervous system.

A problem for me, as a student of human motor behavior, is that I am not particularly interested in those programs. Rather, the kinds of programs that interest me are programs that allow people to throw or kick, perform industrial tasks, or play musical instruments; those programs are not genetically wired in but rather have to be learned. Can we generalize from information about genetically determined programs to make statements about movements that are learned? We hope we can, but we are not sure.

To this point we have been talking about evidence indicating that changes to an ongoing response are very difficult to achieve. It turns out that this generalization is only true for modifications that require a *totally new* movement pattern. It appears that small modifications to patterns already being executed can be achieved somewhat more quickly and easily.

Consider a situation where the individual is holding his/her elbow at right angles (with the forearm parallel to the floor), supporting a light weight from a cable attached to a handle. The individual is monitoring his/her performance via a gauge indicating the angle at the elbow, and the major task is to keep the elbow in a constant position. Suddenly, at a time that is unpredictable to the subject, a weight is added to the hand; the subject is instructed that, should a weight be added, he/she is to continue to hold the elbow at a right angle. This is essentially the protocol used by Dewhurst (1967) and a number of other investigators; Fig. 8.3 contains the important results. From the tracing of the position of the hand,

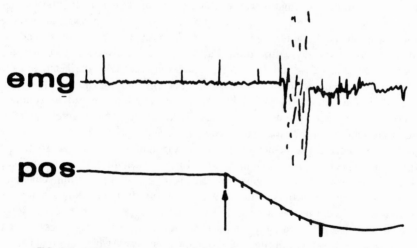

FIG. 8.3.   EMG (top) and limb position (bottom) as a function of time. (The arrow indicates the time of application of the added load, and the two large hatchings indicate 100 msec; from Dewhurst, 1967.)

we see that the hand begins to drop immediately when the weight is added. The electromyogram (EMG) tracing, indicating the level of contraction in the biceps, shows essentially no modification for about 30–40 msec, then there is a single spike, another period of silence, and then a sustained burst of activity that serves to decelerate the downward motion of the limb and bring it back to the horizontal position again. We can clearly see that there is a compensation for the external signal that begins some 50–60 msec afterwards. Because this interval of 60 msec is about one-third of the values we have been discussing with reference to reaction time and movement corrections, there is an apparent contradiction between these findings and the conclusion we drew in earlier sections about the rapidity with which movements could be corrected.

Reflex-Based Corrections

In order to understand the kinds of corrections we see here, we must digress slightly to mention some important neurological mechanisms. One very important structure in this regard is the muscle spindle; a simple description of it and its functioning is presented next.

The muscle spindles are small spindle-shaped (hence the name) structures that lie parallel to and among the fibers of the main body of the musculature. The ratio of the number of spindles to the weight of the muscle in which it is carried varies (in cat) from about 5/gm to 119/gm; apparently, the muscles requiring fine control (e.g., muscles that control the paw) have a larger number of spindles per gram of muscle than do muscles that do not require fine control (e.g., in the legs). Spindles are oriented in parallel with the main body of the musculature, so that stretching the entire muscle by a certain percentage of its length stretches the spindle by approximately the same percentage (see Smith, 1977, and Chapter 2).

The spindle is made up of essentially two parts. In the center of the spindle is a sensory region called the *equatorial region* with stretch receptors located in it. At the ends of the spindle are very small muscle fibers called *intrafusal fibers* (in contrast to the *extrafusal fibers* that are the main part of the muscle in which the spindle is imbedded). These small muscles apparently serve only to exert tension on the sensory region of the spindle and cannot contribute appreciably to the overall tension in the muscle.

The spindle is innervated by two kinds of nerve fibers: sensory and motor. On the motor side, the gamma motoneurons emerge from the ventral (front) horns of the spinal cord and innervate the intrafusal fibers. A number of kinds of afferent (sensory) fibers emerge from the sensory region of the spindle and provide information about stretch that is transmitted to the dorsal (back) horn of the cord. The important feature is that the IA afferents make connection with the alpha motoneurons that innervate the extrafusal fibers, and they do this monosynaptically (i.e., with but a single synapse). They also project to higher levels of the cord and appear eventually to provide information to the cortex about muscle length or muscle velocity.

Returning to the case of the subject holding the weight in the hand, let us examine some of the events that occur when the weight is suddenly increased. The motor program for holding the weight can be thought of as having two kinds of output. First, as we have already discussed, the motor program provides innervation of the extrafusal fibers via the alpha motoneurons, and that is the primary source of force for the overall contraction. But the motor program is also thought to provide excitation of the gamma motoneurons, whose major function is to provide the proper amount of tension on the sensory portion of the spindle, thereby adjusting the rate of firing at a particular muscle length. When the limb is in equilibrium, the amount of tension caused by the direct route to the alpha motoneurons, plus the amount of tension provided indirectly via the innervation of the gamma motoneurons (which then provide additional activity in the alpha motoneurons via the monosynaptic connection from the IA afferents), is just sufficient to hold the limb still and at right angles. When the weight is added, the muscle is stretched, the IA afferent fibers begin to fire more rapidly; the overall level of excitement in the alpha motoneurons is increased, causing increased tension in the extrafusal fibers via the monosynaptic connection. This loop from the spindle to the cord and back to the extrafusal fibers requires about 20–30 msec (depending on the limb studied) and is termed the monosynaptic stretch reflex. It is probably the mechanism responsible for the single spike seen in Fig. 8.3 some 30 msec after the weight is added.

At the same time the stretch reflex is operating, the IA afferents are being projected to higher centers, such as the cerebellum and/or the sensory cortex. These signals are processed and returned to the same level of the cord to cause a stronger, more sustained contraction. This reflex is called the long-loop reflex (or sometimes the transcortical stretch reflex), and its latency is thought to be on the order of 50–80 msec, depending on the limb studied. This reflex is probably responsible for the extra contraction needed to bring the limb back to the horizontal position after the weight is added.

These are by no means the only reflex mechanisms operating in the motor system, as the system is obviously very complex and capable of rapid corrections for errors in a variety of situations. But it should be pointed out that the presence of these mechanisms in no way denies the basic idea of the motor program defined earlier. Simply stated, the program determines the overall pattern of activity, and the reflex mechanisms ensure that this pattern is carried out faithfully, a notion discussed in relation to the control of gait by Grillner (1975). We turn to a discussion of this basic idea in the next section.

Two Kinds of Errors

When the person makes a response (e.g., a shot in basketball), there are really two goals. One of the goals is obvious—to put the ball in the basket. But, in addition, what the subject has to do is translate that goal into terms that mean movement of the relevant body parts. We can think of this as a subgoal. We might imagine that there are a variety of subgoals that one can use that will achieve the overall goal of putting the ball in the basket. Each pattern of movements is defined (by a program) in terms of both space and time, perhaps with the requirement that the limbs be at certain places in space at certain times in order that the movement be correct. Once the person decides what sort of a spatial-temporal goal he/she is going to use in order to make a movement, then presumably the person "calls up" the motor program that is created in memory. We can define two ways that the person can make an error in achieving the environmental goal. One is called an *error in selection*, and the second way is called an *error in execution*. First of all, let's talk about an error in selection.

Errors in Selection. With an error in selection, the subject's problem is that he/she chose the wrong program. The program may have run off perfectly in the sense that the muscles did exactly they were told to do, but the chosen program was inappropriate for the environmental situation. We can think of lots of examples. A batter in baseball expects the pitch to be a fastball, that is, with a nearly straight flight path, and executes a bat swing program appropriate for the fastball. But the pitch turns out to be a curve, and the batter misses the ball because the swing is too early and too high. Or, in basketball, I perceive that the basket is a certain distance away, and I generate a program to shoot that distance; but if I have made an error in deciding about the distance, the ball will miss the basket. In these examples, I can make an error in selection—select the wrong spatial-temporal pattern, the wrong program—and I can execute *that* response perfectly; the problem is that the movement does not achieve the environmental goal (which was the purpose of the response in the first place) because it was inappropriately selected.

Correction for errors in selection then require that the subject perceive that an error in selection is being made during the course of the movement, and it requires that a *new* movement be executed, a new spatial-temporal pattern, a new program; one cannot simply "patch up" the old one. I argued earlier that it requires about 200 msec to initiate a new program. Thus, errors in selection require corrections that have about a 200-msec latency.

Errors in Execution. Consider now errors in execution, where the person may have called up the correct program but something goes wrong in the way the program is run off. The limbs do not move in the way they were intended to, and the person does not achieve the goal—not because the wrong program was selected, but because the muscles did not "do what they were told." For example, in making a response, what if the musculature is a little more fatigued than you expected it to be. You call up the correct program and run it off, but the muscles contract with too little force because they are slightly fatigued. As a result, the response comes out wrong, not because you chose the wrong program, but because the muscles did not carry out the program as commanded. We can think of other examples as well. I lift a milk carton thinking it is full when it really is empty, and smash it into the next higher shelf of the refrigerator. I swing a tennis racket at a ball and a puff of wind hits the racket that slows it down slightly; in this case reflex-based corrections can be made for the fact that the limb is "behind schedule"; as a result, corrections can be initiated to enable the limb to catch up. Corrections for errors in execution require on the order of 50 msec to initiate.

The key distinction between error in execution and an error in selection is that if the subject makes a correction for a error in execution a new program does not have to be issued, whereas with an error in selection it does. For example, consider Dewhurst's (1967) experiment described earlier. The spatial–temporal goal might be verbalized as, "Hold your arm at right angles and resist this weight that's hanging from your hand." It is a pretty simple goal, but nevertheless a goal that is defined in space and time. Now what is the goal when the person has the weight added to the hand? It remains the same. The person can make a correction for that sort of error without having to reprogram a new response to get the limb in position. The old program can be used, corrected for an error in execution with reflex-based mechanisms.

Consider how a horse sleeps standing up? (Does everybody know that horses can sleep standing up?) One explanation for how horses sleep standing up is that they set the muscle spindle system to be compatible with the particular lengths of the muscles that are involved in holding an erect posture. That is tantamount to saying that the horse has specified a spatial and temporal goal and has issued a program to get the muscles to "execute" it. What happens if something goes wrong then, such as a puff of wind moving the horse slightly? If the puff of wind blows the horse forward, the muscles in the back of the leg are stretched (which activates the muscle spindles to a greater extent than they were activated before), which causes a monsynaptic reflex resulting in increased contraction in that muscle; this tends to bring the horse back to the position in which it was before (i.e., the preprogrammed position). So the horse can sleep standing up because of the fact that the system automatically corrects for errors in execution, and it does not have to issue a new program every time the body falls slightly off balance. Perhaps you can use this logic to see how a skilled gymnast might execute a handstand on the still rings.

What happens now with a baseball player when he or she issues a program to hit the ball and then detects that the ball is curving more than expected. In order to make a correction and hit the ball, a *new* motor program must be issued because the old motor program specifies the wrong goal. The person cannot simply make a correction for an error in execution; the spindles ensure that the pattern chosen is carried out as programmed. The reflex-based mechanisms would ensure that the batter will certainly *miss* the ball!

Let me summarize this section with a list of features that differentiate between errors in execution and selection. We have already talked about one of them—how long it takes to issue a correction. For errors in selection, it seems to require about a reaction time of 200 msec, whereas with an error in execution, the answer is something like 30 to 80 msec. There appears to be a wide gap between the latencies of the correcting process for errors in execution and errors in selection.

Secondly, what kinds of things have to happen in order to make a correction for an error in selection? A new program has to be initiated, which requires decision-making mechanisms. The new program has to be selected, "loaded" from memory, and executed. With a correction for an error execution, the same program can continue to run, but some sort of modification based on the muscle spindle mechanism needs to be produced.

A third way that these two kinds of errors and their corrections differ is in the amount of *attention* required for their correction. Is attention required for correction for an error in selection? The answer is, "Yes, and lots of it." We know from earlier chapters that the response-selection and response-initiation stages require attention; if we see a correction as just another response, then "correction-initiation" requires attention. On the other hand, correcting for an error in execution probably does not require attention. That is why a horse can sleep standing up, and that is probably why Henry (1953) showed that subjects could make corrections for positional changes that were so small that they could not even perceive them. It is fortunate that we are built this way because, if you had to pay attention to every little correction that was occurring in all the aspects of the musculature, you would be very busy indeed.

How many corrections can occur simultaneously? For errors in selection, the answer that most scientists who study information processing have come to is one; that is, if we consider a correction as we could any other response (because,

TABLE 8.2
Summary of Characteristics Distinguishing Corrections
for Errors in Selection and Errors in Execution

Characteristic	Errors in Selection	Errors in Execution
Time Required to Initiate a Correction	120–200 msec	30–80 msec
New Program Required?	Yes	No
Mechanisms Involved	Central Mechanisms	Spinal and/or Cerebellar Reflexes
Attention Required?	Yes	No
Number of Possible Simultaneous Corrections	One	Many
Effect of Increasing the Number of Stimulus Alternatives	Increases Correction Time	None

by definition, they both involve new programs), then evidence suggests that subjects can select and initiate only one response at a time (Keele, 1973). On the other hand, with corrections for errors in execution, it is reasonable to assume that there might be many such corrections occurring at a single instant, some from the legs, some from the arms, and some from the neck, etc.; we do not have very good evidence available to demonstrate that more than one correction could occur, but it is consistent with how we understand the reflex-based mechaninsms in the body to operate.

Finally, what if we increase the *number* of possible corrections that the

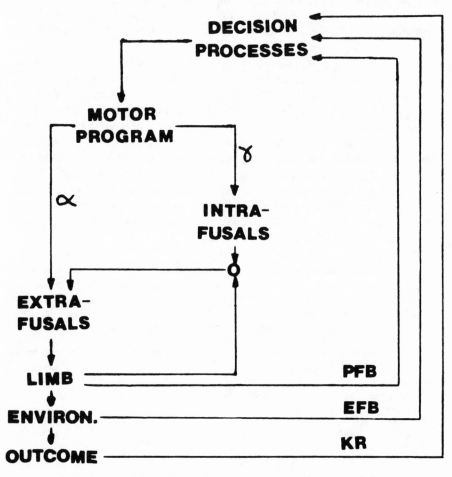

FIG. 8.4. Diagram representing the outside loop for corrections of errors in selection, and the inside loop for corrections for errors in execution. (PFB is proprioceptive feedback, EFB is exteroceptive feedback, and KR is knowledge of results; from Schmidt, 1976.)

subject might be expected to make. Considering corrections for errors in selection, we know from Hick's (1952) work that increasing the number of stimulus and response alternatives in choice-reaction-time situations drastically increases the time to respond when any one of the alternatives does occur. Most motor behaviorists believe that this effect is caused by increasing time spent by the central decision-making mechanisms in resolving the additional uncertainty caused by the increased number of possible actions. On the other hand, there is reason to suspect that the number of possible corrections for errors in execution would not cause increased time to initiate a correction, because decision making is presumably not required in the central mechanisms in order to initiate the correction. The "connection" between the stimulus (the stretching of a muscle) and the response (the increased contraction in that muscle) is presumably more direct for execution errors.

We can diagram all of this in Fig. 8.4. The program sends instructions to the muscles, which causes movement in the limbs. Information from the limbs— vision and kinesthesis, and so forth—is fed back to decision-making mechanisms via the outer loop. This is precisely the loop we talked about during the discussion of the program, and it is responsible for correcting errors in selection. So this loop has an approximately 200-msec loop time. Imbedded within the outer loop we have a loop that can be conceptualized as the spindle loop. When the limb goes too fast, the spindles pick up that information directly and feed back information via the spinal cord straight to the muscles without having to go through these decision mechanisms. These are corrections for errors in execution, and the loop time is something like 30–80 msec.

THE MOTOR PROGRAM REDEFINED

A common definition of the motor program comes from Keele (1968). It says that a motor program is a set of prestructured muscle commands that executes movement in the absence of peripheral feedback. Do movements really operate *in the absence of peripheral feedback?* With the gamma loop, which can operate with a loop time of only 30–80 msec, the first 30 msec of a movement can be feedback free; but immediately thereafter feedback begins to have an influence, but only with respect to correction of errors in execution. If we are content (as Adams, 1976, is) to define motor programs as causing the first 30 msec of a movement, then the existing definition (from Keele, 1968) is acceptable; but the concept should, in my opinion, be redefined to account for the contractions in 200- or 300-msec movements.

I (Schmidt, 1976, 1982) have suggested that the motor program definition should be revised slightly so that it reads this way: A motor program is an abstract structure in memory that is prepared in advance of the movement; when it is executed, the result is the contraction and relaxation of muscles causing movement to occur without the involvement of feedback leading to corrections for errors in *selection*. The change in definition allows us to say that feedback can operate in the movement, but not with respect to being able to initiate a new motor program. Rather, feedback operates at very low levels in the system to correct for minute errors in the way the program is being executed while it is running off.

Feedback and Programming

How does feedback operate in programmed acts? Well, we don't know very much about that, but there are some suggestions from work on the control of gait in lower animals like cats. The control of running and walking and so forth in cats is clearly "wired in" genetically, and it is not learned. Forssberg, Grillner, and Rossignol (1975) had "spinal" cats[2] walk on a treadmill and monitored the behavior of the limbs; there was a continually cycling pattern as the cat walked along. In the stance phase, where the cat is rocking across the "planted" foot, when they tapped the cat on top of the foot, a very small extension of the musculature in the same leg occurred. However, when the foot was tapped just at the point when the cat was ready to lift up the foot to swing it forward, there was a large elevation in the trajectory of the foot during the swing phase, and an extension of the limbs on the opposite side of the body. It is as if the cat were trying to move his foot higher to overcome some object that his foot had struck, like a curb. From an ecological point of view, the cat needs to have programs for running that are modifiable if certain kinds of events occur, like running into a ledge, or encountering uneven terrain. If it could not be flexible, the cat could fall; such behavior is not ecologically effective if one is running from an animal who is trying to obtain a meal.

Can we argue that the response just described is a simple reflex that maps the tap on the foot into leg flexion? No, because, when the authors provided the same tap when the foot was in the beginning of the stance phase, a slight extension response was produced. It is perhaps as if the motor program is like a computer program; in the computer language of FORTRAN, there are steps (called "statements") that are termed *if statements: If* some event occurs, *then* do something else. If the first event did not happen, then the controller goes to the next step in the program. For example, imagine a computer program sorting through the names and addresses of people that are on a magazine subscription list. You might have an *if* statement in the program that would say essentially, "If this person lives in Westwood, CA, then print out the name; otherwise go to the next person." Think of that now in terms of how the human or the animal is

---

[2]A "spinal" animal is one that has had the spinal column completely severed surgically, effectively separating the programs for gait from "higher" decision mechanisms in the brain.

programmed. It seems that the animal has "statements" analogous to that wired into it, so that if certain things occur only at certain times in the cycle modifications are made reflexively. If they do not occur, the program runs off as usual. So you can imagine then that programs are constructed with rather complicated sets of contingencies built into them so that one can have a continually running program that can execute itself slightly differently given that certain things happen in the environment. As Grillner (1975) says, perhaps the reflexes are *prepared* to operate, but have no role unless something goes wrong.

Characteristics of the Motor Program

Duration.   How long does a program govern behavior? The answer to that question is not really well-known, but logically we would expect that the program would have to run for at least 200 msec; that is the loop time for feedback to be able to interrupt it. Data from Shapiro (1977) suggest that the program might run as long as 670 msec, and there is some evidence that the program might run as long as 1300 msec. That means that the program is being carried out with prestructured commands that occupy 1 sec or more. Of course, this does not mean that the program cannot be interrupted during the 1300 msec. When the movement time is very long, like 1300 msec, the performer apparently has a choice (Schmidt, 1980). He can program the response so that all the details of the muscular contractions are handled by the program, and that would be fine if everything occurred as planned. Or, the person can monitor feedback and make corrections as rapidly as three times per second. The advantage of operating with ongoing program control is that one does not have to pay attention to the movement for 1300 msec, and one could attend to "higher-order" aspects of the task (e. g., strategies) while his program carried out the "lower-order" movements. I do not think it unreasonable that a program like running might carry itself out for quite a long time without modification (a few seconds). The point is that motor programs do not have only to do with fast movements, because we can argue that the programs can run far longer than the minimum loop time. Very highly skilled people (athletes and musicians, and so forth) can probably prestructure very long sequences and "pay" attention to other aspects of the movement or to other things.

What happens if something goes wrong? In a long movement, such as jogging, you may trip on a curb or be confronted with a truck. In this case, you can break into the program's execution (which requires attention) to issue a correction. There is very little evidence on this point, but people can perhaps choose to program for long sequences (if the environment is stable) or choose to monitor feedback and issue corrections (if the environment is variable). This relation probably depends on the "cost" of making an error as well (see Schmidt, 1980, 1982, for more on this issue).

Ingredients. What is "in" the motor program? This is a difficult question to answer; but at one level, surely, there must *result* from the program instructions to muscles of the form, "Turn on Muscle A, Turn on Muscle B, Turn off Muscle A, etc.," and this sequence has phasing as well as order information contained in it.[3] At another level, however, it is certainly not clear that the centrally represented program has anything to do with certain muscles, and it is likely that the program is far more abstract that this. There are various lines of evidence that support this position. If we argue that the commands for our signature are stored in a program, then how can we execute tha "same" signature on a check the usual size or on a blackboard some 10 times larger? A quick analysis of these two signatures will show that they use very different limbs and muscles, the smaller signature involving primarily the fingers, with the larger one involving primarily the elbow and shoulder (see Merton, 1972, for more evidence on this point). Also, there is evidence that I can ready the program for an act without knowing which muscles will be used to perform the act; Klapp (1977) showed that prior information about which of two responses (a Morse code "dit" or a "dah," which are different in terms of the duration of the hold component between the press and lift) is going to occur saves the subject time in initiating the movement, even though the muscles to be used (either the thumb or finger) are *not* known in advance. This kind of evidence suggests that the program is defined in abstract terms and is not defined in terms of the particular muscles involved in the action. Clearly, though, in order to move we must eventually define which muscles are going to be activated by the program, and this is presumably done at a later stage in the sequence of operations leading to the response. It does, however, seem that phasing (the timing among the elements in the sequence) is an integral part of the program (see also Schmidt, 1982, or Shapiro, 1977, for additional evidence on this point).

THE ACCURACY OF PROGRAMMED ACTS

I have discussed the idea that the motor program is responsible for producing movement, but have not considered its accuracy in doing this. Subjectively, we all know that even very well-learned responses—presumably with very "strong" motor programs—do not come out exactly as we plan them every time; that is, there seems to be "noise" added to the program's output. Imagine now that the program results in some set of instructions to which are added noise; then the movement that results out in the muscles might not necessarily be what was intended to come out when the program was structured. We have referred to

---

[3]Recent evidence suggests that some simple movements might have programs without any phasing information in them at all. One such movement appears to be unidirectional positioning responses; evidence against phasing in them has been provided by Bizzi (Polit & Bizzi, 1978), Kelso (1977) and by Schmidt (Schmidt & McGown, 1980; Schmidt, 1980, 1982).

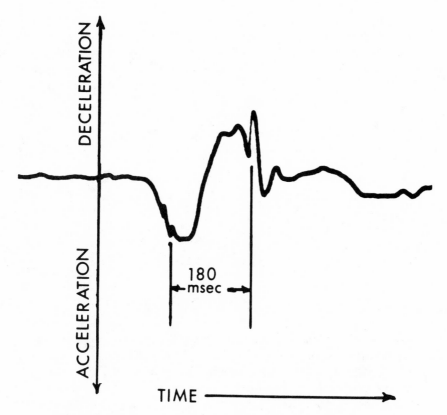

FIG. **8.5.** Accelerometer tracing of a stylus movement (from Schmidt et al., 1979).

these problems as execution errors. How large are these errors in execution? What is the source of noise?

Consider Fig. 8.5 where a record of the accelerations and decelerations (recorded from an accelerometer) from a simple movement I made are presented. The accelerometer was attached to a stylus, and I attempted to move the stylus from a starting point to hit a horizontal target 20 cm away, with a movement time of about 180 msec. In the first half of the movement, there is a pulse of acceleration in the "downward" direction indicating that the object is accelerating toward the target. Then, when the movement was nearly halfway completed, the acceleration stopped, and the curve moved in the "upward" direction indicating deceleration. Movements like this have to have a pulse to get them going that lasts about half the time, followed by another pulse in the opposite direction of equal size to get the movement stopped at its endpoint.

An idealized picture of that force-time curve is given in Fig. 8.6. The area under those curves is called the *impulse* and can be thought of as the aggregate of

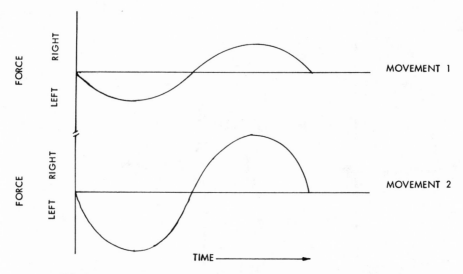

FIG. 8.6. Idealized force-time curves for two movements of equal duration (Movement 1 has half the amplitude of Movement 2).

accelerative and decelerative forces acting on the limb. There are some simple things we can say about these impulses in relation to movement. Consider first only the impulse for acceleration. The speed the limb is going after that initial impulse has ceased its action is proportional to the size of the impulse. If I make the impulse bigger, by increasing the amount of muscular action or lengthening the time over which it acts, the object will be going faster and will have gone farther than if I had generated a small impulse. The distance this object travels is related to the size of the impulse as well.

When I program an act like this, we assume that the muscles do not do exactly what they are programmed to do because of "noise." Sometimes on an occasional trial too much force may have been produced. If this happens, the limb goes too far because too much impulse leads directly to too much distance. If on the next trial the person does not produce enough force, the limb does not go far enough. A key observation, then, is that variations in the impulses are directly related to variations in how far the movement goes. So we can write: σ impulse $\propto \sigma$ distance; that is, the variability of the impulse leads directly to variations in movement distance.

What makes the impulse variable? If the muscle produces too much force or not enough force, then, of course, the impulse is going to be too large or too small, and the movement will be too long or too short. Another dimension that adds to the size of the impulse is how "wide" it is, which is the time dimension. Think back to what I said about the program resulting in a series of pulses that meter out which muscles contract in which order and with appropriate phasing. If the system is in some way variable so that it does not meter out the proper amounts of time, then that also adds variability in the impulse. These two things, basically, influence the size of the impulse and hence its variability, and we need to consider both when we consider variability in how far the movement goes.

If I make a movement to a target, how variable am I going to be at the end? We want to be able to understand the relationship among variables like the amplitude of the movement, how fast the movement goes, its accuracy in terms of the location at the end, and the mass of the objects to be moved. Recently, we (Schmidt, Zelaznik, & Frank, 1978; Schimdt, Zelaznik, Hawkins, Frank, & Quinn, 1979) have generated a mathematical model expressing how these variables relate to each other in movements.

What happens if the movement time is held constant—let's say 150 msec—and the response is made with twice the distance? What does the program have to do to have the limb make this response properly? The program says to the muscles, "Produce a pulse of force in the agonist, then turn it off and turn on the antagonist, and then turn on the agonist again to clamp the movement at the endpoint." (The phasing, or time relations, are structured into this command stream as well.) Because the impulse size is directly related to the distance, then we would say that the height of the curve (i.e., the force) would have to increase by a factor of two.

A very important point is that, when the impulse becomes twice as tall, it becomes twice as noisy at the same time. Let me present some data that support that statement (Schmidt et al., 1978, 1979). The subject sat, holding a lever that was secured so that it would not move. The subject initiated a series of pulses of force, one every 800 msec, and could see the amount of force exerted on a screen. The task was to try to get the dot to shoot exactly to a given level on the screen. What happens to the variability in the force as the subject was asked to produce more force? We might expect that as the amount of force is increased, the amount of variability in the force should increase as well. That's just what happened. In Fig. 8.7, the different levels of force variability are plotted against the amount of force produced. There was a clear linear (nearly proportional) relationship between the two variables. As the subject produced more force, it was produced with more variability.

Returning to the movement, if the program has to produce more force, and in producing more force it becomes more variable, then what happens to how far the limb goes? That aspect becomes more variable as well. If the person has to move twice as far, impulses of twice the height are produced, which are twice as noisy; therefore, the variability in distance moved is twice as large as well. This variability we have called W_e—effective target width—which is the standard deviation of the endpoints of the movement. To sum up, if I double the movement in length holding its time constant, I theoretically double the variability in how far it goes.

Now consider what happens if we change the time of the movement, holding the distance constant. As I make the interval of time shorter, the impulses need to be taller (more force) because the movement has to go more rapidly through

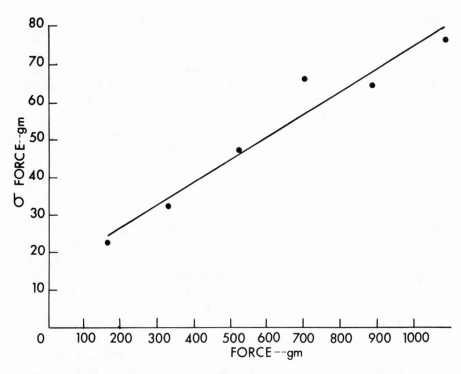

FIG. 8.7.   Within-subject variability in force as a function of the amount of force produced (from Schmidt et al., 1979).

space. In order to move faster, I have to increase the amount of force that I produce, leading directly to changes in the variability of the forces that are produced (and hence impulse variability), because increased force is produced at the "expense of" more variability. But another thing that happens to the program is in terms of the variability of the time dimension. We might suspect that making the interval of time longer would increase the timing variability. The next experiment we performed asked that question.

The subject moved a lever back and forth in time to a metronome and watched the resulting movements of a dot on a screen. The instructions were to move between two large target zones at each end and to use the target zones as a general reference of amplitude. We meausred the impulses by recording continuously the output of the strain gauge mounted to the handle. We measured the durations of the impulses produced, and then computed their variabilities. We asked the people to move in four different movement times: 200, 300, 400, and 500 msec, paced by a metronome. Figure 8.8 shows the important results. The measure of variability in impulse duration is plotted against the average movement time. We see that as the length of the movement time increased from 200 to 500 msec, the variability in the *timing* increased proportionately. Thus, as movement time is shortened, the impulse is "narrower," which tends to make the temporal dimension of the impulse *less* noisy.

To summarize, two opposite things happen when you ask the subjects to change movement time. As you ask the individual to move faster for the same distance, the impulses become "taller," because the movement must be faster through space; and they also become "narrower," because they have less time in which to operate. These effects work to: (a) *increase* impulse variability because of the increased force; and (b) to *decrease* impulse variability because of decreased time over which the impulse operates. The net result (if we were to go through the mathematics) is that W_e, the endpoint variability in the movement endpoint is inversely proportional to the movement time. In general terms, that observation does not surprise us because it says that if we move more slowly we can do so more accurately.

Now let's combine the effect of amplitude and the effect of time into a single expression. We have already said that W_e is directly proportional to the

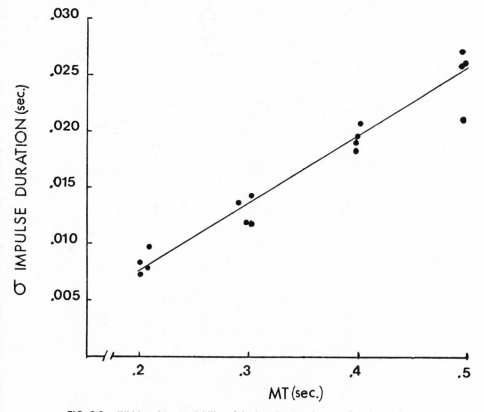

FIG. 8.8.   Within-subject variability of the impulse duration as a function of the movement time (from Schmidt et al., 1979).

amplitude and inversely proportional to the movement time. Thus it follows that the variability of the movement endpoint is proportional to the ratio of the amplitude divided by its movement time. That is,

$$W_e \propto \frac{A}{MT}.$$

In what kind of units of measurement is A/MT expressed? We can see that it is expressed in a measure of distance divided by time—that is, average velocity. We usually measure it in centimeters per second, but you can also use miles per hour, or even furlongs per fortnight.

The implication is that the average velocity of a programmed movement defines how "difficult" the movement is—difficult in the sense of arriving at an endpoint precisely. How does this idea agree with the commonly found phenomenon that the subject trades off speed for accuracy as with Fitts' (1954) Law (see Chapter 6)? If the subject moves rapidly when the target is small, he or she makes too many errors (i.e., too large a W_e), which is unacceptable to the experimenter. How does the person remedy the situation? A is fixed, and the person

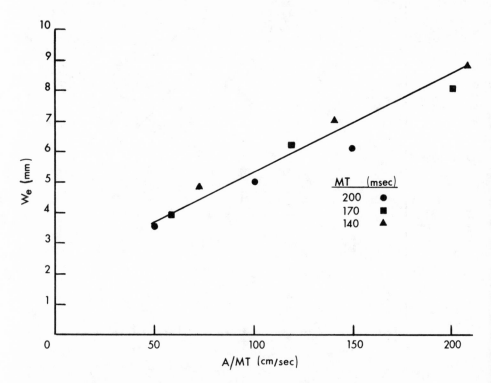

FIG. 8.9.   Effective target width (W_e) as a function of the ratio of the movement amplitude (A) and movement time (MT) (from Schmidt et al., 1979).

can't do anything about that; but the movement time can be changed. By increasing MT, W_e shrinks in proportion to $1/MT$, errors are smaller, and the experimenter is satisfied.

The next thing that we need to ask about is whether we can predict accuracy in moving (e.g., W_e) by knowing how far and how fast we've instructed the subject to move? We have a series of experiments that examine various questions along these lines, and I want to describe one of them. In our method, the person holds a stylus and tries to move it to a dot drawn on a sheet of paper. The task is to hit the dot in a predetermined amount of time. For a particular session, I might ask the subject to move in 150 msec; practice with knowledge of results about movement times is provided. Soon, subjects begin to move at about the right movement time. We specify for the subject the distance (A) of the move (defined as the distance between where he or she starts and the dot), and we specify the movement time (MT). We can therefore compute the theoretical difficulty of the movement as A/MT. Now the question is how the ratio of A and MT relates to the W_e produced in these situations.

Firstly, consider W_e in the dimension parallel to the overall direction of the movement (distance errors). In this experiment, As were either 10, 20, or 30 cm and MTs were 140, 170, or 200 msec. So we have nine data points, one for each

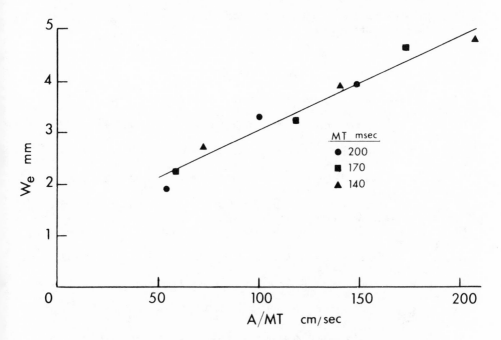

FIG. 8.10.   Effective target width (W_e) in the dimension perpendicular to the overall movement as a function of the ratio of the movement amplitude (A) and the movement time (MT) (from Schmidt et al., 1979).

combination of A and MT. As you can see, in Fig. 8.9, the distance W_es line up pretty closely on a line as the model says it should. One thing worth noting is the three points that have 200-msec movement times. One of the things we expect to happen is that, as the movement times become slower and people begin to use feedback (at around 200 msec), the slope of the line should begin to decrease. Perhaps these data are saying that subjects are just beginning to use feedback when the movement time is 200 msec; this agrees well with the data presented earlier from Keele and Posner (1968). Next, consider the direction errors—errors directly perpendicular to overall movement direction. Figure 8.10 shows a plot of W_e for direction as a function of the ratio of A/MT. Again, we see that error in hitting the target is linearly related to the difficulty of the movement, A/MT.

I'm excited about this line of research. It seems to say that by taking into consideration the fact that programs cause impulses that cause movement, and that when impulses are more noisy the movement is more noisy, we can account for the relationships among such important variables as MT, A, and errors. Motor behaviorists have not been able to do this before now.

ACKNOWLEDGMENT

The project was supported in part by Grant No. BNS 7910672 from the National Science Foundation to the author.

REFERENCES

Adams, J. A. Issues for a closed-loop theory of motor learning. In G. E. Stelmach (Ed.), *Motor control: Issues and trends*. New York: Academic Press, 1976.

Dewhurst, D. J. Neuromuscular control system. *IEEE Transactions on Biomedical Engineering*, 1967, *14*, 167–171.

Fentress, J. C. Development of grooming in mice with amputated forelimbs. *Science*, 1973, *179*, 704–705.

Fitts, P. M. The information capacity of the human motor system in controlling the amplitude of movement. *Journal of Experimental Psychology*, 1954, *47*, 381–391.

Forssberg, H., Grillner, S., & Rossignol, S. Phase dependent reflex reversal during walking in chronic spinal cats. *Brain Research*, 1975, *85*, 103–107.

Grillner, S. Locomotion in vertebrates: Central mechanisms and reflex interaction. *Physiological Reviews*, 1975, *55*, 247–304.

Hawkins, B., Zelaznik, H. N., & Kisselburgh, L. Unpublished manuscript, University of Southern California, 1979.

Henry, F. M. Dynamic kinesthetic perception and adjustment. *Research Quarterly*, 1953, *24*, 176–187.

Henry, F. M., & Harrison, J. S. Refractoriness of a fast movement. *Perceptual and Motor Skills*, 1961, *13*, 351–354.

Hick, W. E. On the rate of gain of information. *Quarterly Journal of Experimental Psychology*, 1952, *4*, 11–26.

Keele, S. W. Movement control in skilled motor performance. *Psychological Bulletin*, 1968, *70*, 387–403.

Keele, S. W. *Attention and human performance.* Pacific Palisades, CA: Goodyear, 1973.

Keele, S. W., & Posner, M. I. Processing of visual feedback in rapid movements. *Journal of Experimental Psychology,* 1968, *77,* 155-158.

Kelso, J. A. S. Motor control mechanisms underlying human movement production. *Journal of Experimental Psychology: Human Perception and Performance,* 1977, *3,* 529-543.

Klapp, S. T. Response programming, as assessed by reaction time, does not establish commands for particular muscles. *Journal of Motor Behavior,* 1977, *9,* 301-312.

Merton, P. A. How we control the contraction of our muscles. *Scientific American,* 1972, *226,* 30-37.

Pearson, K. The control of walking. *Scientific American,* 1976, *235,* 72-87.

Polit, A., & Bizzi, E. Processes controlling arm movements in monkeys. *Science,* 1978, *201,* 1235-1237.

Schmidt, R. A. Control processes in motor skills. *Exercise and Sport Sciences Reviews,* 1976, *4,* 229-261.

Schmidt, R. A. Past and future issues in motor programming. *Research Quarterly for Exercise and Sport,* 1980, *51,* 122-140.

Schmidt, R. A. *Motor control and learning: A behavioral emphasis,* Champaign, IL: Human Kinetics Press, 1982.

Schmidt, R. A., & McGown, C. M. Terminal accuracy of unexpectedly loaded rapid movements: Evidence for a mass-spring mechanism in programming. *Journal of Motor Behavior,* 1980, *12,* 149-161.

Schmidt, R. A., Zelaznik, H. N., & Frank, J. S. Sources of inaccuracy in rapid movement. In G. E. Stelmach (Ed.), *Information processing in motor control and learning.* New York: Academic Press, 1978.

Schmidt, R. A., Zelaznik, H. N., Hawkins, B., Frank, J. S., & Quinn, J. T., Jr. Motor-output variability: A theory for the accuracy of rapid motor acts. *Psychological Review,* 1979, *86,* 415-451.

Shapiro, D. C. A preliminary attempt to determine the duration of a motor program. In D. M. Landers & R. W. Christina (Eds.), *Psychology of motor behavior and and sport III.* Champaign, IL: Human Kinetics, 1977.

Slater-Hammel, A. T. Reliability, accuracy and refractoriness of a transit reaction. *Research Quarterly,* 1960, *31,* 217-228.

Smith, J. L. *Mechanisms of neuromuscular control.* Los Angeles: UCLA Printing and Production, 1977.

Taub, E., & Berman, A. J. Movement and learning in the absence of sensory feedback. In S. J. Freedman (Ed.), *The neuropsychology of spatially oriented behavior.* Homewood, IL: Dorsey, 1968.

Wilson, D. M. The central nervous control of flight in a locust. *Journal of Experimental Biology,* 1961, *38,* 471-490.

9 The Schema Concept

Richard A. Schmidt
University of California, Los Angeles

In the previous chapter we discussed the notion that individuals appear to move (at least in rapid movements) via the use of prestructured motor programs. We saw that the program concept is a very useful one in motor behavior because it seems to account very well for the kinds of movement effects that normally occur. But there are a few problems with the idea, some of which you have probably thought about already. In this chapter, I want to discuss some of these problems, indicating how the motor-program notion has been modified to meet these newer difficulties. Next, we turn to the question of how the performer selects the program for action, and I discuss in some detail one of the theoretical ideas that seems to explain how the performer selects appropriate movement behaviors.

SOME PROBLEMS WITH THE PROGRAM CONCEPT

A first question we might ask is, "How many programs are there?" What if I ask you to make a movement for which you already have a program—throwing a baseball, let's say—and then I ask you to change the speed of the throw. How do you do that? Do you have to have a whole new program? Implicit in the statements I have made in the previous chapter about motor programs is the idea that different responses require different programs; in order for me to have a series of pulses in memory that turn on and turn off muscles at precise times for one kind of throw, I will have to abandon the first program and generate another that does the "new" task that I want to do. How many programs do we need to throw baseballs in the infinite number of ways that we can? An infinite number, under this view. How about when we throw other things—softballs, golf balls? What about all the other ways in which we move, such as speech? MacNeilage estimated that if we think of each sound—called a phoneme—as a specific program, we would need some 100,000 programs just to speak English, considering all the accents and variations we use (MacNeilage, 1970). The idea is that I need a program for every movement or speech sound that I have made or will ever make. That adds up to a lot of programs.

The Storage Problem

One question is, "Where do I put all those programs?" Computer facilities have the same problem in a very literal sense. If we think of all the separate analyses that people on our campus do in the course of a year, and if we had to store all these instructions in the computer, the machine would quickly run short of storage space. To the extent that it is reasonable to think of the human as a computer—which is dangerous to do sometimes—where does the human store all of those programs? Thus, one major objection to the motor-program concept is termed the *storage problem*. It would be helpful if we could think of some other way to conceptualize how people program their movements so we could overcome this difficulty.

The Novelty Problem

Another problem closely related to the foregoing issue is the question of novelty. How do I make a movement that I've never made before? Does anybody doubt that I can do this? Think about a movement that you've not done before: Jump up, touch your right heel with your left palm, and touch your head with your right hand at the same time, and then put your feet in the regular position before you land. I can't imagine why you might have done *that* before. Can you do it? I'll bet that you could, or that you could come pretty close. To the extent that this movement is programmed (that is, you prestructure the commands before you make the movement), where does that program come from? One possibility is that it is already stored in memory from birth; but why would we have evolved to be able to do *that*? I don't think this is the answer. We cannot argue that the program was learned because you have never tried it before. People seem to be able to make novel movements, and the conceptualization of the program presented in the last chapter is inadequate to handle this. This issue has been called the *novelty problem*.

Sir Frederick Bartlett (1932), from England, while talking about tennis strokes, said: "When I make the stroke, I do not, as a matter of fact, produce something absolutely new, and I never merely repeat something old [p. 202]." What did he mean by that? He meant that when I make a tennis stroke at one particular time on the court, it is never completely new with respect to strokes I have done before, because I have a certain (but odd) style to the way I swing the racket that is typical of me. I don't do anything exactly old either, in that I have never done exactly *that* swing before. His point was that, when I make a move-ment, I construct a new movement each time, using knowledge and experience about previous tennis strokes; but because the situation is new (the ball is coming at a different velocity and at a different place on the court with respect to any previous stroke), I have to make a stroke that is not exactly like any I have done before.

These two problems—the storage problem and the novelty problem—have been two that have bothered me a lot ever since I started studying this area. There are some theoretical solutions to these problems, and I want to tell you about one of them. This does not, of course, mean that this one solution is necessarily correct, but it does eliminate these two problems; at the same time it might raise other problems that might be equally objectionable to somebody else.

GENERALIZED MOTOR PROGRAMS

The solution I want to discuss assumes tha the program is *generalized*. This means that I can have one program that can run off in a variety of different ways. There are generalized computer programs to compute means for various numbers of subjects and scores. For example, if I have two scores (height and weight) for each of 150 people, the program will compute the averages of the two measures for the 150 individuals. On the other hand, the next day I might use the *same* program to compute the mean of 100 people for four scores. The program has been structured (written) in such a way that if I supply it with additional information—called *parameters,* which in this case are the number of subjects and the number of variables—then the same generalized program can be run off in a large variety of different ways by giving it different parameters. Think of a program that can compute the mean of from 2 to 10,000 people and from 1 to 500 variables (or scores), and imagine the number of ways that the program could be run (i.e., 4,990,000 ways!).

Generalized computer programs are motivated by exactly the same reasons that we have been discussing here about motor programs. They save space because I have to store only one program in the computer's memory; but they have the slight disadvantage that the user has to supply some parameters in order to run the program in any specific way. I could do it the other way: I could store 4,990,000 separate programs in memory, and I could tell the user of the com-puter that if you have 300 subjects and 100 scores to call up the specific program suitable for that particular combination. Think of all the space that it would take to store all those programs. The solution that the computer scientist uses is to make the program generalized.

You can perhaps see that the generalized program eliminates the storage problem because now I only have to store one program instead of about 5 million, but how does it eliminate the novelty problem? Can you imagine that there is a combination of number of subjects and number of variables that our computer program has never done before? Surely you can. And yet, when I supply those two numbers to it, it easily produces the answers in that particular case; that is, it produces a response that has never been produced before. So, in that sense, the generalized motor-program notion solves the novelty problem. You can produce outcomes that have never occurred before.

So I want to make the case that the generalized-program notion, if you see it in the way the computer scientist does, could perhaps be adapted to be used for motor-skills research. The essence of the generalized-motor-program notion is that there is a program in memory, perhaps to throw a softball or hit a golf ball; and then in order to run the program, I have to specify one or more parameters, perhaps to define the speed of the overall action or the forces used, and so on.

I want to give you some examples of what the parameters might be, along with the evidence for some of these parameters, for motor skills. It turns out that if you look around in the literature there is quite a bit of evidence that supports the idea that motor programs are generalized. Imagine a task like a shuffleboard, where I have a long rod in my hand, the other end of which fits into a depression in a puck. People play this game on cruise ships, by holding onto the rod and shoving the puck with a certain force on a slippery floor so that it will stop at a certain spot. Imagine that you have a program that controls the musculature to perform a 10-m response. Could you use that same program to push the puck twice as far (or half as far)? I would argue that you could by simply speeding up the response, having it run off faster and with greater muscular force so that the puck would glide twice as far before it stopped. So, in this case, the parameters might be force and time. Let's look more closely at the literature to determine what some of the others parameters might be.

Overall Duration Parameter

A leading candidate for a parameter is overall duration (sometimes called speed), and there is quite a bit of evidence to support this view. Armstrong (1970) had people learn arm movements that had a particular pattern in space and time. The pattern was either 3 or 4 sec long and produced a wave like that shown in Fig. 9.1. Armstrong noted that sometimes the subjects arrived at the end of the movement too early. That shouldn't surprise us; but when the subject did arrive, say, 10% too early, the duration of the *whole* movement was decreased by 10%. Imagine that I could put the second (faster) movement tracing on an elastic piece of paper and stretch it by 10% so that it would fit right over the slower one. It appears that there was a generalized program to make these movements back and forth, but that the performer can run the entire sequence off faster or slower. This is evidence supporting overall duration as a parameter for the program.

Michon (1974) studied piano playing, coming to a similar conclusion. The musicians played a sequence of 15–20 notes, keeping the timing constant and

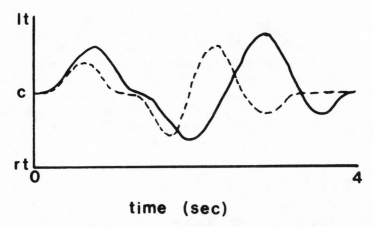

time (sec)

FIG. 9.1. Movement tracing of the pattern (heavy line) and a subject's attempt to reproduce it (dotted line), showing the tendency for the subject to compress the entire response in time (From Armstrong, 1970; upward movements of the trace indicate movements to the left, downward indicate movements to the right.)

correct between notes, but sometimes they would speed up the whole sequence so that all the parts were proportionally too fast. Additional evidence comes from Summers (1975) and from Shapiro (1977), using a series of button presses and movement sequences, respectively; also Viviani (1980) has shown similar processes in handwriting (see also Schmidt, 1982). Notice that Armstrong's movements were 3 sec in duration; you might be surprised, in view of what I said earlier about the duration of the program, that these movements appear to be programmed even though they are so long. This seems to say that programs *can* run for much longer than 200 msec if they are well-learned.

The Overall Force Parameter

Another parameter that we might consider is force. If you have a good understanding of physical principles, you probably realize that if I simply speed up the program without changing the muscular forces, the movement is not going to achieve the proper goal. (See also the section on the accuracy of programmed acts in the previous chapter.) So it would seem that we must have a parameter of changed force when we wish to change the overall movement duration, keeping other things constant (e.g., movement distance). Another way to think of the force parameter is to consider movements in which I throw objects that are of different weights (e.g., a heavy or light ball). Dick Pew, when teaching psychology at the University of Michigan, used to take his class to the Detroit Post Office to study postal workers. The workers, much to our annoyance sometimes, would receive a package off the end of a conveyor belt, look at the zip code to determine where it is to go, and do a perfect 10-m "set shot" into a bin for later delivery. The safety of your grandmother's crystal birthday present depends on the worker doing this properly. What does the person do? He or she would grab the box, "load" in memory a generalized set-shot program, "heft" the box to determine how heavy it is, select the proper parameter of force, and then run the program with that force parameter. In this example, we can perhaps see that the *speed* of various-sized boxes is the same (because their flight distance is the same), but the force requirements to achieve that speed varies directly with the mass of the package. This line of argument at least on intuitive grounds leads to the idea that there must be a separate force parameter.

The Spatial Parameter

The third parameter has to do with the spatial aspects of the response. I am not so sure about this one, but let's consider it as a possibility. Think about the ways that you can throw a baseball: straight overhead, sidearm, three-quarters, etc. In other words, you can adjust the throw by adjusting the angle of your arm to the ground (or to your torso). Thus, a possible parameter might be this type of positional change to support a movement, but there is almost no evidence to show this.

The Movement-Size Parameter

A fourth parameter might be termed *movement size*. Merton (1972) presents records of handwriting on paper versus the "same" writing on a blackboard. As you might imagine, the two are "the same," in the sense that they are both clearly characteristic of the person and recognizable as belonging to that person. Thus, an additional parameter of the program for handwriting might be the size with which the writing is to be performed. Through changes in the forces (even holding timing constant) one can make the desired marks on the paper large or small, although retaining the essential pattern of writing (the signature) (Hollerbach, 1981). This is even more remarkable when we consider that the movements in paper-and-pencil-sized writing involve primarily the fingers and hand, with the heel of the hand being relatively fixed; however, blackboard writing involves the fingers and hand being relatively fixed, with the primary movements coming from the wrist, elbow, and shoulder joints. See also Raibert, 1977, for another example of writing with different limbs. How does the system perform the "same" pattern of movement in these two examples when the joints and muscles used are totally different? The answer is certainly not clear, but this analysis gives some support to the notion that the program does not specify the particular muscles to be involved in the movement (see the previous chapter); it is possible to think of the choice of particular muscles as another parameter that is added to the program to define how the movement will be carried out. These ideas are certainly exciting to consider.

Other Parameters

Here are some other examples about programs and parameters that might be of interest. It is well-recognized by people who study gait that walking, trotting, and galloping in horses or cats are genetically programmed and rather stereotyped. One question you might ask is what does the cat or horse do when it tries to walk faster versus walk slower? It has generally been found that the parameter for changing walking speed is the amount of force that the animal produces horizontally against the ground. Keeping the number of footsteps per minute roughly constant, the animal moves faster through space because each footstep pushes with more force (and velocity against the ground). This is really the force parameter that we talked about before.

GENERATING PARAMETERS: THE SCHEMA

Now let's consider one point of view about what the person does when a movement is made. First, the person must "size up" the situation and decide what program to run; the program must then be retrieved from memory and "loaded" into a buffer (a temporary storage location) and readied to run. But the performer has not solved the problem yet because the initial conditions of the situation must be determined (e.g., the weight of the object, how far away the person is from the bin, whether the person is standing up or sitting down, etc., in terms of the postal worker). There must also be decisions about the parameters of the program to be executed. When all these decisions have been made, then the parameters are applied to the generalized program and the movement is initiated. So parameter selection is part of the problem the performer has before he/she makes a movement. In one sense it requires the person to do more computing, if you will, to generate the proper parameters.

If we understand the notion of a generalized motor program, and we see some evidence here and there for them and for their parameters, the next question we must ask is where the performer obtains the parameter. It's fine to theorize about the person having generalized motor programs and parameters, but a good theory should provide clear statements of the operations that occur when people program; more specifically—and more important, scientifically—can we specify what those operations are and test them to see whether the system "works" in the ways specified? The solution to this problem that I arrived at a few years ago involved the idea that the individual abstracts relationships inherent in his or her past experiences with similar situations, to enable the formation of a *rule* about how to handle similar situations in the future. Many people have considered that such rules are important in various situations (consider, for example, how I recognize that a cat that I have never seen before is, in fact, a cat), and many people (Bartlett, 1932; Pew, 1974) have termed this kind of rule a "schema." I

(Schmidt, 1975a) tried to take this idea about rule formation generated from work in remembering stories and pictures (Bartlett, 1932) and for the categorizing of novel dot patterns (Posner & Keele, 1968, 1970) and generalize it to the production of motor responses. In the remainder of the chapter, I discuss the essentials of this theory; a more complete treatment is found in Schmidt (1975a, 1976b, 1982).

Four Kinds of Information are Stored

The theory states that when we make a response, we briefly store four kinds of information from the response: the parameter for the movement, the outcome of the movement, the sensory consequences of the movement, and the initial conditions of the movement.

Parameters.   After the response is completed, the subject is presumed to store the parameter(s) that was used for the program just completed. (I explain how the subject obtains the parameters in a later section.) These parameters are the same as those discussed in the previous sections—force, overall duration, etc.

Movement Outcome.   The second thing that the individual is assumed to store is the outcome of the response—what happened in the environment. Did the ball go through the basket? Did I hit the baseball with the bat? How far did I throw? In terms of the experiments that we have been discussing so far, this information usually comes from knowledge of results or feedback.

Sensory Consequences.   The third kind of information supposedly stored after the response are the sensory consequences. The sensory consequences are what the response "felt" like after the response was completed. We can think of all the ways that responses produce sensations—they make sounds, they change things in our visual array; I see objects move on which I have exerted force, I feel vibrations, movements of my joints, tension in my muscles, and so on. The sensory consequences are what the response felt like, looked like, sounded like—what I sensed as a result of producing the movement.

Initial Conditions.   The fourth thing the subject is assumed to store after the response is the initial conditions. The postal workers, who are throwing the packages in the bins, "hefted" the package to figure out how heavy it was. The initial conditions refer to things like the weight and shape of objects that I am to move, or to the initial state of my body—whether I'm standing or sitting, upside-down or right-side up.

Schema Formation

Over the course of experience in running a given program, after each response the subject briefly stores these four pieces of information and *abstracts* the relationships among them. The word "abstract" is important, and by it I mean that one generates (or updates) a rule that describes the relationship between these stored pieces of information. Let's consider a simple example of this idea that we can conceptualize in Fig. 9.2. On the X axis is the outcome that the response produced; this is in environmental units such as the number of meters that the shuffleboard puck was pushed, to use an example mentioned previously. On the Y axis is the parameter of the puck-pushing program associated with the outcomes on the X axis; for this example, the parameter is best thought of as some combination of "intensity" (force and time considered together). The particular combination of parameter chosen and outcome produced can be thought of as producing a "data point." The person then does the response again, and another combination of parameter chosen and outcome is produced. This process continues to operate throughout hundreds of such movements made over a lifetime—not always with shuffleboard pucks, but with other kinds of

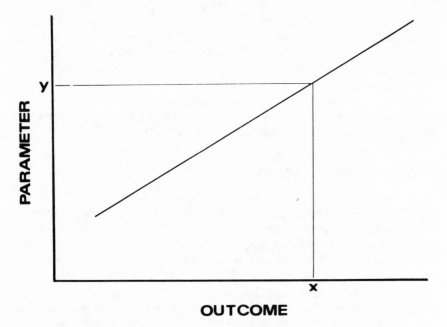

OUTCOME

FIG. 9.2.   Diagram of the recall schema, the relationship between past response outcomes and the parameters that have produced them. If the performer wishes to produce response outcome *x*, the schema indicates that the parameter *y* should be used.

pushing movements as well. Over the course of experience, there begins to emerge a pattern, which can probably be represented by a line, purely for purposes of presentation. This line represents a relationship, a *rule* if you will, that relates the parameters that were called up for the program with the outcomes that the program produced. According to the theory, every time the person makes a new movement, he/she provides one new "data point," and the relation is adjusted slightly. Clearly, if there are 10,000 "data points," and one more is added, the relation is not adjusted very much; but if there are few data points when the level of practice is low, the relation could be adjusted substantially.

After the individual briefly stores all this information after a trial, the rule is updated, increasing the power of the abstraction; the data are then "thrown away," but the updated rule is kept. Eliminating the information from each trial (after updating the schema rule) is important, as it tends to solve the storage problem; it also agrees with our subjective understanding of rule formation—that the instances on which the rule is based are forgotten, whereas the rule itself is remembered. (We certainly don't remember all the long-division problems we have done, but we remember the rule about how to do them; see also Posner & Keele, 1970.)

Now, what about the question of the initial conditions? One way to think of initial conditions is that they represent different lines in our graph, such as are shown in Fig. 9.3. In the shuffleboard example again, the top line might be the schema rule for heavy pucks, the middle line is for medium-weight pucks, and bottom line is for light pucks. Notice that, as the mass of the object increases, the size of the parameter (in terms of force) must increase for a given movement outcome. That's one way to conceptualize how the initial conditions are built into this rule as a result of practice. When I code the initial conditions, I know which of the rules I am using and I add a data point to that rule.[1]

Response Production (Recall)

How does the person make a response? According to the theory, the first step is to "size up" the environment to determine what must be done, which includes decisions about which program will have to be run (e.g., the shuffleboard program, rather than the kicking program). In addition, the subject must decide about the nature of the initial conditions: Is the puck heavy or light? Following

---

[1]Since publication of the schema theory, there has been evidence produced indicating that the initial conditions might not be important for certain kinds of movements. In unidirectional limb-positioning responses, for example, Polit and Bizzi (1978) have shown that deafferented monkeys can move to the correct target, even if the initial conditions (initial location) of the limb has been changed without the monkey being aware of it. Similar data have come from Kelso (1977) and Schmidt and McGown (1980) with human subjects. The evidence suggests that, in these movements, the program specifies an endpoint directly, and the limb moves to it regardless of the particular initial conditions.

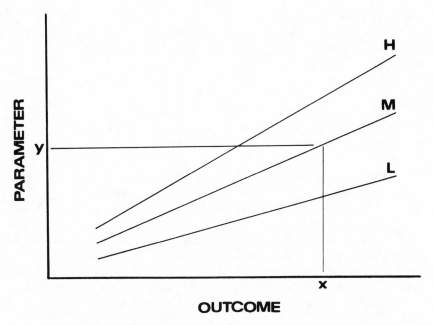

FIG. **9.3.** Recall schemata for light (L), medium (M), and heavy (H) objects. If the performer wishes to produce response outcome x with a medium object, the schema indicates that parameter y should be used.

these decisions, the subject then uses the schema (see Fig. 9.3) for, say, the medium-weight puck and "computes" the parameter for the response that will result in a movement of 30 m. The performer does this by noting (as indicated by the lines in the figure) which parameters are related to 30 m for the rule involved with medium-weight pucks. We can think of this parameter as the subject's best guess about the correct parameter in this situation, given the past experience with similar situations. When all the parameters have been selected for the response, they are applied to the motor program and the response is initiated and carried out.

The Effect of Errors

What does the theory say about the effect of errors? Does it hurt you or does it help you? Some theorists (Adams, 1971) say errors tend to produce weakening in the memory structure for the movement; that is, errors are to be avoided. In schema theory, on the other hand, the object of the performer is to maximize the strength of the schema rule. I can obtain new "data points" whether I achieve my goal in the environment or not, so long as I have the movement outcome (i.e., some form of KR) to associate with the parameters and/or the initial conditions. Thus, one fundamental way that the schema idea is different than other learning theories is in relation to how errors are viewed. I see errors as being just as useful as correct responses, and perhaps more useful because they represent variability in responding.

Recognition Processes

Next, I want to talk about recognition—in particular, how errors are recognized. If you understand how the schema idea handles response production (that is, recall), then you understand how it works for recognition because the idea is almost the same. Consider Fig. 9.4. The quantity on the X axis is the same as before—outcome in the environment. But now we have the sensory consequences of movement on the Y axis. Every time the person makes a movement, he or she stores the outcome and the sensory consequences (among the other things). Assume that the sensory consequences lie on a dimension related to the amount (or intensity) of the sensations from the response; violent, forceful responses produce violent and forceful sensations. Over the course of experience in running the program, a relationship, rule, or abstraction between the sensory consequences of a response and the outcome in the environment is developed.

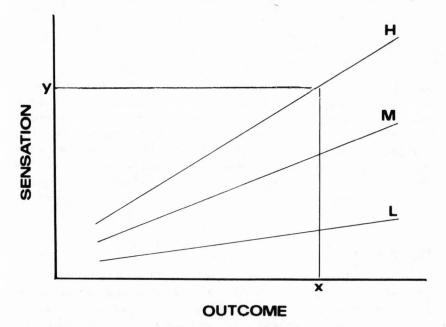

FIG. 9.4. Recognition schemata, the relationship between past response outcomes and the sensations (sensory consequences) that they produced, for light (L), medium (M), and heavy (H) objects. If the performer wishes to produce outcome x with a heavy object, the recognition schema indicates that sensations of intensity y will be received.

When preparing to make a response, along with the parameter(s) of the program, one generates the expected sensory consequences—the best guess about the sensory consequences that will occur if he produces this outcome. Let's say that I ask you to stand up, jump and turn 180°, and land facing the opposite direction. Now close your eyes and imagine what it will feel like to do that. You will probably imagine sensations from your legs, turning, and landing facing the opposite direction; you imagine that what you will see when you are facing the opposite direction is not what you were looking at before. How can you generate this image? The recognition portion of the schema theory says that you can do it because you have had experience doing similar things; that is, you have a recognition schema for determining *in advance* what the response is going to feel like.

How does recognition work in a fast movement? Along with the selection of the program and its parameters (from the recall schema), the performer generates the expected sensory consequences of the movement (from the recognition schema). When the movement occurs and the feedback (the *actual* sensory consequences) returns, the *actual* and *expected* sensory consequences are compared. If those two states match, a message is received indicating that the environmental goal has been achieved. If a mismatch is received, an "error message" is sent indicating that (and in what way) the environmental goal has not been achieved. So we see that the match between the expected and actual sensory consequences is the basis for the subject detecting whether or not an error has been made. Think about that in terms of activities that you have performed. You drive a golf ball, and, without even seeing where the ball went, you can know that it was a "good" shot. The swing felt smooth, the sound of the club hitting the ball was right, the sensations from the club were rhythmical, and everything sounded and felt and looked good. If you play golf at the level I do, you probably receive lots of error messages indicating that performance was not so "good."

What happens in slower movements? According to schema theory, slow movements are handled by the comparison of expected and actual sensory consequences. When the movement is slow, I have ample time to analyze (at a conscious level) my own feedback. Consider a movement in which I am to move a slide down a trackway and stop it at a particular spot. Theoretically, I first generate the anticipated sensory consequences—how the movement is going to feel when it finally reaches the endpoint. Then I issue a motor program that moves the limb part of the distance toward the target. Feedback returns from the limb and is compared with the expected sensory consequences, and I evaluate whether the expected and actual consequences match. If they do not, I move some more. So with this sort of closed-loop mechanism, I can continue making adjustments until the actual sensory consequences and the expected sensory consequences match. Theoretically, then, when those two match I am at the target and I have made a successful response. By this idea, the recall state is the state responsible for producing programmed acts that are quick, and the recognition state is the state either responsible for evaluating fast movements (afterwards) or *producing* slow movements.

As appealing as this idea might be, there have been quite a few experiments in the recent literature that suggest that even very slow movements might be carried out without the involvement of feedback and recognition mechanisms. This seems especially true if the person can select the movement in advance. Thus, even slow movements might be proprogrammed to a much greater extent than we thought before (Kelso, 1977; Kelso & Stelmach, 1976).

Practice Variability

Let's talk about some implications of what this theory means for teaching movement behaviors. One of the implications concerns itself with the amount of variability in practice. From Figures 9.2, 3, and 4, I think you can see that if I "spread out" the outcomes that I produce, I will have a stronger rule; a least in terms of the graphical analogy, the slope and height of the line (the rule) will be more closely defined. One of the major predictions of the theory is that we should produce as many kinds of responses as we can in order to strengthen our recall schemata. The more variety I produce in my responding, the stronger the schema is going to be, and the better I'll be able to produce a novel response in the future.

That hypothesis can be easily tested in the laboratory. Basically, subjects in one group perform a group of responses that vary only minimally along some dimension (like speed or force). Another group of subjects performs the same number of responses, but they are deliberately made to be different from each other. Then all subjects perform a new movement of the same class that they have never produced before. The theory says that the group with more variability in practice should be able to produce that new movement more accurately, because it can generate the parameter more effectively than can the group with minimal practice variability.

McCracken and Stelmach (1977) did just this kind of experiment. Subjects made responses of a slide on a trackway so that the movement time was 200 msec. The movements could be varied in terms of the distance moved in the constant movement time. One group of subjects (the constant group) practiced only one of the movement distances, whereas a second group of subjects (the variable group) practiced with four different distances in a randomized order. As seen in Fig. 9.5, during the practice phase when the groups were practicing either one or four different tasks, there was less error in responding for the constant group than for the variable group; it is perhaps not surprising that we can do one thing more accurately than we can do four things. However, the findings of interest for schema theory concern what happened when the subjects were transferred to a movement distance that they had not performed previously. On an immediate transfer test (on the same day), subjects in the variable group performed the new task more effectively than did subjects in the constant group, supporting the idea that the practice variability in the earlier training period led to

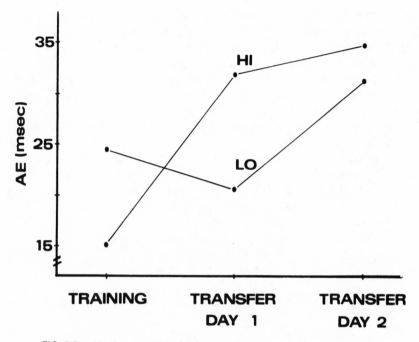

FIG. 9.5.   Absolute error (AE) for the high (HI) and low (LO) variability groups on the training trials, and on transfer trials immediately (Day 1) or 2 days (Day 2) after training (from McCracken & Stelmach, 1977).

increased ability to produce novel responses. After one week, however, this effect was reduced, but the two groups were still slightly different in producing the novel task.

Such effects have also been studied in children (Kelso & Norman, 1978; Kerr & Booth, 1978; Moxley, 1979). Evidence suggests that the variability-in-practice effects are even stronger than they are with adults. Perhaps this observation indicates that much schema learning is completed while we are young, with much less learning accomplished once we have achieved adulthood. This is in keeping with the often-cited notion that motor learning in adults might involve the recombination of old habits rather than the learning of new ones (Schmidt, 1975b, 1982). For a more complete review of this work in both adults and children, see Shapiro and Schmidt (1982).

This evidence has a lot of relevance for certain kinds of physical education. For example, in children's movement-education programs, one common goal is to produce a *capability* for moving in the future; that is to say, instructors are attempting to develop in their participants the capability for making novel movements—movements that perhaps will be important in later life in sport or occupational settings. The instructors usually ask children to attempt a wide variety of movements. For example, the instructor might roll up a mat on a gym floor and ask the children to go over the mat in as many ways as possible. You find the children jumping over with one leg to the other leg, both legs to both legs, backwards, frontwards, and so on.

Theoretically, the instructor is providing high variability of movement outcomes, presumably with the result that students are developing strong schemata. The beneficial effect of this would be that, when children grow up and are asked to jump in some new way—perhaps out of the way of a truck that is going to hit them, or in some sports activity—they can perform the new act more effectively because of their more-varied past experiences. The schema theory was not developed with movement education in mind, but it is interesting that the predictions of a theory aimed at explaining evidence from laboratory settings are so much in line with movement-education practice (see Schmidt, 1976a, for more on movement education and schemata).

ACKNOWLEDGMENT

The project was supported in part by Grant No. BNS 7910672 from the National Science Foundation to the author.

REFERENCES

Adams, J. A. A closed-loop theory of motor learning. *Journal of Motor Behavior,* 1971, *3,* 111–150.

Armstrong, T. R. *Training for the production of memorized movement patterns.* University of Michigan, Human Performance Center (Tech. Rep. No. 26), August, 1970.

Bartlett, F. C. *Remembering: A study in experimental and social psychology.* Cambridge: Cambridge University Press, 1932.

Hollerbach, J. M. An oscillation theory of handwriting. *Biological Cybernetics,* 1981, *39,* 139–156.

Kelso, J. A. S. Motor control mechanisms underlying human movement reproduction. *Journal of Experimental Psychology: Human Perception and Performance,* 1977, *3,* 529–543.

Kelso, J. A. S., & Norman, P. E. Motor schema formation in children. *Developmental Psychology,* 1978, *14,* 153–156.

Kelso, J. A. S., & Stelmach, G. E. Central and peripheral mechanisms in motor control. In G. E. Stelmach (Ed.), *Motor control: Issues and trends.* New York; Academic Press, 1976.

Kerr, R., & Booth, B. Specific and varied practice of a motor skill. *Perceptual and Motor Skills,* 1978, *46,* 395–404.

MacNeilage, P. F. Motor control of serial ordering of speech. *Psychological Review,* 1970, *77,* 182–196.

McCracken, H. D., & Stelmach, G. E. A test of the schema theory of discrete motor learning. *Journal of Motor Behavior,* 1977, *9,* 193–201.

Merton, P. A. How we control the contraction of our muscles. *Scientific American,* 1972, *226,* 30–37.

Michon, J. A. *Paper presented at the Human Performance Center,* The University of Michigan, 1974.

Moxley, S. E. L. Schema: The variability of practice hypothesis. *Journal of Motor Behavior,* 1979, *11,* 65-70.

Pew, R. W. Human perceptual-motor performance. In B. H. Kantowitz (Ed.), *Human information processing: Tutorials in performance and cognition.* New York: Lawrence Erlbaum Associates, 1974.

Polit, A., & Bizzi, E. Processes controlling arm movements in monkeys. *Science,* 1978, *201,* 1235-1237.

Posner, M. I., & Keele, S. W. On the genesis of abstract ideas. *Journal of Experimental Psychology,* 1968, *77,* 353-363.

Posner, M. I., & Keele, S. W. Retention of abstract ideas. *Journal of Experimental Psychology,* 1970, *83,* 304-308.

Raibert, M. H. *Motor control and learning by the state-space model.* Tech. Rep., Artificial Intelligence Laboratory, MIT, 1977.

Schmidt, R. A. A schema theory of discrete motor skill learning. *Psychological Review,* 1975, *82,* 225-260. (a)

Schmidt, R. A. *Motor skills.* New York: Harper & Row, 1975. (b)

Schmidt, R. A. Movement education and the schema theory. In E. Crawford (Ed.), *Report of the 1976 Conference June 3-8.* Cedar Falls, Ia.: National Association for Physical Education of College Women, 1976. (a).

Schmidt, R. A. The schema as a solution to some persistent problems in motor-learning theory. In G. E. Stelmach (Ed.), *Motor control: Issues and trends.* New York: Academic Press, 1976. (b).

Schmidt, R. A. *Motor control and learning: A behavioral emphasis.* Champaign, Il: Human Kinetics Press, 1982.

Schmidt, R. A., & McGown, C. M. Terminal accuracy of unexpectedly loaded rapid movements: Evidence for a mass-spring mechanism in programming. *Journal of Motor Behavior,* 1980, *12,* 149-161.

Shapiro, D. C. A preliminary attempt to determine the duration of a motor program. In D. M. Landers & R. W. Christina (Eds.), *Psychology of motor behavior and sport III.* Champaign, Ill.: Human Kinetics, 1977.

Shapiro, D. C., & Schmidt, R. A. The schema theory: Recent evidence and developmental implications. In J. A. S. Kelso & J. Clark (Eds.), *The development of movement control and coordination.* New York: Wiley, 1982.

Summers, J. J. The role of timing in motor program representation. *Journal of Motor Behavior,* 1975, *7,* 229-242.

Viviani, P. Motor engrams in typing and handwriting. In G. E. Stelmach & J. Requin (Eds.), *Tutorials in motor behavior.* Amsterdam: North-Holland, 1980.

V

DEGREES OF FREEDOM, COORDINATIVE STRUCTURES AND TUNING

Editor's Remarks (Chapters 10, 11 and 12)

Let me introduce the Turvey, Tuller, and Fitch chapters with a conundrum borrowed from earlier discussions of behavioral studies of motor programming (see for example, Chapter 7). It is the claim based on laboratory experiments, that the more elements in a movement sequence there are, the longer it takes to get the sequence started. Reaction time, say the time to lift the finger off a button, increases as the complexity of the program increases. But what do we mean by a complex skill? Does adding on movement elements necessarily implicate a more complicated program? Intuitively, there seems something wrong with this analysis. It's like saying that by adding on to the number of wheels on a cycle (e.g., going from a unicycle to a tricycle) one makes riding more complicated! Years ago, Bernstein—whose work is discussed more fully in Chapters 10 and 11—showed that the sprinter reacts to the starter's gun with the same latency as it takes to lift a finger off a button. Yet, the sprinter has to perform a highly coordinated activity involving a large number of muscles and body segments (plenty of "elements"!). One answer to the dilemma is that the skilled athlete has discovered ways to reduce the degrees of freedom of the motor system, so that the action is performed as a single, functional unit. This goal, of understanding how the very many degrees of freedom of the motor system are constrained to act in a unitary fashion is, and continues to be, a principle focus of Turvey's work. Turvey et al. voice their concerns about current theories of movement because of their failure to embody the concept of constraint: They do not capture the distinction between those acts that do occur and those acts that are physically possible but never will occur. The forms that such "equations of constraint" or "coordinative structures" take and how they modulate—and are modulated by—perceptual information constitute the subject of the final three chapters. The implications of this approach are potentially far reaching for how we conceive the problems of motor control and skill learning: So-called complex tasks that fit existing constraints may be much more easily acquired than the so-called simple tasks we ask subjects to perform in a laboratory.

The problem posed here then is the biological problem of coordination, and Turvey et al. approach it by combining the talents of a powerful duo: Nicolai Bernstein, the Soviet Physiologist who first drew attention to the issues of degrees of freedom and "peripheral indeterminacy" (context-conditioned sensitivity) and introduced the concept of functional synergy (coordinative structure); and James Gibson who conceived "ecological psychology"—the notions that the environment structures the media that surround terrestial creatures, and that it is this structure to which our perceptual systems are sensitive. Needless to say, this saga is a continuing one whose recent developments would occupy the contents of another book (or two). Suffice to say that the proponents of this approach are trying to come to grips with issues such as how coordinative structures develop, how they change over time, the operations underlying their nesting, and the relationship between the "arising of constraints" and intentionality. A tall order that should keep everyone busy for a while.

10 The Bernstein Perspective: I. The Problems of Degrees of Freedom and Context-Conditioned Variability

M. T. Turvey,
Hollis L. Fitch,
Betty Tuller
University of Connecticut
and
Haskins Laboratories

The perspective to be developed in this chapter and the two that follow might be termed the Bernstein perspective after the Soviet physiologist Nicolai Aleksandrovitch Bernstein (1896–1966). In other perspectives, both traditional and contemporary, the contribution of the kinematic and dynamic aspects of movement to its control and coordination are either simply ignored or terribly underestimated. For Bernstein, the obvious fundamentality of these aspects led him to characterize the study of movements in terms of the problems of coordinating and controlling a complex system of biokinematic links. He recognized that the focus of analysis could not simply be the muscular forces provided by the animal but must necessarily include inertia and reactive forces. In a nutshell, Bernstein recognized that any theory that ignores the totality of forces and considers only those contributed by muscles in its functional description of movements would be a theory of the *miming* of movements rather than a theory of movements themselves, for the very simple reason that any coordinated activity requires an environment of forces for its proper expression (Fowler & Turvey, 1978). The purpose of this first chapter is to identify the two major problems that shape the analysis of movement in the Bernstein perspective.

We begin with a view of motor control that was popular in the 19th century and that is depicted in Fig. 10.1. This view assumes an "executive" responsible for the control of movement, whose capabilities are not unlike those of a human being. To put it bluntly, the executive is a scaled-down version of a human being, and traditionally this "little man inside the head" is referred to as the "homunculus." At the disposal of this little man, or homunculus, is a memory bank containing programs for movement, where those programs can be likened to musical scores. To perform a movement the homunculus retrieves a score from

239

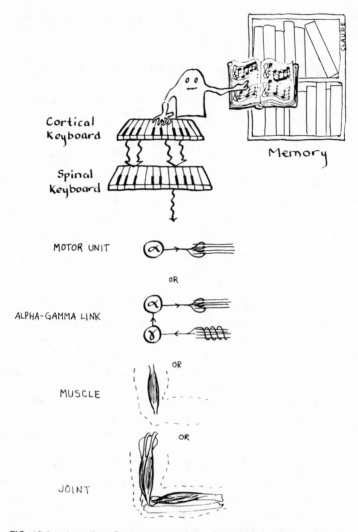

FIG. 10.1. A number of contemporary views of motor control are much like the 19th-century view of motor control depicted here. An executive system, a homunculus, selects from memory a plan for movement (analogous to a musical score) and implements the plan by manipulating the cortical motor strip (analogous to a keyboard). The details of the plan (or the notes in the musical score) might be expressed in terms of: (1) motor units; or (2) alpha–gamma links; or (3) muscles; or (4) joints.

memory and proceeds to "play" the score on the "keyboard" of the cortex, the motor strip. There was already evidence in the 19th century that different locations in the motor strip of the cortex were linked in some fashion to different movement consequences in different parts of the body; it was not very difficult, therefore, to think of the cortical motor strip as a keyboard. Each "key" on the motor strip was thought to cause a specific response in another keyboard, the spinal keyboard, which in turn brought about a certain muscular movement. The idea is much like that of striking a piano key, which, when depressed, causes a specific note by striking a string inside the piano. In this 19th-century view, the nerves that run from the brain into the spine were characterized as pipes through which one could drop balls, or through which one could send commands. If key 1 is pressed, then a command is transmitted to a specific key in the spinal keyboard, causing a particular movement. If key 2 is pressed, a command is transmitted to a different key in the spinal keyboard, causing a different movement, and so on. The job of the homunculus is similar to that of a pianist.

This 19th-century view is an open-loop conception of control: Any given movement is the result of a set program that is insensitive to changes in internal or external conditions. In keeping with the piano analogy, the homunculus plays a chosen musical score but is ignorant of the changes that are occurring as a consequence. No adjustments are made for changing conditions.

Notice also that the homunculus, by pressing the keys, issues a command to each of the units that control the movement; each unit is "addressed" individually. This style of control is called address-specific, or address-individualized, control. But what exactly is being addressed when a key is pressed on the cortical or spinal keyboard? The answer to that question tells us the "vocabulary" of the motor program, or score, because the symbols in the score must relate in one-to-one fashion with the keys in the cortex and the keys in the spinal keyboard. That vocabulary must be the vocabulary that is meaningful for the motor apparatus. Each "note" in the "score" (or instruction in the motor program) could represent, for example, "contract a certain muscle a certain amount!" or "move a particular joint to a particular angle!"

To what, then, do these symbols in the motor score refer? There are several possible candidates. When a cortical key is struck, we can imagine it bringing about a change specifically in a joint, a muscle, an alpha–gamma link, or a motor unit (see Fig. 10.1). To evaluate the candidacy of these entities, let us consider each in turn from the point of view of controlling an arm. We begin with the individual joints.

The shoulder, elbow, radio-ulnar, and wrist joints are schematized in Fig. 10.2. We can imagine the problem of designing an artificial arm that could be attached to, and controlled by, a human being. What sorts of problems does this pose? The shoulder joint can change on three axes: An arm that is fully extended and still can vary its position to the right and left, upward and downward, and it can rotate about its length. At any moment, therefore, the position of the shoul-

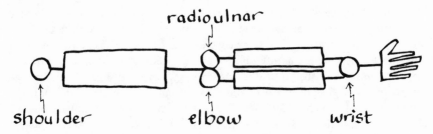

FIG. 10.2.   A schematic of an arm.

der joint is given by its values on three coordinates—the horizontal, the vertical, and the longitudinal. Hence, we say that the shoulder joint has three degrees of freedom that need to be specified to describe its position. This puts a large demand on the homunculus, who, for any particular movement of the shoulder, must assign the desired horizontal value, the desired vertical value, and the desired value on the longitudinal axis for each moment in time.

The elbow joint has only one degree of freedom: The forearm can flex toward or extend away from the upper arm. The radio-ulnar joint has one degree of freedom: The forearm can rotate about its length. The wrist joint can move in both the horizontal and vertical axes—it has two degrees of freedom.

To move the arm via address-specific control, then, where the units addressed are joints, seven values must be sent out at a time: three values to the shoulder joint, one value to the elbow, one value to the radio-ulnar joint, and two values to the wrist. This system of joints has seven degrees of freedom (a more rigorous definition of degrees of freedom is given later).

Now think back to the task of building a functional arm. The job of controlling even a simple movement via the joints already seems quite difficult. But the job gets even harder if the units addressed are smaller than joints. A theorist in motor control might suppose (and this is the more common assumption) that what is being regulated are not the individual joints, but the individual muscles.

There is only one dimension on which an individual muscle can vary: the contractile state. In the case of the shoulder, there are 10 muscles working at the joint (excluding the many stablizers and the biceps and triceps). There are therefore 10 degrees of freedom. At the elbow there are six muscles, and hence six degrees of freedom. There are four muscles that move the radio-ulnar joint, and six that move the wrist. That makes a grand total of 26 degrees of freedom that need to be regulated. If control is in terms of individual muscles, the motor plan must specify 26 values at each moment, one value for each muscle involved, in a language "understandable" to the muscles.

The control problem is greatly compounded for theories that postulate plans written in terms of individual motor units (or, relatedly, alpha–gamma links). There are different numbers of motor units in different muscles, but an extremely conservative estimate would be 100 motor units per muscle (in some muscles there are 6000). That would make 1000 motor units in the shoulder (100 motor units times 10 muscles), 600 in the elbow, 400 in the radio-ulnar joint muscles, and 600 in the wrist. On a conservative estimate, then, there are 2600 degrees of freedom to be regulated at a time.

Remember that the goal of this theoretical excursion is to build an arm that a human being could efficiently regulate, as if, for example, a person has lost an arm and this mechanical arm is to replace it. If this arm is to be controlled by the brain individually specifying values to each motor unit, thousands of degrees of freedom must be continuously regulated for the arm to function properly. If the brain is addressing individual muscles, 26 degrees of freedom must be regulated. If the basic units are joints, then there are only seven degrees of freedom. Obviously, the homunculus would have an easier job if he only had to determine seven values at a time.

We now want to consider whether it is plausible to use address-individualized control, even if there are only seven degrees of freedom to be regulated. As an analogy to the homunculus trying to control the body in this way, imagine a person trying to control a car that had been built according to such a principle. Suppose that when Henry Ford began mass-producing cars, he set them up under the principle of individualized control, where the individual units were the wheels; that is, for any moment in time the driver must independently assign the position of each of the four wheels, possibly by pressing keys that stand for the positions of the wheels. The four wheels are not connected—they are free to vary individually. It would be enormously difficult to regulate such an automobile. Indeed, we might suppose that the accident rate would triple if not eliminate us all!

The lesson is simple: If a task seems very difficult, even impossible for a human, then we ought to assume that it is at least equally as difficult for a scaled-down version of a human, that is, a homunculus. The preceding gives good reason for doubting that the homunculus of Fig. 10.1 regulates the body through an address-specific procedure. Of course, in principle the homunculus could regulate the body by other procedures, but prior to evaluating what they might be, let us take a moment to reexamine the role in which the homunculus has been cast. Does the homunculus notion aid our understanding of the control of movement? In the 19th-century story, in order to understand the coordination of movement, some device in the brain was proposed (a homunculus) that received information about the world and produced appropriate movements. But, notice, that is precisely the problem a student of coordinated movement is trying to understand. *How* can any agent receive information and produce the requisite movements? When trying to explain how it is that a person can, for instance, play tennis, you do not want in your explanation a person inside the head playing tennis. Our understanding of the control and coordination of movement will be directly correlated with the degree to which we can eliminate from our explanation an entity that has abilities approximating those of a fully fledged animal— that is, to the degree that we can trim down the homunculus concept.

A first step in trimming down the homunculus is to notice that some of the work assigned to him/her is unnecessary. He/she was being asked to do a very difficult job of selecting correct configurations from a large number of alternatives. But many of the possible configurations (like combinations of wheel positions for the car) are useless. Suppose the front wheels of the car are at a 90 degree angle to each other. The car could not move. Likewise, paralysis or chaotic movement would occur with many of the possible combinations of muscle innervations. Only some of them are useful; most of them are disastrous and self-defeating. We do not want to assume that the motor system has too many options. We want to do away with options irrelevant to the task, which complicate the problem of control and introduce a greater possibility of error.

To summarize thus far, we have set up a "straw man"—the 19th-century view of how a human or animal produces movement. We have highlighted three of its major features. Firstly, there is no feedback in the account; the system is open-loop and insensitive to changes in external conditions. Secondly, the style of control can be characterized as address-specific, individualized control. The homunculus (and motor program) must specify values for each individual variable. And thirdly, the keyboard model assumes that the vocabularies of the motor program, the cortex, the spinal machinery, and the motor apparatus stand in one-to-one correspondence.

The style of control we have been discussing highlights a particular type of problem that is called the "degrees of freedom" problem: There are too many individual pieces of the body to be regulated separately. What is to be appreciated is that the degrees of freedom problem constitutes a very difficult and fundamental puzzle to be solved by students of movement.

A formal definition can be given for the degrees of freedom of any system: They are the least number of independent coordinates needed to identify the positions of the elements in the system without violating any geometrical constraints. Consider a system of two elements—element A and element B (see Fig. 10.3). If there are two axes x and y (that is, we have a two-dimensional space), then two coordinates are needed to identify the position of each element. Element A must have a value on x and a value on y (for example, x_1 and y_1), and element B must have a value on x and a value on y (for example, x_2 and y_2). For this system of two independent elements (elements that are not connected), two coordinates are needed for each of the two elements, resulting in a system that has four degrees of freedom. This is the least number of independent coordinates needed to describe the positions of the elements of the system.

But now suppose that these two elements are connected by a steel bar, something that does not change in length. Call this connection a line of length L. What this means very simply is that element A and element B are not free to vary independently. So whatever position element A takes, element B must adopt some position that will be determined by the fact that A and B are connected by this link of length L. In fact, there is an equation that states the relationship that

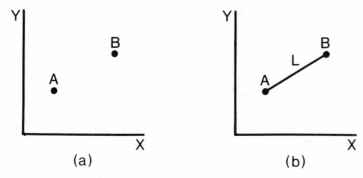

FIG. 10.3. Two simple graphs depicting two simple "systems" each composed of two elements, *A* and *B*, in a two dimensional space, *x* and *y*. System (*a*) has four degrees of freedom, whereas system (*b*), in which the two elements are linked, has only three degrees of freedom.

the coordinates of $A(x_1, y_1)$ and $B(x_2, y_2)$ must maintain: $(x_2 - x_1)^2 + (y_2 - y_1)^2 = L^2$. This equation is an example of an *equation of constraint*. It tells us how *A* and *B* relate.

Notice that when a line connects *A* and *B*, one is no longer free to choose any values of these coordinates. If the coordinates for $A (x_1, y_1)$ are chosen, then only *one* of the coordinates for *B* (say x_2) can be chosen freely; having chosen x_2, y_2 is now determined. This system has only three degrees of freedom. The least number of independent coordinates that are needed is now three, because one of the coordinates is determined by the other three in accordance with the constraints of this particular equation.

In general, the degrees of freedom of any system can be given by the following equation: degrees of freedom = $ND - C$, where *N* is the number of elements in the system, *D* is the dimensionality of the system, and *C* is the number of equations of constraint. By following this equation one can compute the degrees of freedom of any system. In the previous example we were dealing with a system of two elements ($N = 2$), two dimensions—the two axes x and y—($D = 2$), and one equation of constraint ($C = 1$). So the system's degrees of freedom were $(2 \times 2) - 1 = 3$. In the original example of a system without any equations of constraint (where *A* and *B* were not connected), there were four degrees of freedom: $(2 \times 2) - 0 = 4$.

Think of how this equation relates to our formal definition of the degrees of freedom of a system; (that is, the degrees of freedom is the least number of independent coordinates that are needed to identify the positions of the elements of the system without violating any geometrical constraints). By knowing the dimensions of the system, the number of elements, and the number of equations of constraint, the degrees of freedom of the system can be determined.

Let us attempt to pull these concepts together. We are considering one major problem that any theory of the control of movement must account for: How does

the nervous system regulate all its variables? There are many free variables—
they can be the joints, they can be the muscles, they can be the motor units. But
the problem is very straightforward: Regardless of the size of the unit controlled,
how are all those independent units regulated? That is the problem of degrees of
freedom. We have seen that when the variables, or elements, are constrained to
relate in certain ways, the degrees of freedom of the system are reduced.

Now let us consider a second, closely related, class of problems. They are
called the problems of context-conditioned variability. The homunculus in our
19th-century metaphor has an additional control problem that enormously com-
pounds the problem of degrees of freedom. Recall that in the piano metaphor
control is open loop. The homunculus is ignorant of what actually happens as a
result of his/her commands. Unfortunately for the homunculus, his/her commands occur in a context—against a backdrop of ongoing conditions, and their
end results will necessarily be modified by those conditions. In general, the
circumstances in which any particular movement occurs are not completely
fixed, and, in particular, each movement changes the context for the next movement. But with a fixed plan or motor score relating cortical "keys" to muscle
innervation pattern, there is no way to modify the commands to take account of
the changing circumstances into which those commands will be sent. We are
going to explore what the consequences are of not being sensitive to the changes
in context that accompany any movement. These changes allow a fundamental
type of variability into the system. The variability is in the relationship between
muscle states and movements.

Let us step back and see the nature of the problem. The objective is to produce
a certain motor consequence. If it is the case that whenever certain muscles are
brought into play they always produce the same consequence, then a particular
movement can always be produced simply by activating muscle A this amount,
then muscle B this amount, and so on. However, when any given muscle or
muscle group is activated, the actual resulting movement differs with context.
The relationship between muscle excitation and movement is variable and the
variability is owing to context; the variability is context conditioned. A homunculus cannot simply call up muscles without knowing what the context is, because the role played by a muscle is dependent on the context in which the act is
occurring.

Bernstein (1967) has defined three major sources of context-conditioned variability. Consider, firstly, the variability owing to *anatomical* factors. Suppose
that you hold your arm at your side in a position below the level of your shoulder
and you want to adduct your arm (bring it toward the midline of your body). A
good muscle to use would be pectoralis major because its distal insertion is the
humerus, and its proximal insertion is the clavicle. When you activate it, the arm
adducts. If, however, you now hold your arm slightly raised above the horizontal
axis of the shoulder joint and you again want to adduct your arm, activating the
pectoralis major will not work; it will, instead, *abduct* it; that is, it will move

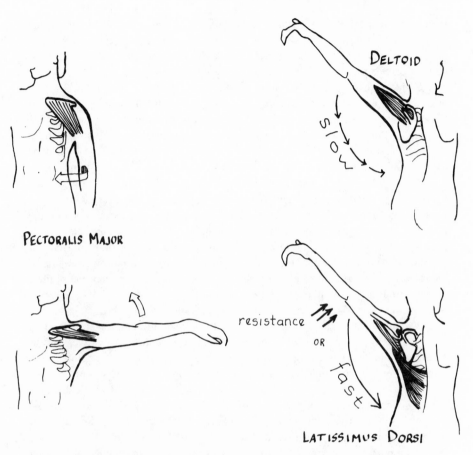

FIG. 10.4. The role of a muscle is context dependent. Given one relation between the angle of pull of the pectoralis major and the axis of the joint, contraction of the muscle adducts the arm (upper-left figure); given another relation, contraction of the muscle abducts the arm (lower-left figure). The deltoid is used to lower the arm slowly (upper-right figure); to lower the arm quickly or against a resistance, the lattissimus dorsi is exploited (lower-right figure).

your arm *away* from the midline of your body. Pectoralis major changes its role as a function of the angle of its pull with respect to the axis of the joint (see Fig. 10.4). The role of the muscle depends on the context.

Consider another very simple example. Suppose that you wanted to move your arm slowly downward against a resistance. The lattissimus dorsi plays an important role in this particular movement (see Fig. 10.4). But suppose you slowly lower your arm with exactly the same kinematic motion, but with no resistance. Now the lattissimus dorsi is not involved at all. You can demonstrate this yourself by palpating the lattissimus dorsi during the two movements. When there is no resistance, the deltoid muscles of the shoulder extend to control the movement of the arm downward (see Fig. 10.4). Although the kinematic details of the movement do not change in the two cases, the muscles that will be used depend on whether there is resistance to the movement.

Consider this problem of context-conditioned variability with respect to the anatomical sources of variability more closely. Most theories of motor control have revolved around a very simple conception of agonists and antagonists working at hinge joints. A fixed agonist and a fixed antagonist can be identified for a simple hinge joint but not for more complex joints, like the shoulder joint or the hip joint. In those joints, which muscles play the role of agonist and which muscles play the role of antagonist are not fixed but change, depending on the trajectory of the movement and the context in which it occurs. Paul Weiss underscored this puzzle in a classic paper written in 1941. He asked how the muscles that are to be agonists and those that are to be antagonists are selected for a given trajectory. When you lower your arm, which of the 10 or 12 muscles of the shoulder joint are to play the role of agonist and which are to play the role of antagonist? These problems are expressions of anatomical sources of variability. The role that a muscle plays is context conditioned.

A second source of context-conditioned variability is what Bernstein termed *mechanical* variability. Imagine that a muscle is excited to a given state, so that there is a particular amount of contraction, which we call X. What we need to appreciate here is that a given innervational state of a muscle does not have a fixed movement consequence. Given X under some conditions, one kind of movement will result; however, under other conditions, X will result in a different movement. The relationship between the muscle's degree of activation and the joint or limb movement that occurs is not fixed. It is ambiguous. Suppose, for example, that your arm is extended at the elbow and that you innervate the brachialis muscle (see Fig. 10.5) to yield state X. As a consequence of X, your arm flexes at the elbow joint. But observe what happens if the context changes. Suppose that the intial position of your arm is flexion at the elbow joint, and you progressively extend the arm at the elbow. If you now set state X for the brachialis muscle, it will not necessarily result in elbow flexion. In fact, depending on how fast the arm is moving, state X in this muscle may stop the arm, it may simply slow down the movement, or it may cause a movement in the direction opposite to the movement, that is, flexion. Notice that depending on the condition of the limb, the value X of this muscle will have different movement consequences. Mechanical sources of variability mean that the relationship between the state of a muscle and the movement consequence is variable—it depends on context.

The pervasiveness of mechanical sources of variability can be illustrated further. An appendage such as an arm or a leg is a biokinematic chain—that is, it consists of several connected links, so that a change in any one link affects the other links. If you actively move only the shoulder joint, the rest of your arm will

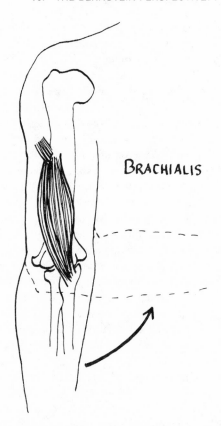

FIG. 10.5.   The brachialis muscle.

necessarily change in certain ways because the joints are linked. These changes generate kinetic energy. The generation of kinetic energy in the distal links—the forearm and hand—works back against the shoulder joint. In brief, the forces operating on a limb are not simply muscular forces. There are nonmuscular forces, such as forces due to gravity, changes in the moments of inertia of the limb, and changes in the reactive forces that one joint exerts against another joint. The recognition that nonmuscular forces greatly influence any movement is devastating for a story in which the command sent to the muscles is ignorant of these nonmuscular forces (as in our 19th-century metaphor). It could, of course, be argued that the commands must be structured so as to overcome the nonmuscular forces. But a different approach is to build a theory that says that movement is controlled and coordinated by allowing muscular forces and nonmuscular forces to complement each other. The nonmuscular forces are to be taken advantage of; they are not to be compensated for. Let us pause for a moment to repeat the story just told before we carry it through to its next step.

We have been looking at the mechanical sources of context-conditioned variability. Fundamentally, we realize that it is impossible to have a program written in terms of contractile states of muscles, because the movement consequences of any such program will be altered by the context of forces in which it is taking place. In most theories of motor control, the biomechanical properties of the body are often just ignored. In an alternative theory of control, the nonmuscular forces are recognized and are treated not as a hindrance to be overcome but as a complement to the muscular forces. In skilled activity, the muscular and non-muscular forces are seen as fitting together like two pieces of a jigsaw puzzle.

Consider this form of control—as Bernstein did—in relation to someone learning a skill. When you are first learning a skill, one of the things that is bothersome is that the parts of your body seem to have a will of their own. You are trying to control one link, but, in controlling one link, other links necessarily change. These unwanted changes follow from the forces generated by the movements of the links. Bernstein realized that in any skilled movement, from dangerous acrobatic routines to simple walking, what actually occurs is that the person or the animal is taking advantage of these nonmuscular forces. A highly skilled performer is in fact *exploiting* the nonmuscular forces and not compensating for them. Ther performer has found a way of ideally relating forces, those that the muscles supply and those that are supplied reactively by the body parts and the environment. An understanding of movement control will include an understanding of how muscular and nonmuscular forces complement each other.

Let us now consider one final source of context-conditioned variability—*physiological* variability. Again, observe the main theme: A fixed relationship cannot be assumed between muscle states and movements. We might imagine that a cortical command is communicated by a transmission line that runs to some location in the spinal cord, where it excites a particular cell or group of cells. This cell or group of cells in turn transmits the command to a muscle, producing a certain degree of muscle contraction. Notice that in this story it is assumed that the relationship from cortex to muscle is rather like a pipe, a passive relay that simply transmits instructions that are then faithfully followed by the motor units. By the very nature of the nervous system, however, it is not possible for instructions coming from the cortex and going to the muscles to be transmitted "faithfully," that is, without modification. The spinal cord does not simply relay instructions from the brain.

What influences other than cortical are exerted on the motoneurons, the final neural links between brain and muscles? Inside the spinal cord are a large number of neural entities called interneurons that interconnect parts of the spinal machinery. Interneurons connect with other interneurons within a segment of the spinal cord and between segments of the spinal cord. These horizontal and vertical connections among interneurons give the spinal cord an integrity and organization of its own. Acting on any motoneuron are inputs from a large number of places in the spinal cord. The state of the spinal cord will determine what actually occurs in the motoneuron. Hence, the signal to the motoneuron does not depend solely on the message from the cortex; the motoneuron is sensitive to, but not subservient to, the signal from the brain.

The point is that we do not want to conceive of the supraspinal mechanisms as dominating the spinal mechanisms: The spinal cord and the brain relate to each other like two diagnosticians, two highly skilled people trying to figure out a problem. It's not that one of them is commanding the other. They relate between themselves like experts, cooperating on a problem.

In this chapter we have considered two fundamental problems in the Bernstein perspective: The problem of degrees of freedom and the problem of context-conditioned variability. Let us conclude by seeing how these two problems relate to skill acquisition.

When you are just beginning to learn a skill, one of the first things you will notice is that you eliminate, as it were, some of your degrees of freedom—put simply, you keep a good part of your body fairly rigid. You do not exhibit the flexibility of the skilled performer. Watch a child learning how to hit a baseball. Initially, he or she stands quite rigid, facing the ball, holding most of the body stiff. This posture simplifies the problem, but it does not allow a very efficient swing. As the child gets slightly better, one of the things that he or she will do is allow shoulder movements into the swing. Several degrees of freedom are "unfrozen." Nevertheless, there is still a ban on many degrees of freedom because they constitute so much trouble for the child. The child is trying to avoid creating too many reactive forces, the forces that are nonmuscular. For example, the beginning batter finds that the swing throws the body off balance—this is a reactive consequence of the movement, a mechanical source of context-conditioned variability. As skill increases, and the child learns to work *with* the reactive forces, he or she will release the ban on the degrees of freedom, allowing additional degrees of freedom to creep in. If the batter's hips rotate, that guarantees a certain rotation in the upper part of the body. The batter does not actually have to push the body through every part of the movement but can exploit the reactive forces to regulate this rotational degree of freedom. Why is the batter attempting to regulate more degrees of freedom? Fundamentally, the skill demands it. A good baseball batter must allow flexibility of the hips, shoulders, and wrists. The additional degrees of freedom are very important in giving power to the swing. In summary, acquiring a skill is essentially trying to find ways of controlling the degrees of freedom and of exploiting the forces made available by the context.

ACKNOWLEDGMENTS

The writing of this chapter was supported in part by the following grants awarded to the Haskins Laboratories: NICHD Grant HD-01994, NIH Grant NS-13870, and NIH Grant

NS-13617. The figures were done gratis by Claudia Carello, to whom the authors are most grateful.

REFERENCES

Bernstein, N. *The coordination and regulation of movement.* London: Pergamon Press, 1967.

Fowler, C., & Turvey, M. T. Skill acquisition: An event approach with special reference to searching for the optimum of a function of several variables. In G. Stelmach (Ed.), *Information processing in motor control and learning.* New York: Academic Press, 1978.

11

The Bernstein Perspective: II. The Concept of Muscle Linkage or Coordinative Structure

Betty Tuller,
M. T. Turvey,
Hollis L. Fitch
University of Connecticut
and
Haskins Laboratories

The puzzle of the control and coordination of movement as seen by Nicolai Bernstein can be expressed succinctly: How can the many degrees of freedom of the body be regulated systematically in varying contexts by a minimally intelligent executive intervening minimally? A reasonable hypothesis is that nature solves this puzzle by keeping the degrees of freedom individually controlled at a minimum, and by using ''units'' defined over the motor apparatus that automatically adjust to each other and to the changing field of external forces (Gel'fand, Gurfinkel, Tsetlin, & Shik, 1971). In accordance with this hypothesis we introduce and explore the concept of muscle linkage or coordinative structure, defined as a group of muscles often spanning several joints that is constrained to act as a single functional unit.

Consider the contrast between a person who is a novice at shooting a gun and a person who is highly skilled. What makes these two people different? Imagine that you aim a gun and try to zero in on a target. And imagine that a light is attached to the end of your gun so that, when you aim, the beam focuses in the region of the target. The beam of light will not remain motionless at one spot, but rather it will wander around the target area. This is because, when you aim, your body in general and your arm in particular are not perfectly motionless. Now, in the case of the skilled marksperson, the light will wander around, but generally it will remain very close to the target; that is, the ''scatter'' is within a limited area around the target. In the case of an unskilled marksperson, however, the light will wander over a wide range around the target. So a skilled marksperson—not surprisingly—keeps the gun on target much better than the unskilled. What we want to know is how the skilled marksperson is able to do this. The question is, how has the person organized the body with reference to the specific problem of aiming a gun. Two differences between the skilled and the unskilled marksperson are evident. Whenever a person lines up to fire the gun, there is some oscillation of the body—the center of gravity is moving. The first thing we can observe about the skilled marksperson is that in comparison with the amateur the oscillatory movement is less. She or he has found some way of "freezing" the muscles, restricting their freedom, so as to keep the body's center of gravity more stable. The second difference we can observe is the following. While aiming the gun, any change of the wrist or shoulder joint will cause the gun to deviate from target. In the unskilled marksperson, movement at one joint is not compensated by a change at the other joint, thus throwing the gun off target. The joints are relatively independent of each other. But in a skilled marksperson, the story is very different. The two joints are constrained to act as a unit such that any horizontal oscillation in the wrist will be matched by an equal and opposite horizontal oscillation in the shoulder (Arutyunyan, Gurfinkel, & Mirsky, 1969). It appears that the joints relate among themselves (see Fig. 11.1) according to some equation of constraint, just as the two points in Fig. 10.3b of the previous chapter relate to each other by the equation of constraint for the connecting line. In the unskilled performer the pieces of the body relevant to the skill vary in a relatively independent fashion, which can be interpreted to mean that no equation of constraint applies. The joint at the wrist is unrelated to the joint at the shoulder, so that whenever there is any oscillation at one joint the other joint follows or remains fixed. In either case the gun moves off target. The difference, then, is that the skilled performer has found a way of constraining his or her muscles to behave as a single unit, that is, as a coordinative structure. And we may suppose that, in part, learning any skill entails a similar discovery of relevant constraints over the muscles used in the skill.

Let us consider another example. When a person breathes, inhaling and exhaling pulls and pushes the spine backward and forward. The mechanics of the body, the biokinematic linkage of head and spine, dictate that the head should move with the spine; curiously, the head is stable throughout the cycle of spinal movements. The stability of the head arises as follows. With inhalation the thoracic region of the spine is pushed backward, but the pelvic girdle and the cervical region move forward by just the degree needed to preserve the head's position (see Fig. 11.2). It appears that there is a functional grouping over the muscles of the cervical-thoracic-pelvic groups (Gurfinkel, Kots, Pal'tsev, & Fel'dman, 1971), because the muscles relevant to inhalation are anatomically quite separate from those relevant to the movements of the hip and anatomically separate from those relevant to the movements of the upper part of the spine. It is as if an equation of constraint has been written over these elements. A change at one joint necessarily entails a particular kind of change at the other. The preceding depicts the control principle identified at the outset of this chapter: Muscles are not controlled individually but are functionally linked with other muscles so as to form autonomous systems—coordinative structures. What pre-

FIG. 11.1.   In a skilled marksperson, any movement at the wrist is matched by an equal and opposite movement at the shoulder. This constraint over the joints keeps the gun on target.

viously was an aggregate of many degrees of freedom becomes a system of fewer degrees of freedom.

If you have ever tried to do a handstand, you can readily appreciate the need for organizing the separate parts of the body. One of the things you are trying to discover in learning how to stand on your hands is a way of linking or constraining those muscles involved so they become just a single entity. A change in one part of the body, the shoulders, must be perfectly matched by a change at the hips. If it isn't, you keep falling over. In part, learning to handstand is discovering the right kinds of constraint over the separate parts of the body. In the discovery of such constraints, effective control of the musculature is achieved through the reduction in the number of degrees of freedom that must be controlled independently. Let us explore this concept further using a detailed example.

FIG. 11.2.   When a person breathes, the backward movement of the thoracic region of the spine is matched by forward movement of the pelvic and cervical regions. This constraint over the relevant muscle groups keeps the head stable.

Imagine an aircraft having two wings, each with one aileron. The ailerons are used to control the roll of the aircraft. On the horizontal part of the tail fin are the left and right elevators that control the pitch of the aircraft. There is also a rudder that controls the aircraft's yaw. The rudder can move to the left or to the right, and the elevators and aileron can be raised or lowered. In short, the plane has five independent parts: two ailerons, two elevators, and a rudder (see Fig. 11.3). For simplicity, assume that these independent parts can each adopt one of nine positions at any time. The zero position is when the part is in its neutral position, for example, flush with the wing in the case of an aileron, flush with the tail fin in the case of the rudder. An aileron or an elevator can go four positions up ($+4$) and four positions down (-4). The rudder can move four positions to the right ($+4$) and four positions to the left (-4).

Imagine that you were the pilot of such a plane and had to control these pieces independently. You have five buttons in front of you with which you must control at any point in time the positions of both ailerons, both elevators, and the rudder. Obviously, controlling such a plane is not going to be easy—rapid adjustments in the flight pattern in order to accommodate to new conditions (say, an evasive maneuver) may prove impossible.

What is needed is a way of organizing the parts of the airplane so as to simplify its control without losing its desirable maneuverability. One way to do this is to link parts of the system together (see Fig. 11.3). Firstly, the aileron and the rudder can be linked into a functional relationship; when the aileron on the left goes up by one position, the rudder goes to the right by one position. This is a simple equation of constraint that says that the position of the left aileron equals the position of the rudder ($La = r$). Next, the right aileron can be linked to the rudder so that when the right aileron moves up the rudder moves to the left. In this case we have an equation of constraint that says that the position of the right aileron equals the position of the rudder but with opposite sign ($Ra = -r$). Think of what we are attempting to do. We are trying to make the airplane manageable. We want the airplane to be something that a pilot could actually fly. Initially, the airplane has five independent parts each capable of assuming nine different positions. A pilot would have great difficulty controlling this system. Now three of those parts have been banded together into a single entity, the aileron–rudder subsystem. The way that a beginner learns a skill is to "freeze out" some of the free variation of the body, so that it is not used, that is, not allowed into the activity. Our task is to make it possible for a pilot to be skillful

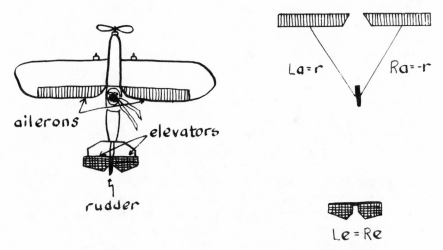

FIG. 11.3. An airplane of five freely moving parts (left) and how they might be linked by equations of constraint (right).

with this plane by likewise "freezing out" some degrees of freedom. This is accomplished by linking the ailerons and rudder with two equations of constraint. Very simply, when the left aileron moves up, the rudder moves to the right by the same amount; when the right aileron moves up, the rudder moves to the left by the same amount. In brief, there are two equations of constraint that apply to the aileron–rudder subsystem of the airplane.

Now let us recall and apply the formula for capturing the degrees of freedom of any system: $ND - C = df$. Remember that N stands for the number of elements. In the system being discussed here there are three elements—the two ailerons and the rudder. The dimensionality, D, of this system is 1; one coordinate or one dimension is needed to identify the position of an element. In other words, each element can move along only one axis going either above zero or below zero. As we just saw, this system now has two equations of constraint, C. So the number of degrees of freedom of the aileron–rudder system is 3 (elements) times 1 (Dimension), minus 2 (equations of constraint), or, in short, a system of one degree of freedom.

The concept that we are pursuing, that of muscle linkage or coordinative structure, suggests that muscles are brought together into similar types of collections; a number of relatively independent muscles are constrained to act as a unit. What does this achieve? In principle, it creates an autonomous (self-regulatory) entity. The skilled marksperson has found a way of organizing the muscles so that, when going into the aiming position, he or she "adopts" a particular equation of constraint over the joints. As in the analogy of the airplane, this constraint means that when the wrist joint goes so many degrees to the left, the shoulder joint must go so many degrees to the right, keeping the gun on target. A particular kind of equation of constraint has been "written," as it were, over the free parts of the body.

Returning to the airplane, the pilot's task can be simplified further by linking the elevators. If the left elevator goes up, the right one goes up by the same amount so that the position of the left elevator equals the position of the right elevator ($Le = Re$). This linkage produces another subsystem and results in an airplane that is even more manageable.

The procedure of making the airplane controllable through linkages can go a step further. The two subsystems, the aileron–rudder subsystem and the elevator subsystem, can be linked by using another equation of constraint. As the organization of the airplane now stands, these two subsystems are free to vary independently of each other; the elevator system can adjust independently of the aileron–rudder system. But they can be related to each other in a precise fashion by writing another equation of constraint. For example, let the positions in the aileron–rudder system always be some constant proportion of the positions in the elevator system, $ar = k(e)$. This simple constraint says that the elevator system must change in some constant ratio of changes in the aileron–rudder system. A link has been forged between the two subsystems. For the five elements that originally comprised five degrees of freedom, we now have four equations of constraint—two for the aileron–rudder system, one for the elevators, and one linking each of these two subsystems—thus leaving us with only one degree of freedom. We see, in short, that as the variable parts of the airplane are linked together the parts are no longer free to vary. Importantly, the procedure of linking can serve to eliminate as possible states those combinations that would result in potentially uncoordinated movements of the airplane (remember the many futile combinations of wheel positions of the car that were discussed in the previous chapter.

Now let us pull the strands of this story together. We have underscored two main problems. The first problem is the large number of degrees of freedom of the body that must be regulated. The second problem is what we have called context-conditioned variability, whether anatomical, mechanical, or physiological in source. When taken seriously these problems can be shown to have strong implications for how coordinated activity is achieved. One implication that we have been examining is that control and coordination cannot be in terms of individual muscles; they must be in terms of something larger—collections of muscles. Moreover, when these collections are constrained, they must compensate automatically to preserve the relationship of muscles within the collection, just as the position of the rudder and right aileron change automatically with a change in the position of the left aileron.

Let us now see how these slowly developing ideas are realized in a fairly complex form of real-life activity—locomotion. In discussing how locomotion is organized, we see the many concepts we have been wrestling with come into play.

Consider the step cycle of a single limb. Various positions of the limb during the step cycle are diagrammed in Fig. 11.4. In position A, the body weight is directly over the foot. In position B, the back leg is extended and the body weight is transferred so that it is centered forward of the foot. Next, the leg flexes as shown in position C, and finally it is extended in front of the torso (position D). So, starting at position A, the leg extends backward, flexes, extends forward and lands, the weight moves over the body, and the cycle starts again. These positions delineate four phases of the single-step cycle (see Fig. 11.5). Going from position B to position C is called flexion (F). Position C to position D marks off the first extension phase (E 1). From position D to position A is the second extension phase (E 2), and from position A to position B is the third extension phase (E 3).

In order to take a detailed look at the step cycle, we also need to distinguish between the support phase and the transfer phase. The support phase is when the leg is supporting the body weight, and it consists of E 2 and E 3. The transfer phase is when the shift from one position of support to the next occurs, and it consists of F and E 1.

Within the constraints imposed by the anatomy of a limb, the muscles of the

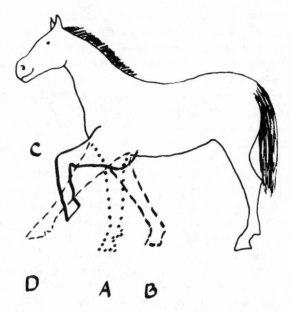

FIG. 11.4.   The step cycle of the single limb. See text for details.

hip, knee, and ankle may relate in many ways. One can jump, squat, or sit and wiggle the leg. But once locomotion starts, a remarkably systematic arrangement over the joints occurs, as can be appreciated by the equations of constraint that coordinate the extensors and the flexors of the limbs.

If you record the activity of the extensor muscles (those responsible for extending the leg) at each of the joints during locomotion, there is a constant

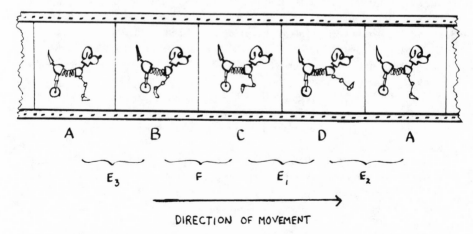

DIRECTION OF MOVEMENT

FIG. 11.5.   The step cycle of the single limb partitioned into phases of extension (E_1, E_2 and E_3) and flexion (F). See text for details.

relationship of the activity among the muscles, regardless of the speed of locomotion (Grillner, 1975). It is as if an equation of constraint is written over the extensors of the limb, preserving this invariant relationship. As the actual amounts of EMG activity in the extensor muscle groups change with velocity, the ratio of activity among those groups does not change. Suppose the extensor muscle group at the hip shows X amount of activity during locomotion, the group at the knee has Y amount of activity, and the group at the ankle has Z amount of activity. No matter how fast the animal is running, although the absolute values of X, Y and Z will change, the ratio of activity among the three muscle groups is always the same.

It is remarkable that, as the animal runs faster and changes gait, very few details of the step cycle undergo any change. This can be seen by breaking the step cycle into its component phases. Consider a simple plot in which the abscissa represents velocity of running and the ordinate represents amount of time spent in each phase (see Fig. 11.6). As the animal runs faster, the time spent in the transfer phase does not change, whereas the time taken in the support phase decreases considerably. In fact, the E 3 phase of support is the *only* part of the cycle that changes significantly (see Fig. 11.7). It gets shorter as the animal runs faster. The flexion activity of the step cycle is remarkably automatic; it will always bring the leg from position B to position C in approximately the same amount of time regardless of running speed. The duration of E 1 and E 2 change only slightly: it is only during the end of extension, at the boundary of the support

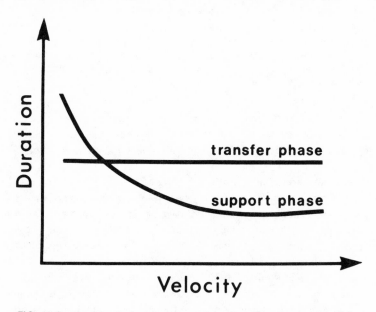

FIG. 11.6. As the velocity of running (*x*) increases, the duration (*y*) of the transfer phase remains essentially unchanged, but the duration of the support phase decreases markedly.

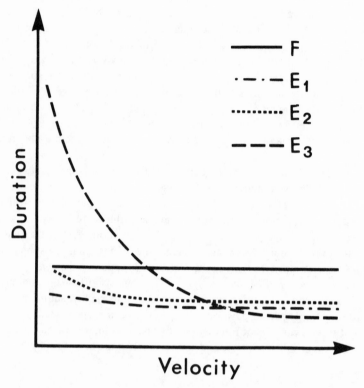

FIG. 11.7.   As the velocity (*x*) of running increases, the durations (*y*) of flexion (F), flexion to extension (E_1), and extension to landing (E_2) do not change. However, the duration from landing to the next flexion (E_3) decreases considerably as velocity increases.

and transfer phases, that some variation occurs. At that point the system can be modified. In fact, what we see is that running speed seems to be increased by applying more force during E 3, causing its total duration to shorten (Shik & Orlovskii, 1976).

Now let us turn to the notion of the nesting of coordinative structures. When we discussed the airplane organization, we wrote two equations of constraint to form the aileron–rudder subsystem and a third equation of constraint to form the elevator subsystem. Another equation of constraint written over the two subsystems allowed the "nesting" of these automatisms. With respect to locomotion, the discussion thus far has been limited to the systematic behavior of a single limb, and how that systematic behavior can be described in terms of muscle linkages—equations of constraint. We now turn to the systematic behavior of two and four legs in the locomoting of a four-legged animal and ask how this systematic behavior might be understood. Again, we find the airplane example to prove useful.

There are a number of gaits, or styles of coordination, available to the four-legged animal. These different styles can be characterized as different nestings of the single-limb step cycles. One style is the alternate-step gait in which the legs are one-half cycle out of phase. This is the gait used by humans for walking and running. When a four-legged animal uses an alternate-step gait, any given limb is always half a cycle out of phase with the other limb of the same girdle. So in an alternate-step gait (see Fig. 11.8), the two limbs at the shoulder are always half a cycle out of phase with each other. In effect, an equation of constraint links the two limbs such that, whatever the position of a given limb, the other limb of the same girdle must be in a specified position as defined by that equation. This is directly analogous to our airplane example—if the aileron is in one position, the rudder must be in some specific position defined by the equation. Experiments have been performed where an animal is running with one leg on one treadmill and the other leg on a faster treadmill; the second, faster limb is running in a shorter cycle than the first, yet the .5 out-of-phase relationship is preserved (Kulagin & Shik, 1970). In alternate-step gaits it is as if an equation of constraint functionally binds the limbs of a girdle, holding the limbs in a specified relationship.

We have considered an equation of constraint linking the muscles of a single leg, and an equation of constraint linking the two limbs of the same girdle. Consider a form of running in which both these equations of constraint are preserved. An additional constraint must hold to coordinate the two girdles. In the trot, the opposite limbs of the different girdles are synchronized so that, for example, the right limb at the hip girdle and the left limb at the shoulder girdle go through their cycles together. The cross limbs of different girdles are syn-

FIG. 11.8.   In the alternate-step gait, any given limb is always one-half cycle out of phase with the other limb of the same girdle.

chronized in trotting, whereas the limbs of the same girdle preserve a half-cycle out of phase relationship between them. As the animal switches into the rack, or pace, the limbs of the same side (and hence different girdles) are synchronized. Think now what that means. To do the trot, the opposite legs of different girdles are linked so as to be in phase; to do the pace or rack, the same-side limbs of different girdles are linked so as to be in phase (see Fig. 11.9).

We now have a family of equations of constraint. In alternate-step gaits only two equations of constraint are used at any one time. One constraint is needed over limbs of the same girdle and one constraint over limbs of different girdles. If we now break the constraint on limbs of the same girdle, just eliminate it, then the animal goes into a gallop. Notice in a gallop, limbs of the same girdle now move approximately in phase with each other, whereas limbs of the shoulder girdle and limbs of the hip girdle move approximately out of phase with each other (see Fig. 11.10). When an animal gallops, it is no longer necessary that the

FIG. 11.9. (Top) In the trot the opposite limbs of different girdles are synchronized.
(Bottom) In the rack, or pace, the limbs of the same side are synchronized.

two limbs on the same girdle be half a step out of phase. However, if you have ever closely watched a galloping animal, you will notice that the animal actually does not land with both limbs simultaneously. One limb lands very slightly before the other. It may be the case that a gallop is actually a synthesis of the two larger constraints—the one that defines the rack (ipsilateral, or same-side limbs synchronized) and the one that defines the trot (contralateral, or opposite-side synchronized). It may be that the combination of these two equations of constraint results in a gallop (see Fig. 11.10).

In these examples, a set of elements (muscles, joints, or limbs) are linked by means of a set of equations of constraint. Linking elements in this fashion reduces the number of degrees of freedom that must be controlled independently. This number is always smaller for a set of constrained elements than for a set of elements that are free to vary independently. Essentially, establishing linkages or constraints produces a system in which effective coordination of elements is possible. We now go a step further and ask: What *kind* of system or device is produced when elements of the motor apparatus are linked by equations of constraint? A major clue is provided by the fact that a coordinative structure is a device which adjusts itself automatically to changing external conditions in the sense of reaching the same final position from any initial position.

There is a very simple and commonplace device that exhibits the property just noted—a mass-spring system. A mass-spring system is simply a spring attached at one end to a fixed support and at the other end to a mass (see Fig. 11.11).

FIG. 11.10.   In the gallop, limbs of the same girdle are in phase with each other. The constraint linking limbs of different girdles appears to be a synthesis of the rack (same-side limbs synchronized) and the trot (opposite limbs of different girdles synchronized).

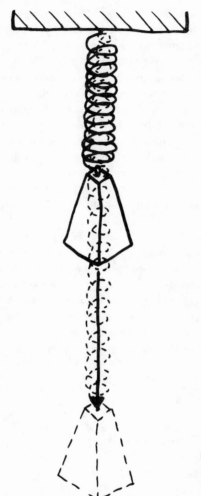

FIG. 11.11. A mass-spring system, consisting of spring attached at one end to a fixed support and at the other end to a mass.

When the mass is pulled it stretches the spring. When let go, the mass (and spring) oscillates eventually coming to rest at some position. When the mass is pushed it compresses the spring; releasing the spring again causes the mass (and spring) to oscillate. However, the system will eventually come to rest at exactly the same equilibrium position as it assumed after the spring was pulled. Given a mass-spring system displacing the mass by pulling or pushing does not affect the final equilibrium position, the length of the spring at rest. Nor is this final equilibrium position affected by the *amount* that the mass is displaced. In sum, the system equilibrates at some constant length of spring regardless of initial conditions.

Notice another characteristic of the mass-spring system: Not only does it get to where it is going regardless of initial conditions, but it does so without any "homunculus" or external controller directing it. The spring adjusts automatically to changes in its context. Picture the situation in which the adjustments of the spring are not automatic but must be controlled directly by the "little man in the head" introduced in Chapter 10. The homunculus sitting outside the mass-spring system must detect the changes in initial conditions and compare the present location of the mass spring to some reference value representing the desired final position of the spring. The homunculus must compute the necessary correction of the mass-spring trajectory and then relay appropriate commands to the mass spring so that the "error"—the distance from equilibrium—is reduced. A system of this sort places an enormous burden of computation on the controller of the spring. Unfortunately, any information that is available to the controller will always arrive too late to be useful. By the time the controller receives information concerning where the spring is in its trajectory, the spring will have already moved into a new position. Thus, the controller would have to correct for more than the discrepancy between where the spring is and where it should be. The controller would also have to correct for the discrepancy between its information about the position of the spring, and the position to which the spring has moved since that information was sampled.

The reality of the mass-spring system, and other oscillatory systems, is that no such "error-correction" is necessary. The system adjusts itself automatically without choice or computation and without increasing the number of degrees of freedom that must be regulated independently. No controller or tracking device is necessary. The parameters of the system, the length and stiffness of the spring and the weight of the mass, uniquely determine the equilibrium position of the mass spring.

Do normal movements of a biological system exhibit the same properties as oscillatory systems? Some experiments suggest that they do: Movements at the elbow (Fel'dman, 1966) and finger movements (Kelso, 1977), for example, act analogous to a mass-spring system. In one experiment subjects moved their forefinger some distance of their own choosing. Their finger was then passively moved by the experimenter to some other location. The subjects' task was to reproduce either the final position or the amplitude of the first voluntary movement. Let us consider this experiment (Kelso, 1977) in some detail.

Suppose that your finger is in a position forming a 180° angle with respect to the palm of your hand (S_1 in Fig. 11.12). You are now instructed to produce a finger movement of your own choosing and let us say that you move the finger to a position that is at a 130° angle with respect to your palm (P/A in Fig. 11.12). This movement can also be described as being of a certain amplitude, that is, a movement of 50°. The experimenter then moves your finger to some starting position different from the original angle of 180°, say 200°, and asks you to reproduce either the final position of a 130° angle, or to reproduce the movement amplitude of 50°. The task is complicated by the fact that two sources of information that are normally available to you have been removed. You cannot see your

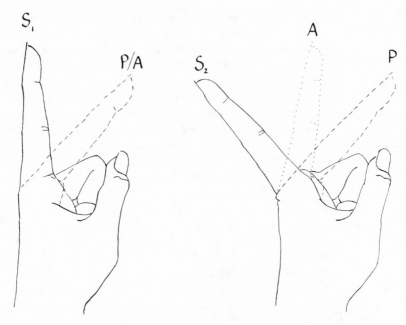

FIG. 11.12.   In the experiments by Kelso (1977), subjects moved their forefinger from an initial starting position (S_1) to some location of their own choosing. Their finger was then passively moved to a different starting position (S_2). The subject's task was to reproduce either the amplitude (A) or the final position (P) of the first movement.

finger, nor can you feel your finger's location. Information from your joint and skin receptors has been eliminated by inflating a cuff around your wrist until the blood flow to the finger is blocked.

So, you attempt to reproduce the amplitude or final position of your previous movement without being able to see or feel what you are doing. As it happens, you will not be very accurate at reproducing the amplitude of your movement. But you will be very accurate at reproducing the final location of your movement. In fact, your ability to reproduce the final position under the conditions of sensory deprivation is as good as when normal skin and joint receptor information is available to you.

The major thing to be appreciated is that your finger movements are not impaired by context-conditioned variability; specifically, they exhibit the property of equifinality. Regardless of where your second movement starts from, you can still reproduce the final position accurately. Moreover, the final position is achieved automatically. It seems unlikely that the distance of the finger from the desired position is computed by a homunculus or other controller with the necessary adjustments relayed as commands to the relevant muscles. After all, no information is available as to where the finger is, and no "error-correction computation" is possible.

To summarize: We have used the analogy of an oscillatory system to illustrate the kind of device produced when muscles are linked by equations of constraint. This device has many advantages over the individual control of free variables. The advantage we have underscored here is that it is able to equilibrate at some invariant position, adjusting automatically for changing initial conditions.

But there are other advantages of this identity between coordinative structure and oscillatory system that may well be of greater significance. We have been speaking of a constrained collection of muscles as a mass-spring system. It happens to be the case that there are a variety of oscillatory mechanisms of which the mass-spring system is just one, and it is a task for science to determine precisely what kind of oscillator best defines a coordinative structure. In these concluding remarks we wish to simply hint at the possibility that coordinative structures are not strictly oscillators of the familiar mass-spring type but oscillators of a somewhat different kind called limit-cycle oscillators (Kugler, Kelso, & Turvey, in press). The reader need not be bothered by the very formal distinctions that mathematicians and physicists draw between these two kinds of oscillators; it is only important for present purposes to note that limit-cycle oscillators have a property of some consequence for understanding the coordination and control of movement that oscillators of the typical mass-spring type do not possess. Limit-cycle oscillators are mutually synchronizing; that is, where two or more limit-cycle oscillators are interacting, they can influence each other's behavior such that eventually they behave as one. This phenomenon of mutual synchronization—or *entrainment* as it is most commonly called—was first observed serendipitiously (that is, by chance!) by Huygens in the 18th century. He noticed that, when two clocks (and a clock, it should be highlighted, is an oscillatory mechanism with *sustained* oscillations) running at different speeds were both hung on the same thin backboard, they became synchronized and kept identical time. Apparently, the ticking of one clock was transmitted through the thin backboard to the other clock, and vice versa, until eventually the two clocks synchronized. This phenomenon of entrainment appears to occur in movement. Consider, for example, a dog locomoting in one of the gaits described previously. If the step cycle of one limb is perturbed for a brief moment so that it is out of phase with the three other limbs, the step cycles of the three other limbs will change, until, within a few, full cycles, all four limbs are again in the phase relations appropriate to the gait (Shik & Orlovskii, 1965). Entrainment may also be manifest as a "limitation" on activity. Witness the difficulty of performing simultaneously two different rhythms, one with one arm and one with the other. There is an impression of one of the rhythms dominating the other or of the two rhythms converging on a compromise rhythm (von Holst, 1973).

At all events, if constrained collections of muscles are instances of limit-cycle oscillators, then the property of mutual synchronization provides a means by which a good deal of coordination among coordinative structures can be maintained "for free," as it were, without burdening an executive system. In short, entrainment as a property of neuromuscular systems would help to resolve the puzzle of Bernstein, identified at the outset of this chapter.

ACKNOWLEDGMENTS

The writing of this chapter was supported in part by the following grants awarded to the Haskins Laboratories: NICHD Grant HD-01994, NIH Grant NS-13870 and NIH Grant NS-13617. The figures were done gratis by Claudia Carello, to whom the authors are most grateful.

REFERENCES

Arutyunyan, G. H., Gurfinkel, V. S., & Mirsky, M. L. Investigation of aiming at a target. *Biophysics*, 1969, *13*, 536-538.

Fel'dman, A. G. Functional tuning of the nervous system during control of movement or maintenance of a steady posture—III: Mechanographic analysis of the execution by man of the simplest motor tasks. *Biophysics*, 1966, *11*, 766-775.

Gel'fand, I. M., Gurfinkel, V. S., Tsetlin, M. L., & Shik, M. L. Some problems in the analysis of movements. In I. M. Gel'fand, V. S. Gurfinkel, S. V. Fomin, & M. L. Tsetlin (Eds.), *Models of the structural-functional organization of certain biological systems*. Cambridge: MIT Press, 1971.

Grillner, S. Locomotion in vertebrates: Central mechanisms and reflex interaction. *Physiological Reviews*, 1975, *55*, 247-304.

Gurfinkel, V. S., Kots, Ya. M., Pal'tsev, Ye. I., & Fel'dman, A. G. The compensation of respiratory disturbances of the organization of interarticular interaction. In I. M. Gel'fand, V. S. Gurfinkel, S. V. Fomin, & M. L. Tsetlin (Eds.), *Models of the structural-functional organization of certain biological systems*. Cambridge: MIT Press, 1971.

Holst, E. von. *The behavioral physiology of animal and man: The collected papers of Erich von Holst* (Vol. 1). London: Methuen Ltd, 1973.

Kelso, J. A. S. Motor control mechanisms underlying human movement reproduction. *Journal of Experimental Psychology*, 1977, *3*, 529-543.

Kugler, P. N., Kelso, J. A. S., & Turvey, M. T. Coordination and control in naturally developing systems. In J. A. S. Kelso & J. C. Clark (Eds.), *The development of movement coordination and control*. London, New York: Wiley, in press.

Kulagin, A. S., & Shik, M. L. Interaction of symmetrical limbs during controlled locomotions. *Biophysics*, 1970, *15*, 171-178.

Shik, M. L., & Orlovskii, G. N. Coordination of the limbs during running of the dog. *Biophysics*, 1965, *10*, 1148-1159.

Shik, M. L., & Orlovskii, G. N. Neurophysiology of locomotor automatism. *Physiological Reviews*, 1976, *56*, 465-501.

12

The Bernstein Perspective: III. Tuning of Coordinative Structures with Special Reference to Perception

Hollis L. Fitch,
Betty Tuller,
M. T. Turvey
University of Connecticut
and
Haskins Laboratories

Following Bernstein, we have in the last two chapters proposed a view of motor control whose strategy is to leave as little explanatory power as possible residing in a "homunculus." In older models, this theoretical entity was asked to make an overwhelming number of decisions (about individual muscle states), requiring an overwhelming amount of information (about the state of the body and the world). The job of dealing with all possible combinations of perceptual states is equal in difficulty to (and just as intractable as) the job of dealing with all combinations of muscle states. Bernstein saw these as complementary problems; it is the perceptual side of the dilemma that we address in this chapter. We have seen how a coordinative structure style of organization can reduce the number of executive decisions that need to be made. Now we want to see how the perceptual information can modulate or tune the coordinative structures without intervention from a super-human homunculus.

Notice that it is not desirable to reduce the degrees of freedom of the muscle system to zero. With no degrees of freedom, an act would be insensitive to changes in its context. It would be a fixed pattern, so stereotyped that adjustments to changes in the environment in which the action occurred would be impossible. The organization that we desire is one that limits the possible combinations of muscle values but still allows some flexibility. Coordinative structures accomplish this: The equation of constraint defining the coordinative structure preserves a relationship among the variables but still allows its variables to take on different values. This reduces the number of degrees of freedom that must be controlled but allows the system to be sensitive to its context. The coordinative structure is flexible and may be "tuned" to its environment.

How might the tuning of a coordinative structure occur? What kinds of information set the specific values of those parameters that are free to vary? In order to be adaptive, the specific values should change with changes in the environment. It is therefore reasonable to look to a system sensitive to the environment—the perceptual system—to provide some of the values.

Before considering how the perceptual system might provide values for parameters of the action system, it would be useful to consider more closely the kind of changes that we would want the perceptual system to regulate. What parameters of coordinative structures may be "tuned" by the perceptual system?

Coordinated movements characteristically exhibit a fixed relationship among the variables of the system but allow the variables to assume different absolute values. We say that coordinated movements exhibit relational (sometimes called structural) invariance over metrical change. The distinction between the relational specification and the metrical specification for a movement is a fundamental one. To use the analogy of the airplane once more, we can see that the relationship among the parts of the aileron–rudder system remains the same $(La = r - Ra)$ no matter how large or small the airplane's movements, but the absolute values (positions) of all the parts change depending on the actual amount of movement. We saw from studies of locomotion that there is a constant relationship among the extensor muscles of a limb, expressed as a ratio of EMG activity, even though the absolute levels of activity in these muscles varied with the velocity of locomotion.

The principle of relational invariance over metrical change has also been demonstrated in the groups of muscles that are responsible for preserving a person's balance. When a person standing in a well-balanced position is suddenly disturbed, he or she will make rapid alterations of the body so that balance is preserved under the new conditions. The muscle activity that occurs in the act of regaining balance after a disturbance shows a familiar characteristic: The absolute amount of activity in the muscles at the hip, knee, and ankle varies, but the ratio of activity among those muscles remains unaltered (Nashner, 1977).

The metrical specification of the level of activity can be considered a tuning of the coordinative structure. Tuning an otherwise invariant structure is an efficient way of producing flexibility with a minimal amount of reorganization. The parameters that we would ask perceptual information to regulate, then, are few.

With the understanding that we are dealing with a system that requires specification of only a minimal number of parameters to produce a maximal amount of behavioral change, let us return to the question of how the perception and action systems might fit together.

Apply our earlier discussion of the homunculus to the relation between the perception and action systems. We do not want a model in which the brain interprets the perceptual information, decides what portion of the information to supply a given coordinative structure, and when to supply it. Instead, the organization of the coordinative structure should be such as to accept only certain information at certain times. A metaphor for this concept that may help is called the piano-roll metaphor. Imagine that you have a roll of player piano music that is unfurling and that a light is shining down on it. No light will shine through most of the unfurling paper, because the paper is opaque. But if there are holes at certain points in the piano roll, the light will get through at these points. The coordinative structure is like the piano roll—it lets the "light" in at only those points where appropriate, according to its own organization. Remember that when an animal runs quickly, many aspects of the step cycle are identical to when the animal runs slowly. The E3 phase at the end of support is the only part of the cycle that changes significantly, getting shorter as the animal runs faster. The shortening of the E3 phase is brought about by the animal allowing more force to be applied during E3, but not during any other phase of the cycle. The energy that is realized as force is like the light in our piano-roll metaphor—continually available but only effective at certain times. The organization of the coordinative structures for the step cycle determines what those times are. The force, and the

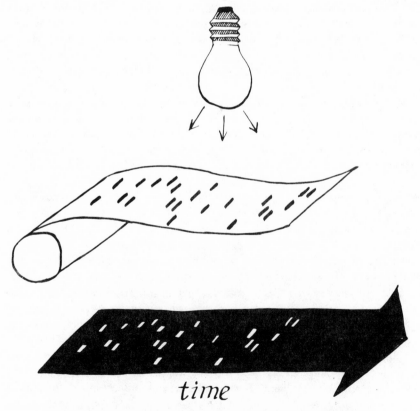

time

FIG. 12.1.   A piano-roll metaphor for the tuning of coordinative structures.

light in our metaphor, are sources of tuning for the modulable aspects of coordinative structures. Generally speaking, information may tune the action system only at the appropriate points.

An example of a mechanical system that uses a similar principle is a pendulum clock (Kugler, Kelso, & Turvey, 1980). The clock is kept running due to the potential energy stored in a hanging weight, which, when it drops, can turn a wheel. The potential energy is always present but is delivered—converted into kinetic energy—only at certain points in the pendulum swing. When the pendulum is at the very end of its arc, it has the least amount of kinetic energy and is most easily affected by outside forces. Because of the way that the pendulum and the wheel with the attached weight are connected, it is just at this point in the pendulum swing that the wheel is momentarily freed. The weight drops, causing the wheel to rotate, which in turn (via that connection) pushes the pendulum back in the other direction. The point is that there is not a separate monitoring device dictating when to deliver force to the pendulum. The organization of the mechanism itself, like that of the player-piano roll or the coordinative structure, allows the continuously available potential energy of the weight, like the light, to have an affect only at those points where appropriate. In conventional physiological terms we would say that a tonic (continuous) source exerts a phasic (periodic) influence.

The light to a perceiver can be a very rich source of tuning information. James J. Gibson (1966, 1979) has described that light in terms of what he calls the optic array. This description takes into account the fact that the light from any source is structured by the various surfaces off of which it reflects. The color, texture, and angle of inclination of each surface will pattern the light in characteristic ways. The result is a reverberating flux of light waves, termed the optic array. Our environment structures the media that surround us, and it is this structure to which our perceptual systems can become sensitive.

The optic array is a more molar level of description of the light than the usual one couched solely in terms of wavelength and intensity. The smallest differentiable unit in the optic array—an optic element, corresponding to a texture element in the environment—is defined as a homogeneous region bounded by a change in wavelength or intensity. But the description does not stop there. The way that these smallest units are constrained, or patterned over space and over time, yields valuable information to a perceiver. If a person moves forward in a stable environment, the total optic array will undergo an outward-flow pattern, or expansion, of the optical texture (see Fig. 12.2). Moving backward causes an inward flow, or contraction, of the optical texture. If a person does not move the body forward or backward but rotates about the longitudinal axis, the borders of the field of view change and the size of the optical texture units stay constant. If a person does not move at all and something in the environment moves toward the person, there will be a local expansion in the optic array and a deletion of optical

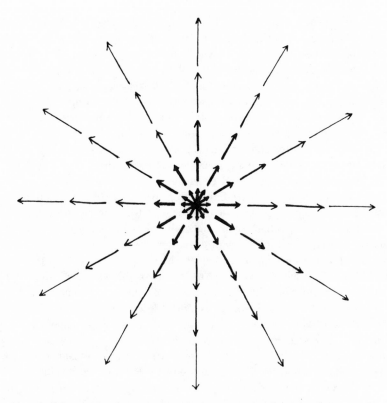

FIG. 12.2.   Flow pattern of optic elements in expanding optic array.

texture from those things behind the approaching object. In principle, there is an invariant pattern of change for every type of movement.

Note that the analysis of the transforming optic array depends on the point of observation. There is a principled difference in the light to each point of observation. In this way, there is information not only about the layout of the surfaces but also about the environment *in relation to the observer*. This latter type of information can be called *exproprioceptive* (Lee, 1978), to contrast with exteroceptive information (about the layout of the environment) and proprioceptive information (about the relation of body parts).

A closer examination of these three types of information is warranted. Exteroceptive information concerns the properties of the environment such as objects, brinks, and surfaces, and how these properties are changing. This type of information is conveyed by local changes in the pattern of the optic array.

Proprioceptive information can also be provided by local changes in the pattern of light. However, the changes in pattern occur in those regions of the visual field that are structured by the observer's body. The expansion of texture elements in the region of the lower arm as the elbow is flexed is proprioceptive information for the actor. Similarly, when a person plays tennis, the tennis racket may be considered an extension of the player's arm. In this way, the visual information regarding the position of the tennis racket with respect to the player's trunk may be considered proprioceptive information. Acquiring a skill such as tennis includes becoming sensitive to this proprioceptive information.

Exproprioceptive information is provided by a third type of change in the optical pattern. When the body moves as a whole within the current layout of the environment, there is global optical change, such as the inward or outward flow of the optical texture. The focus of expansion or contraction indicates the point toward which the observer is heading or from which the observer is retreating. You can think of rules to guide an actor's behavior based on visual exproprioceptive information: To approach, make the global array expand; to steer toward an object, make that object the focus of expansion.

We now turn to some experiments in which expropriospecific information was manipulated. They show us precisely the nature of the optical information that specifies our relationship to the environment. Imagine yourself in a room, standing on a floor that is fixed. However, the room itself is not fixed—the walls and ceiling can be moved. Suddenly the room moves toward you. Although you are standing solidly on the ground, the moving room results in global optical expansion, which normally specifies that you are moving forward. What happens when the optical changes specify that you are moving, but you are actually standing still? You immediately correct for the optical change, falling backward in an attempt to preserve your relationship with the room. If the room is made to swing away from you, the optical change specifies that you must be falling backward. In compensation, you tilt forward (Lee & Lishman, 1974).

What must be understood is that in the course of performing any activity, the perceptual information available is of these three kinds. In order to guide any activity you need to be able to pick up on the properties of the environment, you need to have some appreciation of where your limbs are with respect to each other, and you need to know where you are with respect to the layout of the environment.

Consider exproprioceptive information in the expanding optic array as a source of information for perceptual tuning of the action system. One form of exproprioceptive information that has been quantified mathematically is the "time-to-contact" between an object and an observer. For an object approaching an observer at a constant velocity, time-to-contact is given by the rate of magnification of the optical texture. Obviously, time-to-contact is a variable you would want to be sensitive to, whether you are walking through a crowded room, catching a ball, or driving a car. It has been shown, for example, that this information can be used by a driver to control braking of an automobile (Lee, 1976).

A nice demonstration of the principle mentioned at the
chapter—that of varying a minimal number of parameters to pr
amount of behavioral change—is provided by another example o.
ity that seems to be regulated with regard to time-to-contact. The
of baseball batting. Batters vary how fast they step toward the pit\   ᵤpen
their stance) as a direct function of the speed of the pitched ball; that ᵤ, the faster
the ball, the faster the opening step. This allows the batter to keep the duration of
the swing itself constant. The swing can then be very regular, making maximal
use of reactive forces and employing an invariant relational specification over the
muscle groups involved (Fitch & Turvey, 1978; Hubbard & Seng, 1954).

The importance of visual exproprioceptive information has been shown not
only at the behavioral level for the control of posture (as in the swinging room)
and skilled activity (as in driving and batting) but also at a more physiological
level. Visual exproprioceptive information is effective in biasing reflexes underlying activities. Optical information specific to a cat's orientation to the environment influences the activity in the cat's spinal motoneurons. A large disk of
colored dots was rotated in front of a cat's line of sight to imitate the optical flow
that would result from tilting. When the disk was rotated to the left (indicating a
tilt to the right), the extensor reflexes on the right side of the cat were enhanced
and the flexor reflexes on the left side were enhanced (Thoden, Dichgans, &
Savadis, 1977). Had the cat actually been tilted in the manner specified by the
optical flow, this would have had the effect of righting the cat. These results are
comparable to people's postural changes when placed in the swinging room.

Optical information has also been found to affect muscle reflexes in people. In
one experiment, subjects were asked to fall forward, hands first, onto a platform
(see Fig. 12.3). This platform could be tilted at various angles away from the
body. The electromyographic activity in the triceps, which were used to extend
the arm and brace against the fall, was monitored during the self-initiated fall
toward the platform. When subjects were able to see the platform, the time of the
onset of the EMG activity varied so that it always began a constant amount of
time before impact, no matter how far away the platform was. Only if the
subjects were blindfolded and had no way of knowing when impact would occur
was the muscle response time stereotyped, starting always at the beginning of the
fall (Dietz & Noth, 1978).

Although we have been examining the role of optical information in perceptual tuning of the action system, we should note that the information needed to
tune muscle systems is not tied to a particular sense modality. Experiments on
vision substitution devices for the blind indicate that vision is not the only
modality sensitive to rate of expansion as a specification of impending collision.
One vision substitution system that has been developed transmits a pattern of
intensity differences from a portable television camera to a bank of mechanical
vibrators on a subject's back. This matrix of vibrators acts like a "tactile" array,
changing with the optic array of the camera. Once, while testing this device, the

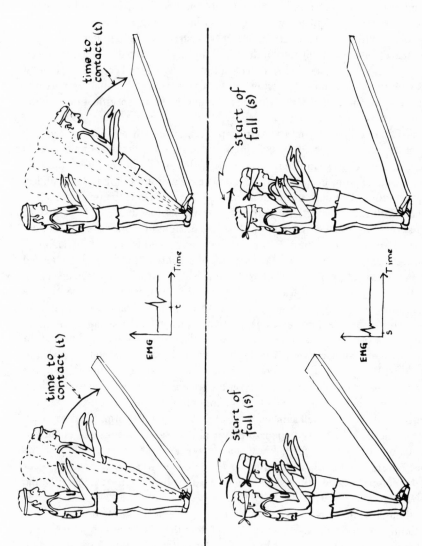

FIG. 12.3. When a person falls forward, visual information about his relationship to the platform (time-to-contact) regulates the onset of EMG activity in those muscles that brace against impact.

experimenter accidentally moved the zoom lens of the camera causing a simultaneous change in all elements of the tactile array on the subject's back. The subject showed a startle reaction, throwing his head back to avoid the "approaching" object (White, Saunders, Scadden, Bach-Y-Rita & Collins, 1970). The expanding tactile array, just like an expanding optic array, specifies that the observer is about to make contact with a substantial surface.

Imminent collison can also, evidently, be conveyed by sound. Hearing has now been implicated as the basis of what was first called "facial vision," a facility that allows a blind person to detect and avoid large obstacles. It seems that sensitivity to the exproprioceptive information is not the exclusive domain of vision. A fundamental understanding is that there may be many sources of tuning information for the muscle systems, and that these sources may all be talking the same "language."

Now consider that not only are the different perceptual systems sources of tuning for the muscle systems but that the muscle systems bias or tune each other. As you turn your head to one side, there is a bias toward extending the arm on the side of the body to which your head is turned, and a bias toward flexing the arm on the opposite side. Of course, you do not see these arm movements—turning the head biases, gives a preference to, a certain type of movement without activating the movement. Turning the head seems to prime the system for extension on the side to which the head is facing and flexion on the opposite side. As one part of the body changes with reference to another part, a tuning or modulation of the spinal organization takes place (Fukuda, 1961).

Another example of this type of tuning comes from experiments with cats. When the cat looks up, stretching the eye muscles, there is a biasing of the spinal cord for the front legs to extend. When the eyes look down, there is a bias set up in the spinal cord for the front legs to flex (Easton, 1972).

We are trying to avoid a theory in which a general-purpose man (or cat) in the head gets information in different languages (from the muscles, the eyes, the ears, etc.), acts as a multilingual interpreter, decides what all the sources of information combined should mean for each specific muscle group, and then sends different messages (in possibly yet another language) to each unit. In the perspective pursued in this chapter and the preceding two, the subparts of the perception and action systems are thought of as pieces of a jigsaw puzzle that are made to fit each other.

Let us examine this fitting together in two large-scale systems. We can call them the posture-preserving system and the transport system. The first defines a class of movements that are concerned with keeping the body upright. Superimposed on these postural movements are movements of the body or parts of the body with respect to parts of the environment. These can be called transport movements.

Any activity is performed in terms of these two classes of movements. You are sensitive to what movements are possible given your postural state; for example, you appreciate that you cannot hit a tennis ball if you are rolling over on the grass. To hit the ball effectively requires that your posture be relatively upright. But every time you move, that movement acts to disturb the upright posture. You must be sensitive to what you can do and still remain upright. You have some understanding of how far you can reach, for example, without falling over. In short, in producing transport movements you are respectful of what can be called the region of reversibility—a region in which for any movement you make that puts you off balance there is another movement you can make that restores your balance. Optical information can potentially provide very fine tuning of the postural system. As we saw, when the whole pattern of light at the eye changes in one overall way, that specifies a change in your relationship to the environment and consequently a change in the region of reversibility. If this expropriospecific information is disturbed, as in the swinging-room experiments, balance is also disturbed. It is very difficult to learn and maintain a new posture (such as a basic Charlie Chaplin pose) when the room is oscillating. Given a system engineered to preserve upright posture, one must choose transport movements that will not violate the region of reversibility.

Think again about performing a skill, such as playing tennis. The player must choose transport movements with respect to the region of reversibility for that act, discovering the postural consequences of different transport movements. A certain action to bring about a forehand stroke will have certain consequences for the player's postural relationship to the environment. What defines the region of reversibility is specific to the skill at hand. The transport movements must be tailored to the posture-preserving system.

Likewise, the posture-preserving system is tailored to the transport movements. Whenever you make any transport movement, it is anticipated by adjustments in the rest of the body that guarantee that the movement will not disturb overall balance. When you raise your arm from the shoulder, the first sign of activity in the relevant arm muscles is preceded by changes in activity of leg and back muscle groups (Belenkii, Gurfinkel, & Pal'tsev, 1967). Different transport movements are preceded by different postural adjustments. Any transport movement is anticipated by *exactly* those adjustments that will preserve posture.

Thus, the transport and postural systems constrain each other. The relation between these systems is not that one commands or dominates the other, but they relate in a fashion that we would call free dominance. They operate cooperatively. We submit that a good deal of skill acquisition focuses on discovering the relationship between these two systems: You must develop some sensitivity to the region of reversibility for a given task and to the postural consequences of any transport movement. On the basis of this developing sensitivity, you learn to perform skills like tennis and gymnastic routines.

To conclude, what we sought to do in this chapter was to show how perception may be organized in a way that complements the organization of the motor apparatus in the performance of acts. Such complementation is a further step in the direction of pruning the duties of the homunculus, a task that we have identified with Bernstein's goal of understanding how the many degrees of freedom of the body are systematically regulated in action, without substantial reliance on an intelligent executive system.

ACKNOWLEDGMENTS

The writing of this chapter was supported in part by the following grants awarded to the Haskins Laboratories: NICHD Grant HD–01994, NIH Grant NS–13870, and NIH Grant NS–13617. The figures were done gratis by Claudia Carello, to whom the authors are most grateful.

REFERENCES

Belenkii, V. Yi., Gurfinkel, V. S., & Pal'tsev, Ye. I. Elements of control of voluntary movements. *Biophysics*, 1967, *12*, 154–161.

Dietz, V., & Noth, J. Preinnervation and stretch responses of triceps bracchii in man falling with and without visual control. *Brain Research*, 1978, *142*, 576–579.

Easton, T. A. Patterned inhibition from single-eye muscle stretch in the cat. *Experimental Neurology*, 1972, *34*, 497–510.

Fitch, H. L., & Turvey, M. T. On the control of activity: Some remarks from an ecological point of view. In Landers & Christina (Eds.), *Psychology of motor behavior and sport*. Champaign, Ill.: Human Kinetics, 1978.

Fukuda, T. Studies on human dynamic postures from the viewpoint of postural reflexes. *Acta Oto-Laryngologica*, 1961, Suppl. 161.

Gibson, J. J. *The senses considered as perceptual systems*. Boston: Houghton–Mifflin, 1966.

Gibson, J. J. *An ecological approach to visual perception*. Boston: Houghton–Mifflin, 1979.

Hubbard, A. W., & Seng, C. N. Visual movements of batters. *Research Quarterly*, 1954, *25*, 42–57.

Kugler, P. N., Kelso, J. A. S., & Turvey, M. T. On the concept of coordinative structures as dissipative structures: I. Theoretical lines of convergence. In G. E. Stelmach & J. Requin (Eds.), *Tutorials in motor behavior*. Amsterdam: North-Holland, 1980.

Lee, D. N. A theory of visual control of braking based on information about time-to-collison. *Perception*, 1976, *5*, 437–459.

Lee, D. N. On the functions of vision. In H. Pick & E. Saltzman (Eds.), *Modes of perceiving*. Hillsdale, N.J.: Lawrence Erlbaum Associates, 1978.

Lee, D. N., & Lishman, J. R. Visual proprioceptive control of stance. *J. of Human Movement Studies*, 1974, *1*, 87–95.

Nashner, L. M. Fixed patterns of rapid postural responses among leg muscles during stance. *Experimental Brain Research*, 1977, *30*, 13–24.

Thoden, U., Dichgans, J., & Savadis, Th. Direction specific optokinetic modulation of monosynaptic hindlimb reflexes in cats. *Experimental Brain Research*, 1977, *30*, 155–160.

White, B. W., Saunders, F. A., Scadden, L., Bach-Y-Rita, P., & Collins, C. C. Seeing with the skin. *Perception & Psychophysics*, 1970, *7*, 23–27.

Epilogue: Two Strategies for Investigating Action

J. A. Scott Kelso
Haskins Laboratories and
The University of Connecticut

When one thinks about it, much of this book has to do with questions of the following type: When animals and people move about in their environment in an apparently purposeful fashion, what is lawful about their behavior? And, if there are identifiable, law-like regularities in their acts, how do we—as students of motor behavior—understand them?

In the early chapters of the book there is represented a single set of solutions to these questions. Such solutions revolve around hypothetical constructs like the perceptual traces, reference mechanisms, and comparators that are common in cybernetic, closed-loop systems, or the motor programs and schemata that have their origins in computer technology. We can call this set of solutions "artifactual," in the sense that acting humans are compared to machines (servomechanisms and computers) provided with means of control and regulation. I think it is quite clear that this class of model has dominated research and thinking in the 1970s and is certainly well-represented in the chapters by Stelmach, Schmidt, and Keele. Along with promoting a great deal of laboratory activity, the artifactual approach has allowed us to conceptualize the underlying "processes" that may guide human activity. I have little doubt that the artifactual approach will continue to play a major role in movement science for many years to come. It embodies many attractive features that appeal to the scientist, not least of which as is its apparent testability. Questions like: Is feedback important?; which modality (vision or proprioception) is more powerful for regulating activity?; are recall and recognition fundamentally different motor memory processes?; what is "contained" in the motor program?; how abstract is a motor schema's representation?; do we program movements or muscles?; and so on, all seem relevant to an understanding of movement. Most of these issues and many related ones have been adequately discussed at various points in this book.

In this final note, however, I want to offer a different perspective on problems of movement that follows on from some of the ideas introduced in later chapters by Michael Turvey, Betty Tuller, and Hollis Fitch. I do this because I think that it is sometimes very useful not only to question the current zeitgeist of the times but to sensitize the reader to a point I made at the beginning of the book; namely, that there is seldom any absolute truth in science. Just because an approach is popular does not mean that it has captured the guts of the problem. In the case of movement there is the obvious possibility that the solutions offered for the control and regulation of machines may have very little to do with the regularities that animals display when they move. The assumptions that one starts off with about the workings of animals as machines may be revealed as erroneous once a fuller understanding of the relationship between animal and environment becomes available.

Even at this point—as the 1980s are upon us—there are grounds for questioning the validity of the artifactual perspective. One concern is worth highlighting—even though philosophical in nature—if only because it is often ignored by psychologists and neuroscientists. It goes like this. When trying to understand complex systems such as how an animal's movements are controlled, we often create some analogous device (like a program or a perceptual trace) and ascribe to the device a principal role in the control process. These devices are what we call *representations* in that they represent or embody—usually in the animal's brain—the activity about to be revealed in the animal's movements. Consider the idea of a motor program, for example, defined as an abstract representation of a movement sequence stored in memory. One problem with this view is that a program necessarily implicates a user (with goals and interests) very much like the animal that science is trying to explain. Philosophers refer to this problem as an infinite regress, and to be quite blunt there is simply no easy way around it (Dennett, 1978; Searle, 1980). Similarly, we can talk about the referent values in servomechanisms, but where, one asks, do these referent values come from? If the response is that these values are simply the output of higher-order servomechanisms, then again an infinite regress is created. Someone or some thing must put the referent value in there to begin with. In psychology and the neurosciences this intelligent controller is sometimes called the homunculus (if male!), or feminicula (if female!), or more neutrally, the "ghost in the machine" (Koestler & Smythies, 1969).

Now all this probably means very little to the person doing experiments on discrete limb movements, or the coach trying to improve athletic performance, or the teacher of movement education, but it has serious implications for the theorist who is trying to provide a principled account of motor behavior. It means simply that there cannot be an adequate account of action in psychological or physiological terms until: (1) the presence of the "ghost" is explained; or (2) alternative accounts are offered in which the ghost is banished forever. Because I (and everybody else) am unable to say anything sensible about strategy (1), let me pursue strategy (2), in a rather more concrete fashion.

What I am saying amounts to this: In trying to understand complex behavior, movement science often attributes a large portion of that behavior to an intelligent executive component. It ascribes the order and regularity evident in an animal's action to a device that contains said order and regularity. Conventional movement science asks: What is the nature of the prescription for action?, and in doing so ignores how the prescription could have got there in the first place. Thus, the prescription is given elevated status as an entity that is independent of, and causally antecedent to, systemic behavior.

The strategy that my colleagues and I adopt and that is briefly elaborated here contrasts sharply with the action-as-prescription approach.[1] Its tack is as follows: How can I understand the order and regularity that I see when people and animals generate actions as a necessary *consequence*—an a posteriori fact—of the way the system is designed to function? Or, said another way, what are the constraints on the system that allow actions to arise?

Let me unpack what I mean with an example. Imagine that you the reader were interested in accounting for the schooling of fish. What we know intuitively about fish-schooling phenomena is that all the individual fish are collectively coordinated in a highly coherent manner. The "system" with very many degrees of freedom (its individual components) behaves as an organized, seemingly wholistic unit. Most observers would agree that the schooling of fish is not due to a "teacher" or dominant individual that instructs the other elements in the system what to do and hence governs the collective behavior of the school. It also seems unlikely that the behavior of individual fish is referred to a "reference value" that regulates the collective. A search for the "executive" or the "internal referent" would prove to be quite fruitless. These would be *special mechanisms* introduced by the unknowing observer to explain a phenomenon that is poorly understood.

---

[1]The recent history of this alternative approach and its applications can be gleaned by the interested reader from a series of papers starting with Turvey (1977), Turvey, Shaw, and Mace (1978), and Fowler (1977). The broader theoretical framework is developed in Kugler, Kelso, and Turvey (1980), and relevant empirical data is presented in a companion paper (Kelso, Holt, Kugler, & Turvey, 1980). The dynamics perspective as applied more specifically to motor systems is available in Kelso (1981) and is elaborated for speech production by Fowler, Rubin, Remez, and Turvey (1980). The common dynamic properties between speech and other motor activities is emphasized in Kelso, Tuller, and Harris (in press). An important theoretical extension of the approach to naturally developing systems is provided in a very recent paper by Kugler, Kelso, and Turvey (1982). The framework may also afford insights into certain neurological disorders (Kelso & Tuller, 1981), as well as sign language (Turvey, 1980). Moreover, it can motivate a principled approach to problems of human interlimb coordination (Kelso, Holt, Rubin, & Kugler, in press), limb localization (Kelso & Holt, 1980; Kelso, Holt, & Flatt, 1980), as well as ongoing investigations of speech production (Tuller, Harris, & Kelso, 1981; Tuller, Kelso, & Harris, 1981; Zimmerman, Kelso, & Lander, 1980).

In fact, the highly coherent behavior of fish schooling can be accounted for with a fairly small set of key variables. One of these is "density" as defined through the metric of fish length. When the average distance between nearest neighbors is greater than one fish length, spacing between fish is random, not schooled (Okubo, 1980). Observations of many fish schools reveal that "attraction" between fish is specified by a critical distance that seldom exceeds 16–25% of the mean body length of the fish.[2] Under normal, stable conditions, individual fish rarely allow themselves to be separated from others by more than 40% of their body length. Interestingly, fish tend to form a "tighter" school (i.e., the critical distance decreases) when nearby shelter such as seaweed or rocks is absent. This type of gregarious behavior may have ecological significance, in that "close packing" reduces the chance of an individual fish being caught by a predator. (The predator, like Caesar of Gaul, seems to operate on the principle of divide and conquer.)

Now the details of collective fish behavior may seem far removed from the issues germane to the student of motor behavior, but I think there is a message here that is important. It has to do with the way we approach complex problems. In the case of the ecologist studying coherence phenomena such as fish schooling, we can see that considerable insights into the problem are gained by determining the necessary and sufficient conditions for organization to occur. Schooling is a *consequence of* certain crucial variables such as critical density and diffusion gradients. These variables are common in the analysis of physical systems and are constrained by a *contextual occasion* (are sharks nearby?; where can I hide?). The point is, and I apologize for belaboring it, there is no a priori *prescription* for the complex organization that we call schooling. Instead, this example motivates an alternative strategy for investigating action—one that rejects the introduction of special mechanisms before the laws of dynamics have been fully explored. Put another way, what can we, as students of movement, explain "for free" by considering the causal and logical support for action? And, by doing this, can we trim away the ghost in the machine? Therein lies the rub for the movement scientist, the brain theorist, the cognitive psychologist, the molecular biologist, and anyone else seeking to understand intelligent behavior.

REFERENCES

Dennett, D. C. *Brainstorms: Philosophical essays on mind and psychology*. Montgomery, Vt.: Bradford Books, 1978.

---

[2]Note that the idea of a critical value is very different from the reference value in a servomechanism. Critical values are a common feature in natural systems with many degrees of freedom. For example, consider fluid phenomena in which water is enclosed between two cylinders that can be rotated in opposite directions. At slow rotation speeds the water flow is laminar and smooth; beyond a critical value of rotation, however, the flow becomes turbulent, progressing to still higher forms of organization such as vortices. (For further examples in natural systems, see Haken, 1977, and for examples in movement, see Kelso, 1981; Kugler, Kelso, & Turvey, 1982.)

Fowler, C. *Timing control in speech production.* Bloomington: Indiana University Linguistics Club, 1977.

Fowler, C. A., Rubin, P., Remez, R. E., & Turvey, M. T. Implications for speech production of a general theory of action. In B. Butterworth (Ed.), *Language production.* New York: Academic Press, 1980.

Haken, H. *Synergetics: An introduction.* Heidelberg: Springer-Verlag, 1977.

Kelso, J. A. S. Contrasting perspectives on order and regulation in movement. In J. Long & A. Baddeley (Eds.), *Attention and performance* (IX). Hillsdale, N.J.: Lawrence Erlbaum Associates, 1981.

Kelso, J. A. S., & Holt, K. G. Exploring a vibratory systems analysis of human movement production. *Journal of Neurophysiology,* 1980, *43,* 1183–1196.

Kelso, J. A. S., Holt, K. G., & Flatt, A. E. Towards a theoretical reassessment of the role of proprioception in the perception and control of human movement. *Perception & Psychophysics,* 1980, *28,* 45–52.

Kelso, J. A. S., Holt, K. G., Kugler, P. N., & Turvey, M. T. On the concept of coordinative structures in dissipative structures: II. Empirical lines of convergence. In G. E. Stelmach (Ed.), *Tutorials in motor behavior.* New York: North-Holland, 1980.

Kelso, J. A. S., Holt, K. G., Rubin, P., & Kugler, P. N. Patterns of human interlimb coordination emerge from the properties of nonlinear oscillatory processes: Theory and data. *Journal of Motor Behavior,* in press.

Kelso, J. A. S., & Tuller, B. H. Toward a theory of apractic syndromes. *Brain & Language,* 1981, *12,* 224–245.

Kelso, J. A. S., Tuller, B. H., & Harris, K. S. A 'dynamic pattern' perspective on the control and coordination of movement. In P. MacNeilage (Ed.), *Motor control of speech production.* Springer-Verlag, in press.

Koestler, A., & Smythies, J. R. *Beyond reductionism.* Boston, Mass.: Beacon Press, 1969.

Kugler, P. N., Kelso, J. A. S., & Turvey, M. T. On the concept of coordinative structures as dissipative structures: I. Theoretical lines of convergence. In G. E. Stelmach & J. Requin (Eds.), *Tutorials in motor behavior.* New York: North-Holland, 1980.

Kugler, P. N., Kelso, J. A. S., & Turvey, M. T. On coordination and control in naturally developing systems. In J. A. Scott Kelso & J. E. Clark (Eds.), *The development of movement coordination and control.* New York, London: Wiley, 1982.

Okubo, A. *Diffusion and ecological problems: Mathematical models.* Berlin, Heidelberg: Springer-Verlag, 1980.

Searle, J. R. Minds, brains and programs. *The Behavioral and Brain Sciences,* 1980, *3,* 417–461.

Tuller, B. H., Harris, K. S., & Kelso, J. A. S. Articulatory motor events as a function of speaking rate and stress. *Haskins Laboratories Status Report on Speech Research,* 1981, *SR-65,* 33–62.

Tuller, B. H., Kelso, J. A. S., & Harris, K. S. Phase relationships among articulators as a function of speaking rate and stress. *Haskins Laboratories Status Report on Speech Research,* 1981, *SR-65,* 63–90.

Turvey, M. T. Preliminaries to a theory of action with reference to vision. In R. Shaw & J. Bransford (Eds.), *Perceiving, acting and knowing: Toward an ecological psychology.* Hillsdale, N.J.: Lawrence Erlbaum Associates, 1977.

Turvey, M. T. Clues from the organization of motor systems. In U. Bellugi & M. Studdert-Kennedy (Eds.), *Signed and spoken language: Biological constraints on linguistic form.* Verlag Chemie, 1980.

Turvey, M. T., Shaw, R. E., & Mace, W. Issues in the theory of action: Degrees of freedom, coordinative structures and coalitions. In J. Requin (Ed.), *Attention and Performance* (VII). Hillsdale, N.J.: Lawrence Erlbaum Associates, 1978.

Zimmermann, G., Kelso, J. A. S., & Lander, L. Articulatory behavior pre and post full-mouth tooth extraction and alveoloplasty: A cinefluorographic study. *Journal of Speech and Hearing Research,* 1980, *23,* 630–645.

Glossary

This glossary is included for the purpose of defining terms that may not be clear in the body of the text. Initials of the authors identify the definitions.

Additive effects: The effects on the dependent variable when independent variables affect different stages of processing such that the total deficit is equal to the sum of each stage's deficit. (GES)

Afference: The conduction of information from peripheral sensory receptors towards the brain via nerve fibres. (GES)

Closed-Loop: A mode of system control in which feedback from action is compared against a reference of correctness to compute an error signal, which serves as a stimulus for future action. (RAS)

Coding: The act of transferring information from one processing stage to another so that the receiving stage optimally comprehends the information. (GES)

Dependent variable: The factor which is observed and measured to determine the effect of the independent variable. It is considered dependent because its value depends upon the value of the independent variable. (GES)

Detection: The result of stimuli impinging upon sensory receptors-sensation; also the first stage of information processing. (GES)

Difficulty: For rapid movements, the ratio of movement amplitude and movement time (A/MT), or the average velocity. (RAS)

Effective target width (W_e): The variability of a set of aiming responses about their own mean. (RAS)

Effector: The structure(s) through which any response or action is ultimately evidenced; may refer to the entire set of efferent pathways of the nervous system or just the body's musculature. (GES)

Efference: The conduction of information via nerve fibres from the brain to the periphery, usually to effectors such as muscles. (GES)

Errors in execution: An error in movement where the action that was planned and programmed was not carried out faithfully. (RAS)

Errors in selection: An error in movement where the action chosen was inappropriate for the environmental situation. (RAS)

Expected sensory consequences: An image of the sensation anticipated if a particular action should be carried out; the major output of the recognition schema. (RAS)

Factorial design: The most common means by which two or more independent variables are manipulated, such that their respective levels are crossed with each other. (GES)

Floor effects: An experimental or testing artifact by which the distribution of scores are artificially raised or skewed by having the lower performance levels attracting a disproportionate frequency of scores than the equivalent higher performance levels. (GES)

Generalized motor program: A motor program that can be carried out in a variety of ways depending on the parameter(s) specified. (RAS)

Impulse: The aggregate of forces acting over time to produce acceleration of the limb; the area under the force-time curve. (RAS)

Independent variable: The factor which is measured, manipulated or selected by the experimenter to determine its relationship to an observed phenomenon. It is considered independent because the experimenter is interested only in how it affects another variable. (GES)

Initial conditions: The state of the environment or of the subject prior to action. (RAS)

Interaction effects: The effect on the dependent variable when independent variables affect more than one stage or the same stage of processing, such that the total deficit is greater or smaller than if separate stages were affected. (GES)

Kinesthesis: That information derivable from the stimulation of the joint and muscle spindle afferents, subsumed under proprioception. (GES)

Knowledge of results: KR is the information a performer receives (most often) from external sources regarding the nature or success of the completed act. (GES)

Labeling, Imaginal: Cognitive process aiding retention through construction of images of the to-be-remembered item. (GES)

Learner variables: Those aspects of the learner or performer which affect the individual's ability to learn or perform (e.g., motivation, attention). (GES)

Motor program: An abstract memory structure prepared before the movement which, when executed, results in movement without the involvement of feedback requiring a correction for an error in selection. (RAS)

Movement outcome: The result of a movement in the environment; usually defined by knowledge of results. (RAS)

Muscle spindle: A spindle-shaped structure located parallel to the main fibers in the muscle that is responsible for signalling changes in muscle length; the primary receptor in the gamma system. (RAS)

Open-loop control: A mode of system control in which instructions for action are prepared in advance and carried out without modification from feedback. (RAS)

Parameter: An abstract value provided by the recall schema and applied to the generalized motor program that defines the way in which the program is to be carried out. (RAS)

Passive movements: Those movements which are initiated by any external forces acting on the body or parts of it. (GES)

Perceptual organization: A cognitive process that assimilates items presented for memory representation into a meaningful relationship, resulting in a stronger, stable representation. (GES)

Perception: Those processes (detection and recognition) by which meaning is derived from information supplied by receptors about the external world. (GES)

Proprioception: Movement information derived from the sensory receptors excluding vision and audition, e.g., kinesthetic, tactile, vestibular, etc. (GES)

Recall: Task which requires a subject to generate from memory any item or response that has been previously encoded there. (GES)

Recall schema: The relationship between the sensory consequences, the initial conditions, and the outcomes in the environment; serves as a basis for selecting the parameter(s) in novel movement. (RAS)

Recognition: Task which requires a subject to determine whether a stimulus is a member of a set of stimuli presented previously, requiring matching of information stored in memory. (GES)

Recognition schema: The relationship between the sensory consequences, the initial conditions, and the outcomes in the environment of past movements; serves as a basis for determining tbe expected sensory consequences. (RAS)

Reductionism: Approach to research which attempts to reduce phenomena to their basic elements or isolate them from extraneous events to discover their basic laws. (GES)

Rehearsal: The act of practicing either physically or mentally the task to be performed. (GES)

Reinforcement: An event, the occurrence of which strengthens a response in close temporal proximity to a stimulus. A positive reinforcement is a pleasant stimulus (e.g., a reward), a negative reinforcement is an unpleasant stimulus (e.g., physical punishment). (GES)

Response complexity: A term difficult to define, but in general refers to those aspects of a response that involve greater degrees of accuracy, force and movement alteration; increasing complexity most often increases difficulty, however the reverse is not true. (GES)

Response execution: The fourth stage of information processing, in which instructions from the response selection stage are carried out, resulting in observable motor performance. (GES)

Response selection: That stage of processing which acts on the information from previous stages to choose an appropriate response from all possible alternatives. (GES)

Retention: The ability to either encode and/or recover items from memory. (GES)

Sensory consequences: The sensations produced by action, including vision, audition, and proprioception. (RAS)

Task variables: Those aspects of performance which are attributable to the nature of the task (e.g., using one hand or two, hitting a small or large target). (GES)

Contributors' Biographical Information

Steve Keele obtained an undergraduate degree in Psychology from the University of Oregon in 1962. Very shortly after graduation he entered the University of Wisconsin Psychology Department and obtained the Ph.D. degree four years later in 1966. After two years of postdoctoral study with Michael Posner at the University of Oregon's Psychology Department, he joined the faculty there and now is a Professor of Psychology at Oregon.

During that early postdoctoral period, Dr. Posner encouraged Dr. Keele to review the psychological literature on motor behavior. The time was indeed ready for a review, for the resulting *Psychological Bulletin* paper, "Movement Control in Skilled Motor Behavior," published in 1968, came just when information processing analyses of movement and skill were beginning to mushroom in psychology and physical education. In the ensuing years, the information processing analysis of motor control became a dominant one in those areas. But now new trends are apparent as scientists from many disciplines—physiology, ethology, biomechanics, medicine and others, as well as psychology and physical education—are building an interdisciplinary understanding of motor control. Some of these new developments are reviewed in Dr. Keele's chapter, "Behavioral Analysis of Movement," in the *Motor Control* volume of the *Handbook of Physiology*.

In addition to his interests in motor behavior, Dr. Keele has been interested in the psychological investigation of attention and, together with Trammel Neil, has recently published "Mechanisms of Attention," a chapter in the *Handbook of Perception, Vol. 9*.

J. A. Scott Kelso is a native of Londonderry, Ireland and was educated at Foyle College and later at Stranmillis College, Belfast where he graduated with

293

honors in 1969. After a short bout of teaching mathematics and english at Coleraine Academical Institution (and coaching rugby football and cricket), Kelso emigrated to Calgary, Alberta in 1971. At the University of Calgary, Kelso pursued studies in psychology and physiology under the guidance of Dr. Barry Kerr obtaining a bachelor's degree in 1972. An offer of a research assistantship in Dr. George Stelmach's laboratory at the University of Wisconsin, Madison was duly accepted, and a Ph.D. followed under Dr. Stelmach's tutelage in late 1975. While at Wisconsin, Kelso was fortunate to gain research experience in the Departments of Neurology where he conducted his masters degree work with William Wanamaker, M.D., and Psychology where he worked on perception with Dr. William Epstein. In 1976 Kelso was appointed Assistant Professor and Director of the Motor Behavior Laboratory at the University of Iowa. In September 1978 he moved to the exciting environs of Haskins Laboratories where he currently holds a senior research staff position. Kelso also holds an associate professorship in The Departments of Psychology and Biobehavioral Sciences at The University of Connecticut in Storrs. He collaborates closely on problems of movement control and coordination and speech production with a number of colleagues, including Michael Turvey, Katherine Harris, Carol Fowler, Betty Tuller and Michael Studdert-Kennedy. Kelso has published widely on these topics in a number of journals, both psychological and neurophysiological. His 1977 paper in the *Journal of Experimental Psychology: Human Perception and Performance* entitled "Motor control mechanisms in human movement reproduction" showing "equifinality" in the absence of conscious position cues was significant in bringing to light the currently popular "mass-spring" style of control. In 1979, with his students David Goodman and Dan Southard he introduced a new paradigm in *Science* for studying human interlimb coordination. Kelso reviews for over 20 scientific journals and is currently Co-Executive Editor of the *Journal of Motor Behavior*. Between 1976 and 1978 Kelso represented the U.S.A. in international rugby football on a number of occasions. Recently he was invited to manage a group of Yale rugby players on a Tour of Zimbabwe (formerly Rhodesia), a trip that represented one of the first efforts on the part of the U.S. to establish normal relations with the new government there.

Richard A. Schmidt attended public schools in southern California and later enrolled at the University of California, Berkeley, where he studied a variety of engineering and mathematics-related subjects. Around 1960, his interest and success in gymnastics (third in the NCAA championships on the rings in 1962) led him to pursue a career in physical education, with early experiences with Franklin Henry at Berkeley creating an interest in motor behavior and skill acquisition. After teaching high school for a year, Schmidt entered the University of Illinois where, in 1967, he received his Ph.D. under A. W. Hubbard, with powerful influences from Jack A. Adams. At this time, Schmidt was beginning to become interested in theoretical aspects of motor behavior, particularly in the notion of motor programs, and mechanisms of anticipation.

Following the Ph.D., he joined the faculty at the University of Maryland, where in 1969 he founded the *Journal of Motor Behavior*—a research journal devoted to motor control and learning. In the 1970's, he moved to the University of Michigan, and later to the University of Southern California. Presently he is with the Department of Kinesiology, UCLA, where he is Professor and Director of the Motor Control Laboratory. In the 1970's, his research interests in motor programs and learning led to the creation of the schema theory, in which previously separate notions about motor performance and motor learning were combined. Recently, Schmidt and his colleagues have developed an impulse-variability model for accuracy in rapid, programmed actions, a mathematical model based on sources of variability in motor-program output. His research interests in human performance complement and are complemented by a 25-year pursuit of excellence in sailboat racing, as well as in relatively new interests in marathon running.

George E. Stelmach was born in Harvey, Illinois and attended the University of Illinois from 1957-61. While at Illinois he majored in Physical Education and played football. From 1961-63 he taught and coached at Thornton Fractional High School, Lansing, Illinois. Realizing that very little information was available on the acquisition and retention of motor skills, he decided to give up his teaching position and enroll in Graduate School at the University of California, Berkeley where he received his masters and doctoral degrees. It was during his graduate school days that he came in contact with Dr. F. M. Henry who changed his life considerably. In his years at Berkeley, Dr. Henry clearly demonstrated the need and the importance of motor skill research but more importantly he planted the seed of scientific inquiry that has guided him over his professional career.

In 1967 Dr. Stelmach accepted a position at the University of California, Santa Barbara where he taught Kinesiology and Motor Learning. In 1971, he accepted a position at the University of Wisconsin, Madison where he has remained ever since except for semester leaves at University of Texas, Austin and the National Center for Scientific Research in France, at Marseilles. During the Spring of 1981 he was a Senior Research Fulbright Scholar in the Netherlands.

Dr. Stelmach is on the editorial board of seven Psychological journals and is the book series editor for Advances in Psychology. Dr. Stelmach has over 60 publications on motor skill research and has edited three books Motor Control: Issues and Trends, Information Processing in Motor Control and Learning, and Tutorials in Motor Behavior.

Dr. Stelmach has diverse research interests that cross a broad spectrum of Motor Behavior that includes attention, learning, control and memory. Dr. Stelmach's task for this text, was to review Information Processing, Adams closed loop theory, and Short-term motor memory research as it applied to Motor Skills.

Michael T. Turvey was born in Surrey, England and obtained his under graduate education at Loughborough College where he graduated with first class honors in 1963. It is not surprising that one of his major academic interests is the link between perception and action because Turvey captained the Loughborough Athletic Team and represented Great Britain in the triple jump. Turvey emigrated to the USA and pursued his studies at Ohio State University, first receiving a Masters Degree in Physical Education and then a Ph.D. under Delos Wickens in human experimental psychology in 1967. Since that time he has been a professor at the University of Connecticut, becoming a Full Professor in 1974; he has also been a Research Associate at Haskins Laboratories since 1970. Turvey has received a number of honors that attest not only to his scholarship but also to his inspirational teaching. With respect to the former he was the recipient of an Early Career Award by the American Psychological Association and also a John S. Guggenheim fellowship. In 1980–1981 he was a Fellow at the Center for Advanced Studies in Behavioral Sciences in Palo Alto, California. Attesting to his teaching excellence was the profferment of a University of Connecticut Alumni Award in 1975. Turvey's *Psychological Review* papers in 1973 and 1977 are considered classics in the area and they also represent a great shift in his theoretical orientation—from an information processing perspective to the ecological view. It is fair to say that he is now one of the chief proponents of the late James J. Gibson's ecological psychology.

Betty Tuller and **Hollis Fitch** were both graduate students of Turvey's. Dr. Tuller graduated in 1980 and is currently a Sloane Fellow at Cornell Medical College in New York City. She is also a Research Associate at Haskins Laboratories where she pursues problems of movement coordination with special reference to speech. Dr. Fitch also graduated in 1980 and currently works on problems of language and speech perception at the Institute of Defense Analysis in Princeton, New Jersey.

Author Index

Numbers in *italic* indicate pages with bibliographic information.

Subject Index